ACK

MW01615178

Mountain biking would not ~~be possible~~ without the help of so many people within our communities. I'd like to thank all the countless individuals within the Forest Service, the BLM, the Gunnison County Trails Commission and the Crested Butte Mountain Bike Association who help build, maintain and keep access to all our wonderful trails. So many others have given their time and physical and monetary support it would be impossible to name them all, so thanks to all the volunteers who help with our trails, you know who you are! Thank you to all the mountain bike shops of our area and many other businesses who offer services to all in very seasonal economies, and also donate prizes and bodies to trail work days. Keep up the good work everybody!

I'd like to thank my husband Rob, my folks Roy and Loretta, and all my friends who have supported my efforts writing this book. Thanks to Peter Vanags, Gene Bollig, Xavier Fane, Alison White, Tom Stillo and B & B Printers for their contributions to this book.

And thanks to mother nature for the fine scenery we enjoy every day!

Cover Photo by Tom Stillo, Trail 403
Back Cover Photo by Rob Mahedy, Hartman Rocks

Graphic Design by Gene Bollig
Printing by B&B Printers, Gunnison, CO
Maps by Peter Vanags

©2006 • Holly Annala

1

AREA OVERVIEW

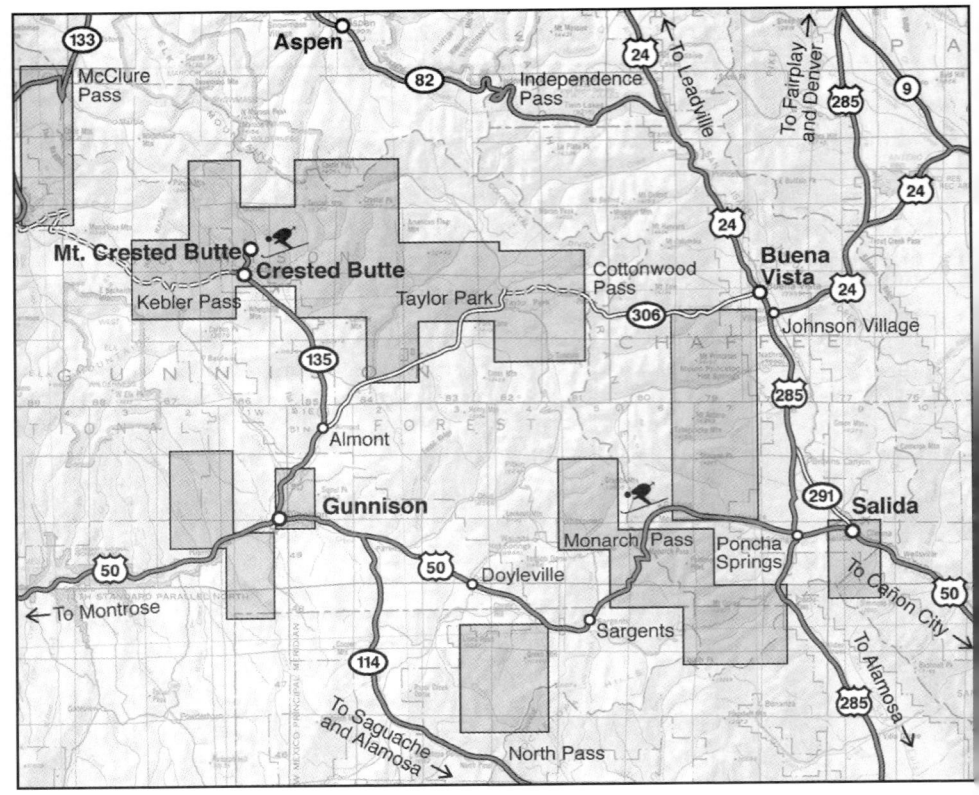

THE RIDES

Introduction:

CRESTED BUTTE AREA TRAILS:

Beginner and Easy Intermediate Rides

Intermediate Rides

Advanced Intermediate and Expert Rides

Expert to Epic Rides

GUNNISON AREA TRAILS:
Beginner and Intermediate Rides

Advanced Intermediate to Expert Rides

Expert to Epic Rides

SALIDA AND MONARCH CREST AREA TRAILS:
Intermediate and Advanced Intermediate Rides

Advanced Intermediate and Expert Rides

Local Services

WELCOME TO CRESTED BUTTE, GUNNISON AND SALIDA, COLORADO,

home to some of the best mountain biking found anywhere! These mountain towns offer trails for every level of mountain biker. Enjoy spectacular views, lots of fresh air, easy to challenging terrain, lots of wildflowers, and miles of excellent singletrack! This book is written for folks who want to experience the great singletrack, but also includes a quick rundown of the areas' dirt road rides. It fits right in your pack for easy reference out on the trail. The trail descriptions help you decide on a ride that fits your ability, desires, and time schedule. Have fun out there!

Here are a few considerations before heading out on the rides:

High Altitude: The town of Crested Butte is at an altitude of 8,885 feet, Gunnison is at 7,700 feet, and Salida is at 7,100 feet. Many of the rides climb above 10,000 and up to 12,000 feet or more. Before attempting the higher and more strenuous rides, plan on spending a few days here riding shorter rides and taking it easy if you are from a lower altitude or not accustomed to mountain biking on a regular basis. Drink extra water before, during and after rides. Know your limits and respect them, too! If you aren't feeling well, it could be the altitude. Take the day off and rest, and see a doctor if needed.

Weather: A storm can blow in quickly in the mountains, so check the weather before starting your day and plan a ride accordingly. Get started as early as possible, (7:00 or 8:00 a.m. is perfect for long rides) so you can be off the high ridges and peaks when afternoon thunderstorms roll through, as they often do, even when the day starts out clear. If the weather looks threatening, ride near town and stay lower. Save that epic ride for a clear day! Be prepared with warm clothes and raingear. Plan exits from long rides in case the weather turns stormy.

Route Finding: Take this guide and an accurate map with you on every ride. Know how to read the map and use a compass. Each description lists which map or maps are best for the individual ride. Before heading out on a ride, read the entire description and plot it out on your map before starting. Keep track of surrounding landmarks and know the destination of spur trails if you might ride them. Hire a local guide if you are afraid of getting lost. Work your way up to the longer and more primitive rides as you get to know the area and its' landmarks. Always stay on the marked trails, the terrain is rugged and you could get in worse trouble by bushwhacking.

Trail Conditions: Check with a local bike shop for current trail conditions before setting out on rides. (And help support their business while in town!) In the spring many of the trails don't melt out until well into June or even into July. After rainstorms, many of the trails stay wet and slick for several days. Don't ride muddy trails, and walk around muddy sections! Riding muddy trails speeds erosion, and it generally isn't all that fun to push your bike through the mud. Often a big snowstorm in October will close higher trails for the winter. Gunnison's Hartman Rocks is a great alternative for earlier and later season rides and rides after storms. Salida has S Mountain riding that is even open in the winter. Check with Salida bike shops for information on the trails in this area.

Clothing and Gear: Make sure you always carry a jacket even on the shortest rides. It can cool off quickly here in the mountains, and high points where you want to take a break to enjoy the views are often breezy and cool. On all day rides and cooler days, bring leggings or tights, a warm wool or polypro shirt, a good waterproof jacket, and full finger gloves. Gore-tex pants are a good idea to bring on long rides in the cooler seasons, as the temperature can drop 20 degrees if a storm rolls in. Being caught in a severe rain or snowstorm is not unusual even in the summer months here. Always wear a good fitting helmet! Camelbak-type packs are the best for carrying enough water and all your gear and food. On epic rides or long rides in unfamiliar areas, throw in a headlamp and a warm hat that fits under your helmet. Bring a basic first-aid kit, as well.

Water and Food: Always take extra water and food! Even on the shortest rides in this book, you will probably want a snack and some water. On the epic rides take a full 100 oz. camelback, two full waterbottles or a water filter, and a pack full of high energy food: sandwiches, fruit, nuts, etc. Sugary foods are not enough for longer rides. Drink extra water at high altitude, and eat often to retain your energy. A water filter is a good addition to your pack for epic explorations, and is lighter weight than the extra water bottles. It is not a good idea to drink unfiltered stream water, as you risk getting giardia or similar digestive ailments. Check your maps and get local bike shop advice to make sure there are year round streams on the epic ride you have planned.

Tools: Always take along basic tools and know how to use them. It's a long walk home, even from the shortest rides. Carry a good pump, an extra tube, a patchkit, a tire patch, Allen wrenches, a chain tool, lube, and a rag and stiff brush to clean up your chain if it gets dry or muddy. Also bring a lighter in case of the unfortunate event of getting lost and needing to build a fire.

Maintenance: Keep your bike in good running order at all times! Check it over before every ride to make sure everything is tight and in good shape. Keep your chain clean and lubed. If you don't know how to do this, take it to a shop regularly, get a good book or take a clinic and learn to be prepared.

Maps: When setting out on a ride, bring this book along to help you find your way. The maps in this book may not be exact to scale, so also bring along an up to date and more detailed map or maps for the area on each ride. I recommend the best map or maps for each ride in its' overview. The best up to date maps for the Crested Butte area are the Latitude 40 Crested Butte/Taylor Park (new in 2005,) and the 5th Edition Latitude 40 Recreation Topo Map Aspen/Crested Butte/Gunnison. The latter covers a larger area but isn't as detailed, both are quite accurate. National Geographic/Trails Illustrated Crested Butte/Pearl Pass is quite detailed but covers a smaller area around Crested Butte. It has a few inaccuracies, so beware. The Alpineer Bike Trail Map is good for rides close to Crested Butte, but doesn't cover as large an area or as many rides and isn't very detailed. Specific National Geographic/ Trails Illustrated maps are suggested for many of the rides that are farther from Crested Butte and the newer versions are fairly complete and accurate. Buena Vista/Collegiate Peaks, Salida/St. Elmo/Shavano Peak, and La Garita/Cochetopa Hills are good maps and cover most rides between Gunnison and Salida and Buena Vista. A few important trails and intersections are wrong or omitted on these maps, always doublecheck your information. The Crest Trail by Absolute Bikes is the only complete map for many of the Monarch Crest Trail area rides. It is put out by locals and is easy to use and accurate. It has a picture flow for the rides, which helps riders with potentially confusing turns. Hartman Rocks in Gunnison is the only map out for that area, and covers the main area for the rides and is accurate. It is a little hard to use because of the dark color and difficulty differentiating road and trail.

Here are a few considerations for riding:

Stay in control at all times to avoid an injury to yourself or others, or a serious mechanical. Some of the rides are quite isolated, and you may not see another person if you need help. Stay with marked trails if you do end up walking back. The destination of important spurs along the routes are described in most trail descriptions. If you do not know the destination of a spur trail, don't take it! Stay with the main trail. Always carry a map!! Keep in mind that there are new user created trails every year, so not all roads and trails are on the maps in this book or any larger map.

Respect private property, trail closures, and wilderness areas, and stay on existing roads and trails. Sections of many trails travel across private property, respect the owners by staying on the trail and passing quietly. Respect no trespassing signs. Close all gates behind you. Don't ride in wilderness areas, it is illegal and carries a heavy fine. If you are caught, your bike may be confiscated. Most trails in wilderness are too rough or steep to ride anyway. Don't ride closed trails. It is against the Gunnison National Forest Travel Plan to ride off trail or create new ones, and carries a heavy fine. Responsible use helps keep our trails open! It is also against the forest plan for four-wheel vehicles to drive on singletracks. If you see any of this damaging activity, report it to the Gunnison Forest Service Office, see listing in back of book.

Respect other users and create a feeling of peace on the trails. Always yield the right of way to horses and other animals! Don't ride quickly up on horses, let them know you are coming and ask permission to walk past, or dismount to let them pass if they are coming toward you. Don't chase or spook livestock or wildlife. Let them get off the trail before passing. Always yield the right of way to hikers, and to motorcyclists as well. It is easier for mountain bikers to step off for a moment. If a motorcyclist drives off the trail to go around every mountain biker, soon we'll only have doubletracks. Be polite to other mountain bikers, and let them pass. Uphill riders have the right of way. Step to the side to let others pass, do not ride off the sides of the trail. This creates erosion and side trails. Ride past others who step off the trails for you at walking pace. Practice no trace etiquette while out on the trail. Watch out for small animals and birds, they tend to be hard to see until the last minute. Keep your speed down in tall vegetation to avoid running them over. Pack out your trash and leave no trace that you've been there. Don't squash vegetation with your bike or yourself.

I suggest riding the bike path or dirt roads to the rides instead of driving to trailheads if possible. A road warm-up is good for getting in shape and improves your riding ability on the trail, and is more environmentally friendly than driving. If you do drive to a trailhead, slow down! Pass other riders and hikers slowly. The Mountain Express bus system will carry your bike up to Mount Crested Butte for free, this can shorten several rides by three miles and 800 feet of climbing. Check at the four-way stop in Crested Butte for pickup times and information, or call 349-7318.

Protect yourself during hunting season (mid-September through November) by wearing hunter orange and staying on popular trails. Find out from the Forest Service where most hunters will be during your stay.

Disclaimer:

Finally, I assume you know: how to ride your bike, your limits and when to turn back, basic navigation and route finding, basic bike repairs, and what to do in case of an emergency. This book is simply a trail guide, intended to help you pick out and find rides. It is not meant to replace basic knowledge of mountain biking and backcountry travel, maps, navigation skills, or just plain common sense. Inaccuracies may be present within the ride descriptions, always double check the information with other accurate resources including trail signs and detailed maps of the area where you are intending to ride. The author, the producer, the designer, and the publisher of this book, and anyone mentioned in or associated with this book are in no way responsible or liable for anyone using this book and the suggested routes within this book. Mountain biking is a hazardous sport with unforeseen risks and dangers, including but not limited to: getting lost, injured, heat stroke, hypothermia, and even death. Cyclists must assume responsibility for themselves. Be careful out there, be responsible, and have fun!

How to use this book

I have listed the important statistics and a description for each ride, so you can decide which rides suit your abilities and skill level. Here is a short explanation of all the elements listed.

Distance: As close as possible in tenths of miles, and also a breakdown of singletrack, dirt road, and paved road in miles. Loop, out and back, or shuttle ride is also listed here. Please note that due to differences in maps, computers, weather, etc., that the distances might be slightly different than what your computer reads. I have described important points in the trail with landmarks as well as mileage to help you find the routes even if you don't ride with a computer. Use maps, a compass, trail signs, landmarks, and this guide to help you be sure of your location.

Time: A general guide. The time listed is a range for the level of rider that matches the rides difficulty rating, or a rider of a higher level of expertise. If a trail is an listed as an expert ride, the time range is for expert riders. If the ride is listed as an intermediate level ride, the fastest time would apply to an expert rider and the longer time would apply to an intermediate rider, and so on. Ride times can fall greatly in either direction of this range due to weather, trail conditions, mechanicals, long rest breaks, or your physical condition, to name a few factors. Read into the description and make appropriate time allowance based on your knowledge of your own level of riding and experience. Always allow extra time for a ride.

Difficulty: A general rating. Read the remainder of the description to get a better idea of how tough the ride is. Distance, steepness and length of climbs, and amount and degree of difficulty of technical obstacles, as well as the difficulty following the trails are considered in the rating. Beginner and easy intermediate rides are for those with little experience mountain biking on singletrack. Intermediate rides are for riders who have ridden a fair amount of singletrack, are in fairly good physical condition, and have a good knowledge of how to handle their bike in moderately technical situations. They have also ridden rides longer than 20 miles. Advanced intermediate rides are a step up in difficulty from intermediate. A strong intermediate rider would probably do fine on several of the expert rides, but I suggest starting with intermediate rides to gauge the difficulty ratings before setting out on expert rides. The expert rating is for experienced riders who can handle several hours in the saddle and technical trails. Some rides rated expert may not be so long, but have a lot of challenging technical riding involved. Rides rated Expert to Epic are for strong and experienced expert riders only. They are long, rough, and difficult to follow. These rides challenge the strongest of riders with long climbs at high altitude and continuous technical singletrack. They are for the adventurous rider who can truly ride all day, and doesn't mind carrying their bike. The trails with the expert to epic rating are often rough or in poor condition.

INTRODUCTION

Technical Skill: Beginner, intermediate, advanced intermediate, expert. Also to give you more of an idea of what the ride holds as far as rocks, deadfall, exposure, creek crossings, etc. The beginner rating has little or no technical riding, intermediate has moderately hard obstacles and just a few of them, advanced intermediate has more or harder obstacles or longer distances of technical riding. Expert can be quite difficult technically, have continuous sections of technical riding, or many technical sections.

Aerobic Effort: Whether the ride demands easy, moderate, moderately high, high, or strenuous aerobic output. If you are from a lower altitude, a ride may seem more difficult to you than the aerobic rating suggests. Most rides in the Crested Butte area challenge even experienced riders because of the length of the climbs and the altitude. If you are concerned about the difficulty of the ride, start by riding shorter, easier rides first. The Lower Loop, Snodgrass, and Strand Hill are wonderful rides and a great way to start your riding experience here!

Elevation: Top: The highest elevation on the ride in feet. **Gain:** The gain in elevation in feet.

Season: This is a general guide. Please visit a local bike shop to find out if trails are in good condition and dry before riding them, regardless of the time of year. Snow often keeps trails closed later in the spring than usual, or closes them with an early fall flurry. Heavy or prolonged periods of rain common to the mountains here can affect trail conditions for several days.

Finding Route: Easy, moderate, or difficult, or variations of these ratings. This rating assumes you carry this book and at least one of the maps suggested in the description for the ride, and have a basic knowledge of route finding.

Maps: The map or maps that best illustrate the ride. See maps heading on page 5 for more information on specific maps.

Description: a short general overview of the ride.

Point by Point Mileage: Measured with an accurate cylcocomputer. These could be slightly off for various reasons, so I have included descriptions of landmarks along the routes to help you decipher where you are if you don't have a cyclocomputer on your bike or if your numbers don't match the description. Some of the mile points have (approx. mileage) after, this is to alert you to a possible greater difference. Again use several resources to be sure of where you are.

Farris Creek

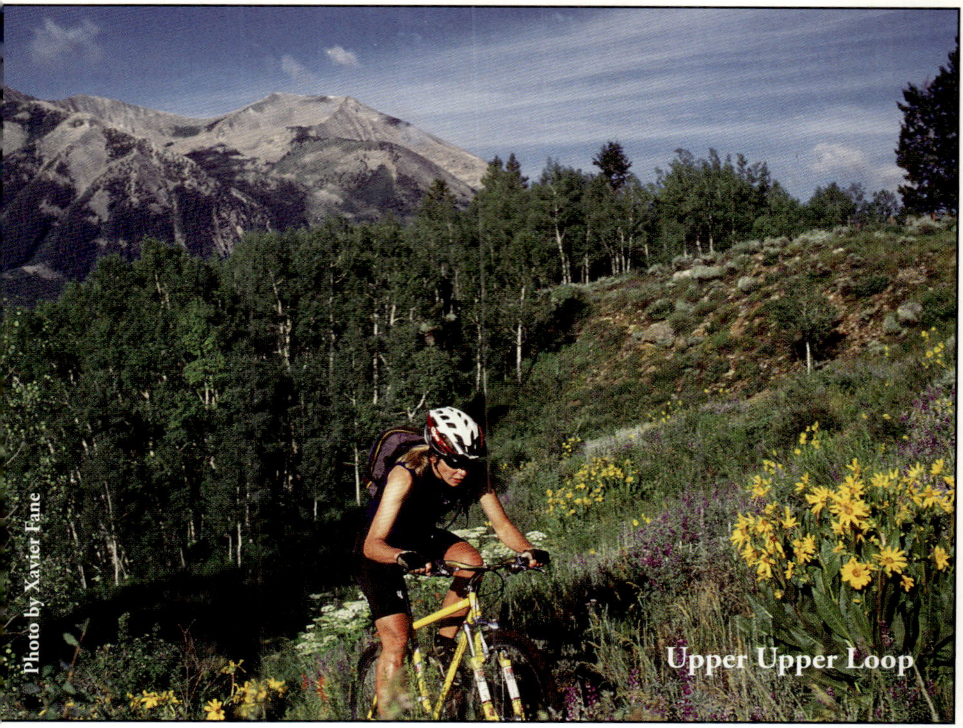
Photo by Xavier Fane
Upper Upper Loop

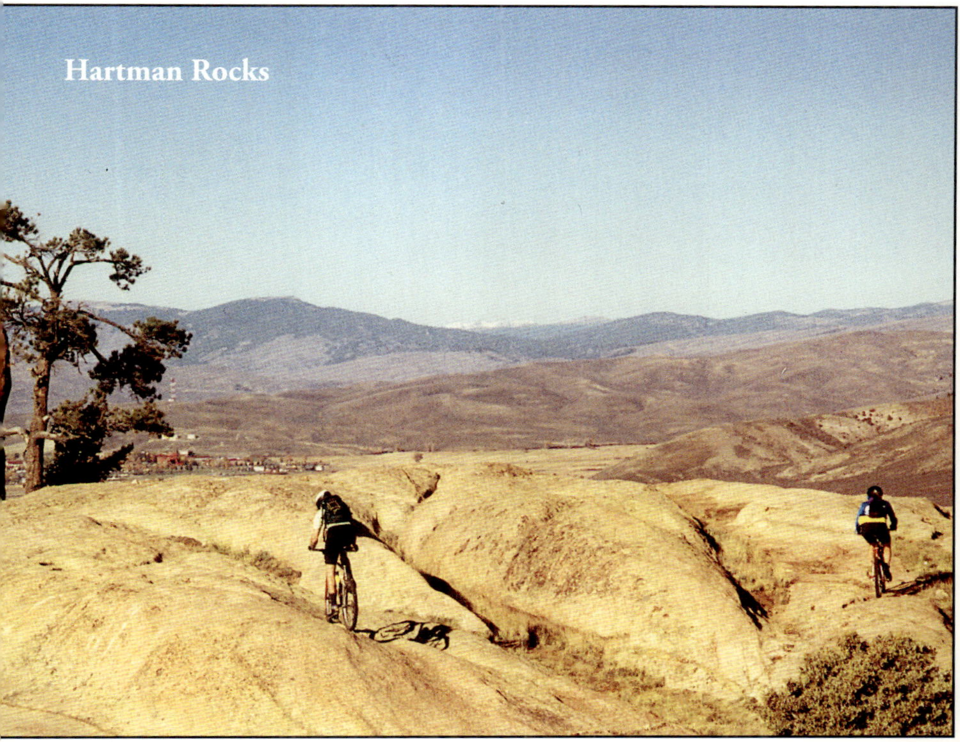
Hartman Rocks

Hartman Rocks

Photo by Xavier Fane

Photo by Alison White,

Teocalli Ridge

Dyke Trail

Photo by Xavier Fane

Deer Creek Trail

Photo by Xavier Fane

Trail 401

Photo by Xavier Fane

Photo by Xavier Fane

Lower Trail 401

Strand Hill Trail

Photos by Alison White

Snodgrass Trail

Photos by Alison White

Upper Upper Loop

Lower Loop

Photo by Xavier Fane

April Gulch Loop-West Beaver Creek Trail

Photo by Holly Annala

MAP LEGEND

····················	singletrack trail	**TH**	trailhead
·—··—··—··—	4 wheeler / ATV track	**P**	parking
- - - - - - - -	doubletrack jeep road	**A**	campground
============	dirt road	**I**	restroom
═══════════	paved road	•—•	gate
▬▬▬▬▬▬▬	highway	⋈	bridge
▪▪▪▪▪▪▪▪▪▪▪▪	bike path	■	building / structure
—·—·—·—·	fence / chairlift line	FS, FSR	Forest Service road
▬ ▬ ▬ ▬ ▬	wilderness boundary	CR	county road
			Ski Area

C.B.M.B.A

TRAIL ACCESS & MAINTENANCE

Founded in 1983, the Crested Butte Mountain Bike Association (CBMBA) is the oldest mountain bike club in the world. The volunteers and members of CBMBA are passionate about mountain biking; however, riding mountain bikes is not the focus of CBMBA. CBMBA is active in advocating responsible riding, trail access issues and cooperation and cohesion among all user groups. CBMBA understands that without periodic repair, our trails would gradually fall victim to consistently harsh winters, multiple uses and spring runoff.

Monthly trail work events (in conjunction with the United States Forest Service) in the summer provide local and visiting mountain bikers the opportunity to halt erosion and perpetuate a cycle of sustainable trails. Volunteers can always count on an abundant supply of food, raffle prizes and beer (afterwards) from our sponsors. To join the 130-member strong CBMBA or to inquire about trail work day plans, please call (970) 349-6817 or check out our website: WWW.CBMBA.ORG

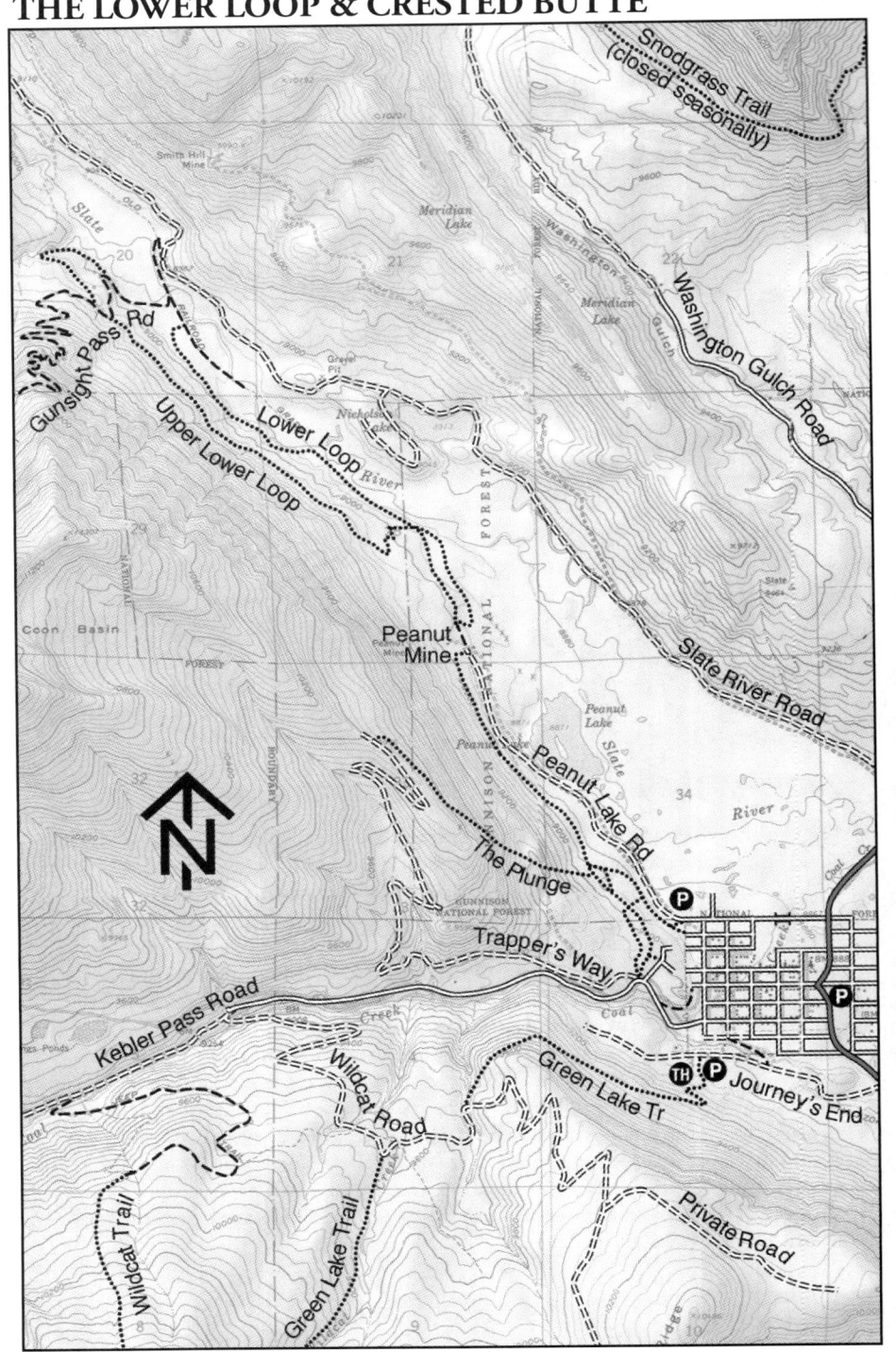

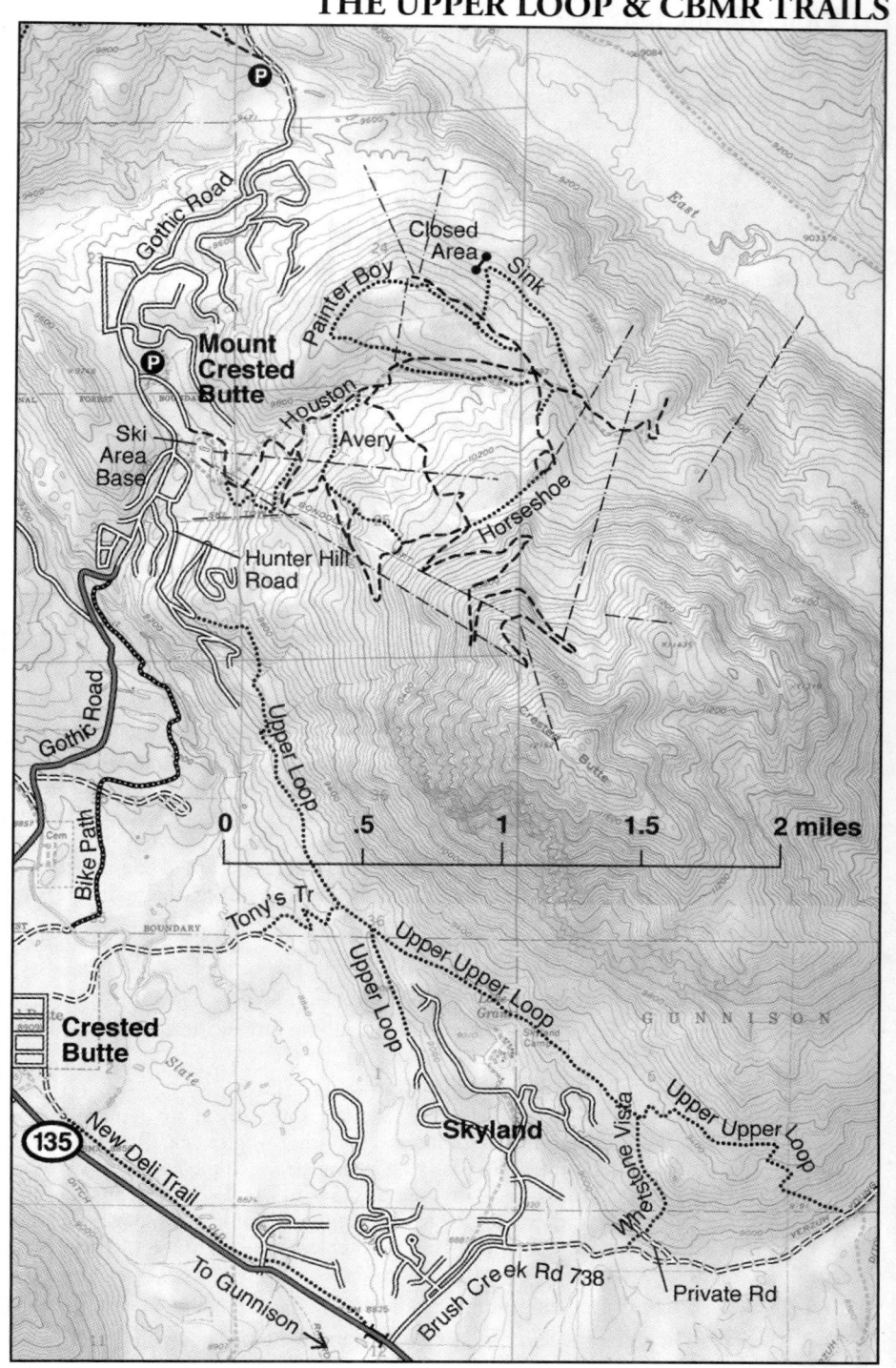

Gothic Road

P

Closed Area

Sink

Painter Boy

P

Mount Crested Butte

Houston

Avery

Horseshoe

Ski Area Base

Hunter Hill Road

Upper Loop

Gothic Road

Bike Path

| 0 | .5 | 1 | 1.5 | 2 miles |

Tony's Tr

Upper Upper Loop

Upper Loop

Upper Loop

G U N N I S O N

Crested Butte

Skyland

Whetstone Vista

Upper Upper Loop

135

New Deli Trail

Brush Creek Rd 738

Private Rd

To Gunnison

THE LOWER LOOP
Ride Information

See map page 18

Description: The Lower Loop is a short, mostly singletrack loop that starts right in the town of Crested Butte and has very little elevation gain. It has beautiful views of Paradise Divide and the Slate River Valley. It offers beginning singletrack riders and folks not yet used to the altitude a nice singletrack ride, but riders of all levels will enjoy the break from the big climbs here in the mountains. There's a nice overlook of Oh-Be-Joyful Creek on the Gunsight Bridge Loop at the far end. This is a great introduction to singletrack in the Crested Butte area, and also good for a short day. On the return to Crested Butte, there are several side trails near town, try any of them because they all lead right back to town. (With the exception of the Plunge, at mile 8.7 of the description.) The loop described here is easy intermediate. For an easier loop, ride out County Road 4 to Peanut Mine and continue on the trail until mile 4.3 of the description below, turn right and return to town on Slate River Road.

Distance: 9.9 mile loop, 1.7 miles of paved and dirt road and 7.2 miles of singletrack.

Time: 1-2 hours

Difficulty: Easy intermediate

Technical Skill: Easy intermediate.

Aerobic Effort: Low

Elevation: Top: 9,150' **Gain:** 475'

Season: Late May through October

Finding Route: Fairly easy. There are several unmarked trails between Kebler Pass and Peanut Lake Road, but these trails are close to town and it is easy to find your way back if you get off the main trail.

Map: Latitude 40 Crested Butte/Taylor Park Trails

Location: Start at the four-way stop at the corner of Elk Avenue and Sixth Street (Highway 135) in Crested Butte. There is plenty of parking behind the visitor center. If you have a dog or children that will go on the ride, there is a parking area on County Road 4 at the beginning of the ride. To get to the parking, drive west on Elk Avenue and turn right on First Street. Continue to Butte Avenue. Turn left and continue on to County Road 4 and another 1/10th of a mile to the parking area on the right.

Mileage Log:

0.0 From the four-way stop, ride north on Sixth Street toward the ski area. Please ride on the bike path or shoulder.

0.2 Turn left onto Butte Avenue and follow it all the way to the end and the start of County Road 4.

0.8 Arrive at the end of Butte Avenue and the start of County Road 4. Just past the homes and the start of the dirt road is an unmarked singletrack to the left. Take it and climb briefly to intersect another singletrack. Turn right and contour on this flat trail, and pass a steep singletrack to the left in 1/10th of a mile. Just keep heading north on the trails toward Paradise Divide if you want to avoid looking at these directions constantly. (Or ride out County Road 4 past Peanut Lake and Peanut Mine to intersect the beginning of the Lower Loop there.)

1.1 Begin to climb gradually alongside a fence.

1.2 Stay right along the fence, passing a singletrack to the left.

1.3   Top out and join another singletrack. Turn right and descend.

1.4   At the bottom of the hill stay left and continue out the valley toward Paradise Divide. The spur to the right connects to County Road 4.

2.2   Turn left on County Road 4 when the singletrack ends and ride straight through the mine.

2.4   Stay right, passing a private road on the left, then arrive at the beginning of the Lower Loop. Descend right and then go right or left at the fork. Left is wider and easier, and right is slightly longer and narrow. The trails join at the next junction.

2.8   Arrive at a four-way junction. Continue straight ahead on the flat Lower Trail.

3.3   Ride through a narrow rock area and past a bench, turn left and ride uphill between two tight trees. (Straight dead-ends at the Slate River.)

4.2   Turn left onto the gravel road.

4.3   Stay left as the road forks. (Right leads to the Gunsight Bridge and up to Slate River Road if you want to exit the easier way.)

4.4   Just as you enter the forest, turn right on the unmarked Gunsight Bridge (GB) loop singletrack.

4.9   After climbing a steep hill and riding up to the Oh-be-Joyful Creek overlook, turn left and head back on the return trail. It is directly across from the overlook. A trail also heads up the creek, but quickly becomes unrideable.

5.1   Stay right and climb two short hills, passing a building to the left and mining debris.

5.4   Turn left and ride downhill briefly on Gunsight Pass Road.

5.5   Turn right on the Upper Lower singletrack, by the BLM sign and stair/fence.

7.1   Arrive back at the four-way intersection of the Upper Lower and Lower. Ride straight ahead onto the narrow singletrack.

7.5   Back at the beginning of the Lower Loop. Continue through the mine.

7.8   Just after the cattleguard, turn right and head back the way you came on the singletrack.

8.7   Stay right at the intersection of two singletracks above the house. (You climbed up the left fork earlier.) Next, stay left, passing the Plunge Trail coming in on the right, then stay right at the next intersection. Ride straight ahead on the flat singletrack toward the aspens and below another house.

9.0   (approx. mileage) Cross a singletrack just in the aspens.

9.1   (approx. mileage) Cross a singletrack.

9.2   Arrive at Kebler Pass Road. Turn left and ride down the shoulder to town.

9.4   Turn left on First Street and ride back to Elk Avenue, turn right and continue to the visitor center.

9.9   Back to your car! 🚲

BIKE PATH TO THE UPPER LOOP
See map pages 18-19
Ride Information

Description: This is a short, fun trail right out of Crested Butte. The Upper Loop and Tony's Trail have beautiful views and some smooth, rolling singletrack. There are beautiful flowers along the entire loop early in the summer. It is a nice ride for those still acclimating to the altitude, or for a short afternoon loop, or for intermediates learning to ride singletrack. Ridden in reverse starting with Tony's Trail, The Upper Loop is great singletrack access to the Snodgrass Trail, Trail 401, and rides on the ski area. Turning right on the Upper Loop at the top of Tony's Trail offers singletrack access to Whetstone Vista, The Upper Upper Trail, and Brush Creek area rides (Strand Hill, Farris, Teocalli Ridge, Deer Creek.)

Distance: 7.2 mile loop: 2 miles of singletrack and 5.2 miles of bike path, paved road, and dirt road.

Time: 1-1½ hours

Difficulty: Intermediate

Technical Skill: Intermediate with short sections of expert rutted, rocky descent on the Upper Loop. Some of this rocky section is bypassed by a short section of smoother trail.

Aerobic Effort: Moderate

Elevation: Top: 9,450' **Gain:** 575'

Season: Late May through October

Finding Route: Easy

Maps: Latitude 40 Crested Butte/ Taylor Park Trails or Latitude 40 Aspen/Crested Butte/ Gunnison or National Geographic/Trails Illustrated Crested Butte/Pearl Pass

Location: Start at the four-way stop in Crested Butte at the corner of Elk Avenue and Highway 135 (6th Street.) There is a large public parking area here.

Mileage Log:

0.0 Ride toward Mount Crested Butte on Highway 135 (6th Street). Stay to the right on the bike path.

0.2 Turn right on Teocalli Avenue. Ride two blocks and onto the bike path that starts on the left. Follow it toward Mount Crested Butte, along the Slate River.

0.6 Turn left and cross a large bridge over the Slate River and continue on the concrete path. Cross a low wooden bridge over a marsh area and begin climbing toward the ski area.

1.2 Cross a private road and continue up the bike path toward the ski area.

2.7 The bike path crosses Gothic Road. Cross carefully and continue up the bike path.

3.1 Turn right, cross Gothic Road again, and ride up Hunter Hill Road.

3.2 Turn right again on the continuation of Hunter Hill Road. Follow this down past the condominiums and then up again.

3.8 On the next corner look for the signed Upper Loop Trail off to the right. Watch for other users, this trail is quite popular. When the trail splits, take the right if you want to avoid more technical areas. This is just a short bypass.

5.1 After a descent, arrive at the signed Tony's Trail, by a huge boulder. Turn right here and zip down through the meadows on this smooth trail.

5.8 Ride through the gate and reach the end of Tony's Trail. Turn right on the dirt road and ride back toward Crested Butte.

6.8 Ride onto the paved Elk Avenue and follow this back to the four-way stop.

7.2 Back to the four-way stop! 🚲

SKYLAND TO THE UPPER LOOP & TONY'S TRAIL
See map pages 18-19 ———————————————— **Ride Information**

Description: This is a short, easy singletrack loop right out of the town of Crested Butte. The Upper Loop has beautiful views and Tony's Trail has wonderful wildflowers for much of the summer. Tony's is a smooth, rolling singletrack descent. This is a good loop for those acclimating to the altitude or learning to ride singletrack. The trails in this area open fairly early for the Crested Butte area. Ridden in reverse, Tony's and the Upper Loop to Skyland are good access to the Brush Creek area rides (Strand Hill, Farris Creek, Teocalli Ridge and Deer Creek.)

Distance: 6.5 mile loop: 2.5 miles of pavement, 2 miles of singletrack, and 2 miles of dirt road.

Time: 1-1 ½ hours

Difficulty: Easy Intermediate

Technical Skill: Easy Intermediate

Aerobic Effort: Moderate

Elevation: Top: 9,150' **Gain:** 275'

Season: May through October

Finding Route: Easy

Maps: Latitude 40 Crested Butte/ Taylor Park Trails

Location: Start at the four-way stop at the corner of Elk Avenue and Highway 135 (6th Street) in Crested Butte. There is a large public parking lot behind the visitor center here.

Mileage Log:

0.0 Ride east on Elk Avenue away from the main downtown area. Turn right on 9th Street and follow it several blocks and past Red Lady Avenue and behind the school, where it turns to dirt. This dirt road eventually narrows to a singletrack that parallels the highway. Follow the singletrack over a private paved road and continue to the end.

2.0 Turn left on Highway 135 and cross the Slate River.

2.2 Turn left on Brush Creek Road 738. This turn is marked by the Crested Butte Country Club sign. Be sure to stay on the shoulder of this sometimes busy road.

2.7 Turn left on Skyland Drive.

SKYLAND TO THE UPPER LOOP & TONY'S TRAIL
Ride Information

3.1 Turn left on Country Club Road and follow it to the dead-end.

3.7 Start up the signed Upper Loop at the dead end.

4.1 Turn left at the intersection, staying on the Upper Loop.

4.4 Arrive at the signed intersection with Tony's Trail, right by a big boulder. Ride down the mostly smooth switchbacks through the sage meadows. There are nice flowers here all summer.

5.1 Ride through a gate, and to the end of Tony's. Turn right on the dirt road and ride back toward Crested Butte.

6.1 Ride onto the paved section of Elk Avenue and follow it straight back to the four-way stop.

6.5 Back to the four-way stop. ☙

TONY'S TRAIL, THE UPPER UPPER LOOP, WHETSTONE VISTA
Ride Information ———————————— *See map pages 18-19*

Description: These are short, very nice trails through sage meadows and aspen groves, right out of Crested Butte. There are many ways to link up these few trails, as all are good riding in either direction. The first loop option starts with a short dirt road spin and an enjoyable, moderate climb up Tony's Trail and the Upper Loop to the Upper Upper Loop. Tony's is loaded with flowers most of the summer. The Upper Upper Trail begins as a moderate singletrack climb through the aspens, but becomes more and more technical as it climbs. The entire trail is rideable for expert level riders, but challenging! Descend a short, steep section on The Upper Upper Trail, then spin home on Brush Creek Road to finish off the loop, or turn right to climb Whetstone Vista back to the Upper Upper for more singletrack. Whetstone Vista is a bumpy, but fun climb and a great way to return to Crested Butte on singletrack. A second loop option is to turn right at mile 3.7 on the Whetstone Vista Trail and skip the most technical part of the climb on The Upper Upper Trail. Whetstone Vista is a bumpy but moderate descent. From here return on Brush Creek Road or ride through Skyland to the Upper Loop to return to Crested Butte. Another option that many folks prefer is to ride the Upper Upper in the reverse of what is described here, either as its own loop from Brush Creek Road or after riding Strand Hill, Farris Creek, Teocalli Ridge, Trail 409 or Trail 409.5. It is a challenging but short grunt to the top, and a fun, technical descent. All these trails are lower and face mostly south, so they dry out more quickly in the spring or after rain than most of the other Crested Butte Trails. They also are nice in the fall as they travel through large aspen groves. Have fun exploring!

Distance: 9 mile loop: 5-8 miles of singletrack and 1-4 miles of dirt and paved roads.

Time: 1-2 hours

Difficulty: Tony's Trail is intermediate, the Upper Upper is expert, Whetstone Vista is advanced intermediate.

Technical Skill: Tony's Trail is intermediate, the Upper Upper is Expert, Whetstone Vista is advanced intermediate. The Upper Upper is rocky and technical, Whetstone Vista is quite rocky also, but more bumpy than technical.

TONY'S TRAIL, THE UPPER UPPER LOOP, WHETSTONE VISTA

Ride Information

Aerobic Effort: Moderate, high for a short distance on the Upper Upper Loop.

Elevation: Upper Upper: Top: 9,400' **Gain:** 575'

           Whetstone Vista: Top: 9,300' **Gain:** 450"

Season: May through October

Finding Route: Easy

Maps: Latitude 40 Crested Butte/Taylor Park Trails is the best; The 2002 Alpineer Bike Trails Map or The 5th edition Latitude 40 for Aspen/Crested Butte/Gunnison or the 2001 National Geographic/Trails Illustrated Crested Butte/Pearl Pass are good.

Location: Start at the four-way stop in Crested Butte at the corner of Elk Avenue and Highway 135 (6th Street.) There is a large public parking area here behind the visitor center.

Mileage Log:

0.0   Ride east on Elk Avenue, away from the main business area of town. Follow the street as it turns to a dirt road, crosses a big off-angle cattleguard, and curves around to cross the Slate River.

1.4   Turn left on signed Tony's Trail, shortly before the end of the road. Go through the gate and close it behind you. Climb up the gradual switchbacks through the sage.

2.1   Turn right at the T-intersection with the Upper Loop.

2.4   Turn left at the signed intersection of the Upper Upper Loop and begin climbing. (The Upper Loop, right, continues down to Country Club Drive in Skyland. This is the easier option to Brush Creek Road.)

3.7   Stay left and pass the Whetstone Vista Trail. The most challenging part of the trail is still to come! (Or turn right and descend Whetstone Vista Trail to Brush Creek Road.)

4.4   Summit of the Upper Upper!

5.0   End of the Upper Upper Trail on Brush Creek Road. Turn right and ride toward Crested Butte.

5.7   Pass the Whetstone Vista Trail, staying on Brush Creek Road. (Or turn right and climb back to the Upper Upper Trail, turn left and continue back to the Upper Loop, turn right and retrace your tracks back to Tony's Trail and Crested Butte.)

6.9   Turn right on Highway 135 and cross the Slate River. Look for the singletrack on the right that will take you back to Crested Butte.

9.1   Back to the four-way stop. 澶

CRESTED BUTTE MOUNTAIN RESORT TRAILS
Ride Information ———————————————— *See map pages 18-19*

Description: The trails at Crested Butte Mountain Resort were built especially for mountain biking and are fun, easy to link loops. Most of the trails are good ridden in either direction, with the exception of Hard Corp, Avery, Buckley, and Waterfall. There are nice views from the trails on the ski area, and lots of aspens make it a nice fall color ride. Because of recent development at the ski area, it has lost some of its' best trails and will also lose the Sink Trail, but there are still a few fun trails for a day's riding. Crested Butte Mountain Resort is undergoing massive changes, on-mountain and at the base area. They are awaiting Forest Service approval of plans, including adding many more trails. The plans include cross-country, downhill and freeride additions. This summer the resort plans to continue the bike program so the lifts will be running, the trails will be marked, and the Pinnacle and Wildflower Rush races will be held. Stay posted for upcoming changes. If you are starting this ride from Crested Butte, I suggest riding the bike path or Tony's and the Upper Loop to the ski area to avoid traffic on busy Gothic Road and to get a little more riding in. Add 45 minutes-1½ hours and 6½ miles roundtrip if you ride from town, depending on the route you take. The Mountain Express Bus will carry your bike up to the base area as well, check the posted bus schedule at the four-way stop on the corner of Elk Avenue and Highway 135 (6th Street) for pickup times, or call 349-7318 for more information. Read ahead through several mileage points at intersections to avoid a lot of stopping.

Distance: 6 mile loop, 3 miles singletrack, 3 miles dirt road.

Time: 1 hour

Difficulty: Intermediate to expert, depending on the trail you descend.

Technical Skill: Intermediate to expert

Aerobic Effort: Moderate

Elevation: Top: 10,650' **Gain:** 1,300'

Season: Mid-June through October

Finding Route: Moderate, well signed in the summer. It is hard to get lost from the ski area, you always end up at the bottom.

Maps: Latitude 40 Crested Butte/Taylor Park Trails, CBMR Summer Trails Map.

Location: The ski area base is located at the town center of Mount Crested Butte. To get here, I suggest riding up or taking the bus. The area is under construction currently and it is difficult to find a spot to park. Make your way around all the construction to the base of the lifts.

Mileage Log:

0.0 Begin riding up Houston, the dirt road that traverses the base of the slopes. It starts by the Brown Labrador Pub. Pass a couple singletracks and road spurs, continue climbing the main road until the first major fork.

0.6 Turn left at the road fork, and continue climbing. Pass a faint singletrack that cuts to the right, then more prominent singletracks to the left and right and descend a little.

0.8 Pass the Avery singletrack on the right, just past a forested area.

1.1 Pass the Painter Boy Lift on the right, stay left on the road.

1.2 Turn left onto the Painter Boy Trail and cut across the ski slope and under the Painter Boy lift. Climb.

1.6 Stay right, passing a less used spur singletrack to the left.

2.0 The trail forks, turn right. This is just before a doubletrack. Follow this smooth singletrack into the woods.

2.3 The singletrack forks, stay right.

2.4 End of the singletrack on the road. Turn right and ride briefly on the road to the four-way intersection. Ride straight across and climb. (Straight across and to the right is a singletrack that leads back down to the Painter Boy Lift. Take this for an intermediate descent that ends at the base of the Painter Boy Lift.)

2.6 Pass a singletrack on the left. Continue climbing on road.

2.8 Turn right at a road fork and climb.

3.1 Turn left onto a road, just before climbing up to the Keystone lift tower.

3.2 Turn right onto the rocky Horseshoe singletrack, just inside the forest.

3.4 Intersect Aspen Park Road on a corner and junction with a side road from the right. Ride straight ahead and down. Be aware of downhillers crossing the road in 2/10ths of a mile on The Waterfall Trail. (Or take this shortcut to Twister Lift and The Hard Corp Trail. Waterfall has a short section of walking for most riders.)

4.0 Turn right at the next road intersection and descend to the Twister Lift base.

4.2 Just before the lift, cut sharp left onto a singletrack in the dark woods. This is a fun and challenging descent on Hard Corp.

4.5 Turn right on the dirt road at the bottom of Hard Corp and ride around a corner to the next singletrack on the right.

4.6 Turn right on the Avery Trail.

4.9 Turn left at the fork in the trail just before the creek, then cross a bridge.

5.0 End on the Houston service road, turn left and continue descending. Pass two singletracks, left and right, as you ride up a short hill and straight ahead onto a flat singletrack on the left side of the road. It intersects the Aspen service road immediately, turn left and climb a few feet on the road. Turn right onto the Buckley singletrack. Descend this fast, switchbacking trail.

5.6 Stay right with the switchback and continue down the mountain. Right leads to a dead-end. Stay with the singletrack all the way to the base.

5.7 Stay left with the singletrack.

5.8 Cross a service road and continue to the base area.

6.1 Back to the bottom of the ski area. 🚲

THE GREEN LAKE TRAIL
Ride Information See map pages 18-19, 54-55

Description: The Green Lake Trail is a challenging, nearly all singletrack ride right out of Crested Butte. It begins with meandering narrow singletrack through beautiful aspen groves. The second half is a continuous, often technical and steep climb to Green Lake that will challenge even strong climbers. The Green Lake is a beautiful spot, right below Mount Axtell, perfect for a chilly swim on a hot day. Descent is by the same route. See Carbon and Green Lake Trail for a much longer loop that includes the Green Lake Trail.

Distance: 10.8 mile out and back, 7.4 miles of singletrack, 3.4 miles of dirt and paved roads.

Time: 2-3 hours.

Difficulty: Expert

Technical Skill: Expert.

Elevation: Top: 10,613' **Gain:** 1850'

Season: Mid-June through mid-October

Finding Route: Moderate.

Maps: Latitude 40 Crested Butte/Taylor Park Trails or the 5th edition Latitude 40 Aspen/ Crested Butte/Gunnison.

Location: Start at the four-way stop at the corner of Elk Avenue and Highway 135(6th Street.) There is a large public parking area here behind the visitor center.

Mileage Log:

0.0   Ride west up Elk Avenue to 2nd Street, and turn left. Ride straight across Sopris and Whiterock Avenues to the Nordic Center.

0.5   Right behind the Nordic Center building is an old road climbing up the hill to the left. Follow this to the top.

0.7   Turn right onto the dirt road (Journey's End Road) and ride past a few houses.

1.0   Turn left into a parking area. A green sign marks the beginning of the Green Lake Trail. Start up the switchbacks through the aspens.

2.0   Turn left onto a steep doubletrack.

2.3   Turn right onto the singletrack (The road is blocked off.)

2.7   Turn right on Trapper's Crossing dirt road. This is a private road, please be respectful. Follow this gradual road down and around a corner, then up until you see the green sign marking the continuation of the Green Lake Trail.

3.1   Turn left on the Green Lake Trail. Here the trail begins to climb more steeply, and is quite continuous.

4.9   Cross an unmarked singletrack. Continue straight ahead. (Left leads to the Carbon Trail and right leads to Splains Gulch and Kebler Pass Road via a rocky trail then a road. See Carbon to Green Lake for more information on a left turn here.)

5.4   Reach the Green Lake. When ready to return, retrace your tracks back to Crested Butte.

10.8   Back to the four-way stop. ☁•

TRAIL 401 and TRAIL 403

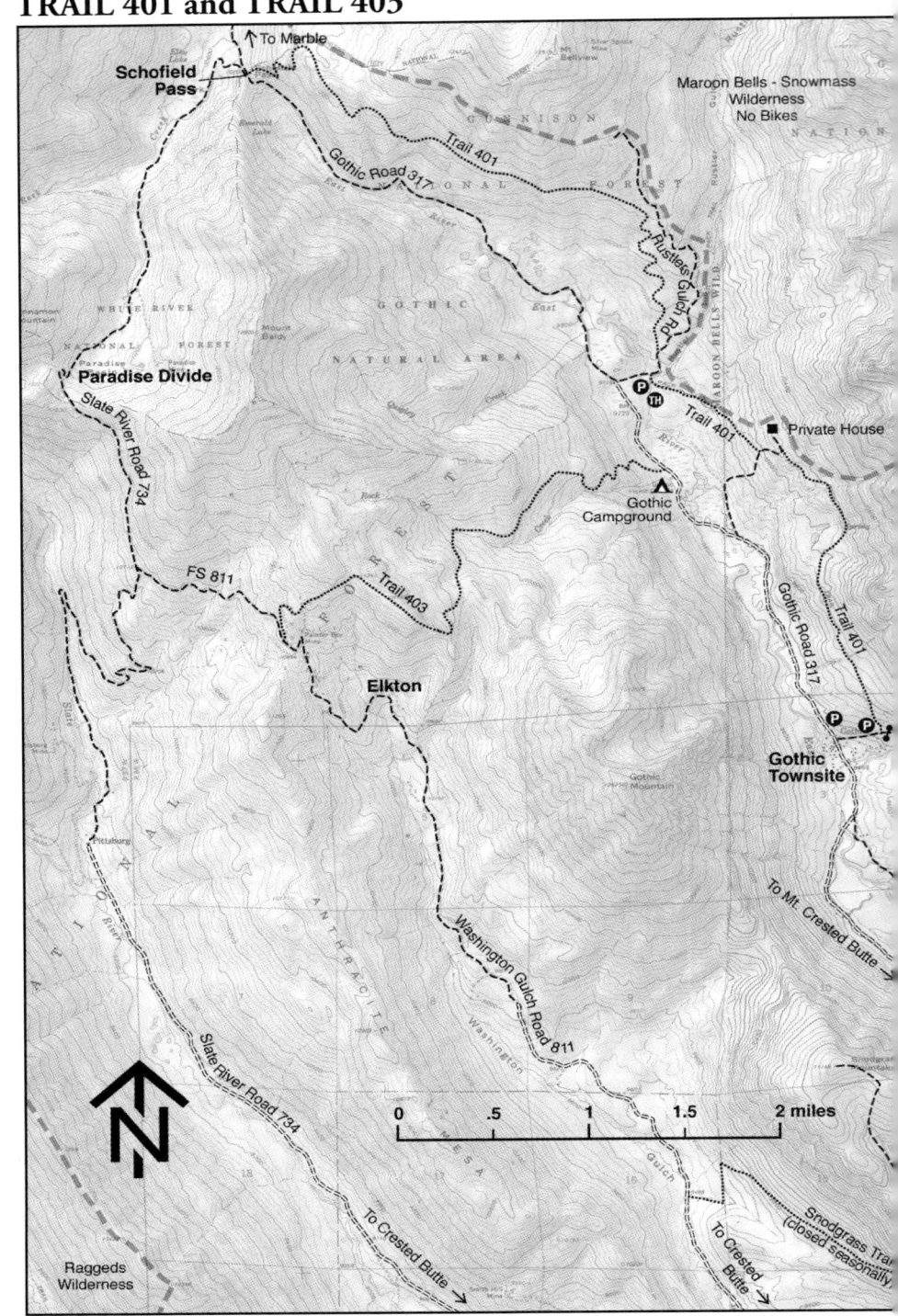

Description: Trail 401 is probably the most famous trail in Crested Butte, and for good reason. This is a classic ride with smooth, fast singletrack, spectacular views, and lots of tall wildflowers in late June and July. Most of the climbing is on the dirt Gothic Road and moderate, but the last mile of the road and the beginning of the singletrack are steep and challenging, especially because of the altitude. The descent is all singletrack and winds gradually around Belleview and Avery Mountains, offering breathtaking views for nearly the entire ride. The second half of Trail 401 offers a smooth climb through aspen groves and flower filled meadows and a smooth, speedy descent through the aspens. The second half is a great intermediate option by itself or for those riders not accustomed to the altitude or such big climbs. Both sections are good riding in reverse, the lower section an intermediate ride, the upper section being challenging but all rideable for expert level riders. The upper section can be ridden in reverse a couple weeks before the northern section of the climb off Schofield Pass is open in the early summer, see option 2, below. The lower section opens earlier as well. The loop described here is from town, but riders can drive to The Copper Lake Trailhead and shorten the ride by 19 miles of dirt and paved road, see option 1, below. The mileage for this option is in parenthesis starting at mile 9.5. Don't miss Trail 401 on your trip to Crested Butte!

Distance: 33.4 mile loop from town: 8.4 miles of singletrack, 10 miles of pavement and cement bike path, 15 miles of dirt road. 14.4 mile loop from the Copper Creek Trailhead, 6 miles of dirt road and 8.4 miles of singletrack. The Mountain Express public bus can be taken to Mount Crested Butte to shorten the ride by 3 miles. (For more information on the bus, call 349-7318 or check the four-way stop for pickup times.)

Time: 3½-6 hours from town, 2-3 hours from the Copper Creek Trailhead.

Difficulty: Advanced intermediate

Technical Skill: Advanced intermediate

Aerobic Effort: High

Elevation: Top: 11,350' **Gain:** 3,300'
    Gain from Copper Creek Trailhead: 2,180'

Season: Late June - early October for the loop. In big snow years, the north part of the trail may not be melted out until July. Check with a local bike shop before riding it to find out trail conditions.

Finding Route: Easy, 401 is marked at all junctions.

Maps: Latitude 40 Crested Butte/Taylor Park Trails or 5th edition Latitude 40 Aspen/Crested Butte/Gunnison or the Alpineer Bike Trail Map

Location: Start at the four-way stop in Crested Butte at the corner of Elk Avenue and Highway 135 (6th Street.) There is a large public parking lot here behind the visitor center.

Mileage Log: *Note: The numbers in the parenthesis ( ) starting at mile 9.5 below, are the mileage points if riders start at the Copper Lake Trailhead.*

0.0   Ride north toward Mount Crested Butte on Highway 135 (6th street.)

0.2   Turn right on Teocalli Avenue. Ride 2/10ths of a mile and turn left onto the signed dirt bike path. Follow this along the Slate River.

0.6   Turn left and cross a bridge over the Slate River. The cement path swings around to the left and toward Mount Crested Butte. Cross a flat wooden bridge over a marsh and start climbing.

TRAIL 401
Ride Information

1.2   Cross a private road, and continue climbing straight ahead on the bike path.

2.7   Junction with Gothic Road. Cross carefully and continue up the bike path until it ends, then continue up the road. Continue on Gothic Road all the way to Schofield Pass (11 more miles past the ski area.)

5.2   Pass the Snodgrass trailhead on your left. From here the road levels, then descends about 3 miles to cross the East River.

8.9   Ride through the town of Gothic and then climb and descend a short hill.

9.5   (0.0) Pass the Copper Creek Trailhead. Continue (or begin riding if you drove out) on Gothic Road 317, riding through the mostly level valley and crossing the East River again.

11.0   (1.5) Pass Washington Gulch Trailhead and the end of Trail 403 on the left.

11.6   (2.1) Pass Rustlers Gulch Road on the right. The climbing becomes steeper now, with small breaks.

14.0   (4.5) After riding through a narrow pass that often holds snow late into the summer, descend a short distance and then ride up again. Emerald Lake is below to the left. Just a short climb more to the top of the road.

14.8   (5.3) Reach the top of Schofield Pass. Turn right on Trail 401 across from the Schofield Pass sign and continue climbing. Look for the Maroon Bells when you ride into meadows up higher.

16.3   (6.8) Summit of the upper section of Trail 401, and a wonderful spot to eat lunch and view all the surrounding peaks. From here, head right and descend. (Left leads to the Maroon Bells Wilderness Boundary.) This is a beautiful section of smooth singletrack with great views and lots of wildflowers! There are a few technical sections, so be aware.

18.5   (9.0) (approx. mileage) Enter the dark woods, cross a rutted section, then ride down a rocky hill and begin more switchbacks. The Rustlers Gulch Road is just to your left as you descend, stay right with the singletrack. This is great fun through the aspens, and in late summer the plant life is nearly as tall as you. Be alert, as this is a popular trail with both people and animals.

20.4   (10.9) End of the upper section of Trail 401. Turn right and descend Rustlers Gulch Road for 2/10ths of a mile. When the road flattens out, look for the signed continuation of Trail 401 to the left, just before the road crosses a wide creek. (If you choose not to ride the second half of 401, continue across the creek and rejoin Gothic Road in 1/10th of a mile.)

20.6   (11.1) Turn left onto the continuation of Trail 401. Ride into the woods and cross a side creek on a wooden bridge, and begin climbing through the meadows.

21.1   (11.6) Cross another creek on a log footbridge, and continue climbing through the forest.

21.8   (12.3) Turn left and climb as the trail ends on a dirt road. Soon the red rock face of Avery Peak comes into view. (There is a small, but hard to see, sign to your left on this turn.)

22.0   (12.5) Trail 401 splits off to the right and climbs. An old sign points toward Virginia Basin and Trail 401. (The road continues left through a fence and to a house.) Cross a rock slide shortly and climb a bit more, then begin a mostly smooth, but occasionally rocky descent through open meadows and aspen groves.

23.4 (13.9) End of the second section of Trail 401 at the Copper Creek/Trailriders Trailhead. Turn right on the road and descend.

24.0 (14.5) Arrive at Gothic Road. Turn left, retracing your tracks back to Crested Butte if you rode out.

33.4 Back to the four-way stop (via the bike path.)

Option 1: To shorten the ride by 19 miles, drive to The Copper Creek Trailhead (mile 9.5) and park here. Ride Trail 401 as described from here. Mileage points for this option are in parenthesis.

Option 2: To ride Trail 401 as an out and back from Rustlers Gulch, ride or drive to mile 11.6 and park. (Or there is better parking at Copper Creek Trailhead, mile 9.5.) Turn right and ride 1/10th of a mile and cross a wide creek, go left and climb steeply up the road for 2/10th of a mile to the signed Trail 401. Turn left and ride up as far as the trail is dry, then turn around and ride back down. This is a challenging and all rideable singletrack climb to do before the northern section of the trail is melted out. This is not a great option once the trail is open from the top because of the many fast riders coming down. Ride the second half of Trail 401 either before or after the upper section, or both! 🚲

See map pages 30, 18-19

Description: Trail 403 is popular with locals for its descent: steep and technical in spots and fast and smooth in others. The entire ride boasts wonderful wildflowers in the summer and wonderful views of the Ruby Range, the Maroon Bells, and Gothic Mountain from the top of the road climb and the singletrack. Later in the summer the flowers on the descending switchbacks are over your head as you swoop down the hillside. The loop combines a long road climb up Washington Gulch that becomes quite steep at the end, a moderate singletrack climb and challenging descent, and a long, fast road spin back to Crested Butte. The ride is fairly quick for as long as it is because of the amount of road. For more singletrack, add on the Snodgrass Trail at the beginning or end, or ride Trail 401 or Deer Creek after descending to Gothic Road. See options, below.

Distance: 26 mile loop from town: 4 miles of singletrack, 9 miles of pavement and concrete bike path, 13 miles of dirt and forest road.

Time: 2½-4 hour loop

Difficulty: Expert

Technical Skill: Expert. Steep, rutted and technical descent.

Aerobic Effort: High

Elevation: Top: 11,400' **Gain:** 2,900'

Season: July through September

Finding Route: Easy

TRAIL 403
Ride Information

Maps: Latitude 40 Crested Butte/Taylor Park Trails or 5th edition Latitude 40 for Aspen/ Crested Butte/Gunnison

Location: Begin at the four-way stop in Crested Butte at the corner of Elk Avenue and Highway 135 (6th Street.) There is a large public parking lot here behind the visitor center.

Mileage Log:

0.0 Ride north toward Mount Crested Butte on Highway 135 (6th Street.)

0.2 Turn right on Teocalli Avenue. Ride 2/10ths of a mile and turn left onto the signed dirt bike path. Follow this along the Slate River.

0.6 Turn left and cross a bridge over the Slate River. The cement path swings around to the left and toward Mount Crested Butte. Cross a flat wooden bridge over a marsh and start climbing.

1.2 Cross a private road, and continue climbing straight ahead on the bike path.

2.5 Turn left on a faint dirt trail and ride up to Gothic Road. This trail is after the bike path descends to a level area, and the path comes right up next to Gothic Road. Cross Gothic Road, turn left briefly then turn right on Washington Gulch Road. Ride gradually up the valley. Pass Meridian Lake on the left and the Meridian Lake subdivision on both sides of the road.

5.7 Pass the Snodgrass Trail on the right.

10.2 Pass the Elkton Cabins on the right. The toughest part of the climb is just after you pass the last cabin.

10.6 At the summit of road climb is a parking area and campsite to the left. Just past this, turn right on the signed Trail 403 singletrack and begin climbing. (If you begin to go down on the road, you have gone too far.) The trail climbs gradually, goes through an old mine site, and then switches back twice.

11.3 The trail climbs steeply, then turns right for a more gradually contouring reroute. The wildflowers are quite beautiful here in July!

11.6 Swing right at the ridge where beautiful views open before you and continue climbing. There is a nice view and lunch spot off to the left at the summit of the singletrack, just ¼ mile farther.

12.0 Summit of singletrack climb. After a break, continue straight ahead on the singletrack, and down some loose, steep switchbacks. Ride down through dark sections of forest, across streams, and through beautiful meadows. The last section of the trail starts with very rutted and steep singletrack, and descends several switchbacks through plants as tall as you!

14.8 Reach the end of Trail 403. Ride through a campsite, turn right on Gothic Road and spin back toward Crested Butte. (Or turn left to ride Trail 401, see options, below.)

16.9 Ride through Gothic. Slow, pedestrians and traffic! Begin a gradual climb after crossing the East River on the south end of Gothic.

20.6 Pass the Snodgrass Trail on the right, and roll down to the pavement. Continue downhill through Mount Crested Butte (or ride the Snodgrass Trail).

23.1   Turn left onto the bike path just before a sharp corner.

25.8   Back to the four-way stop.

Option 1: Combine Trails 403 and 401 for a big day of climbing (4,800' total.) After descending to Gothic Road at the end of Trail 403, turn left and climb up to the summit of Schofield Pass (just over 3 ½ miles) to Trail 401. Turn right and follow the trail description for Trail 401 from mile 14.8, all the way back to the Copper Creek Trailhead and down to Gothic Road. Turn left and spin back to Crested Butte. This adds 11.5 miles and 2 hours to your ride. Or just ride the second half of Trail 401 after riding Trail 403, a much easier option: Again turn left when you reach Gothic Road, and ride 6/10ths of a mile to Rustlers Gulch Road and turn right. Ride 1/10th of a mile, cross the wide creek and turn right onto signed Trail 401. This adds 2 miles and ½ hour to your ride.

Option 2: Add the Snodgrass Trail to your ride for a little more singletrack. You can ride it from Gothic Road to Washington Gulch in either the beginning or the end of the ride. This adds 3.4 miles and about ¾ hour to the ride if ridden in the beginning and 3 miles and ½ hour if ridden at the end. 🚲

Trail 403

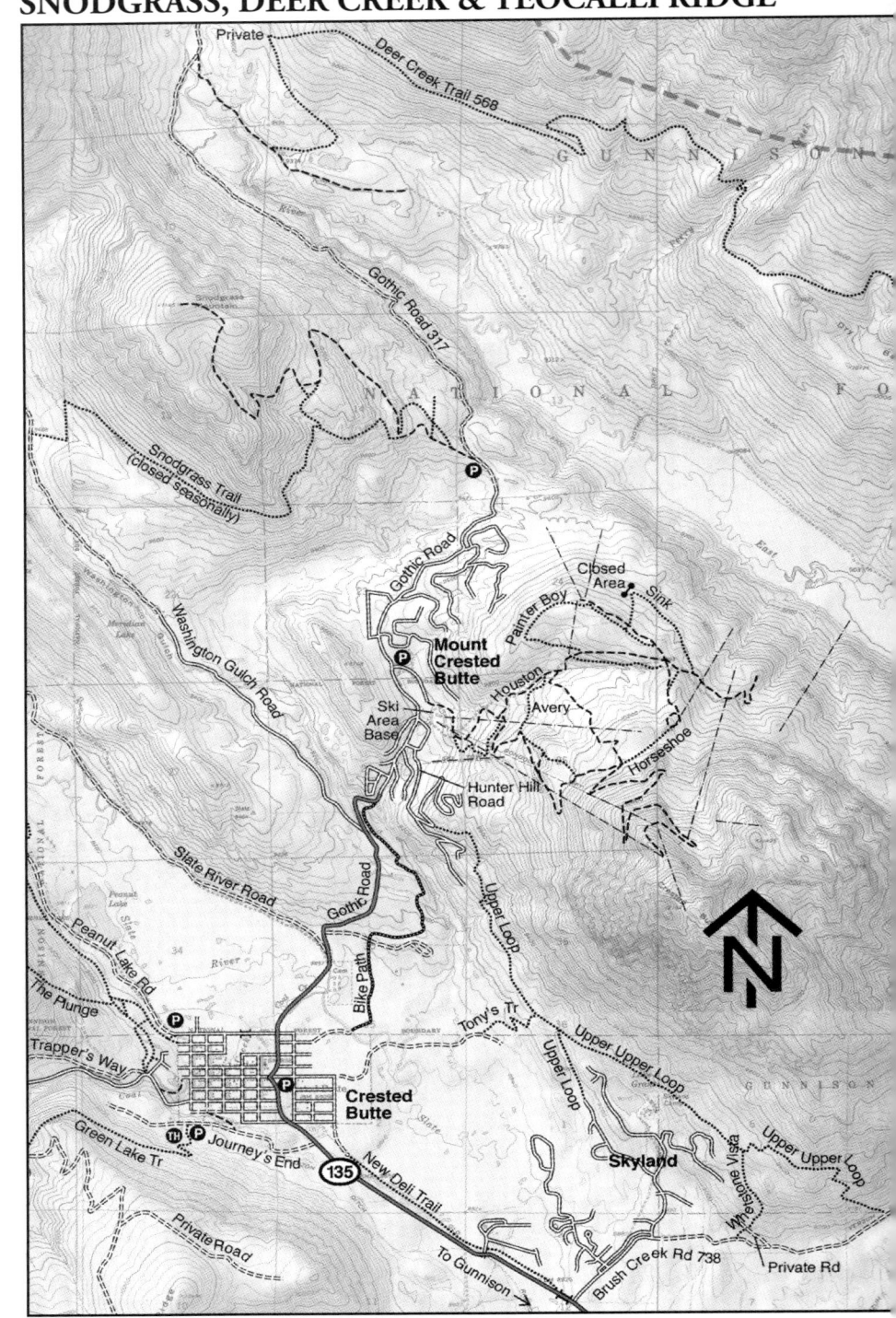

CANAL, STRAND HILL, FARRIS CREEK & 402 TRAILS

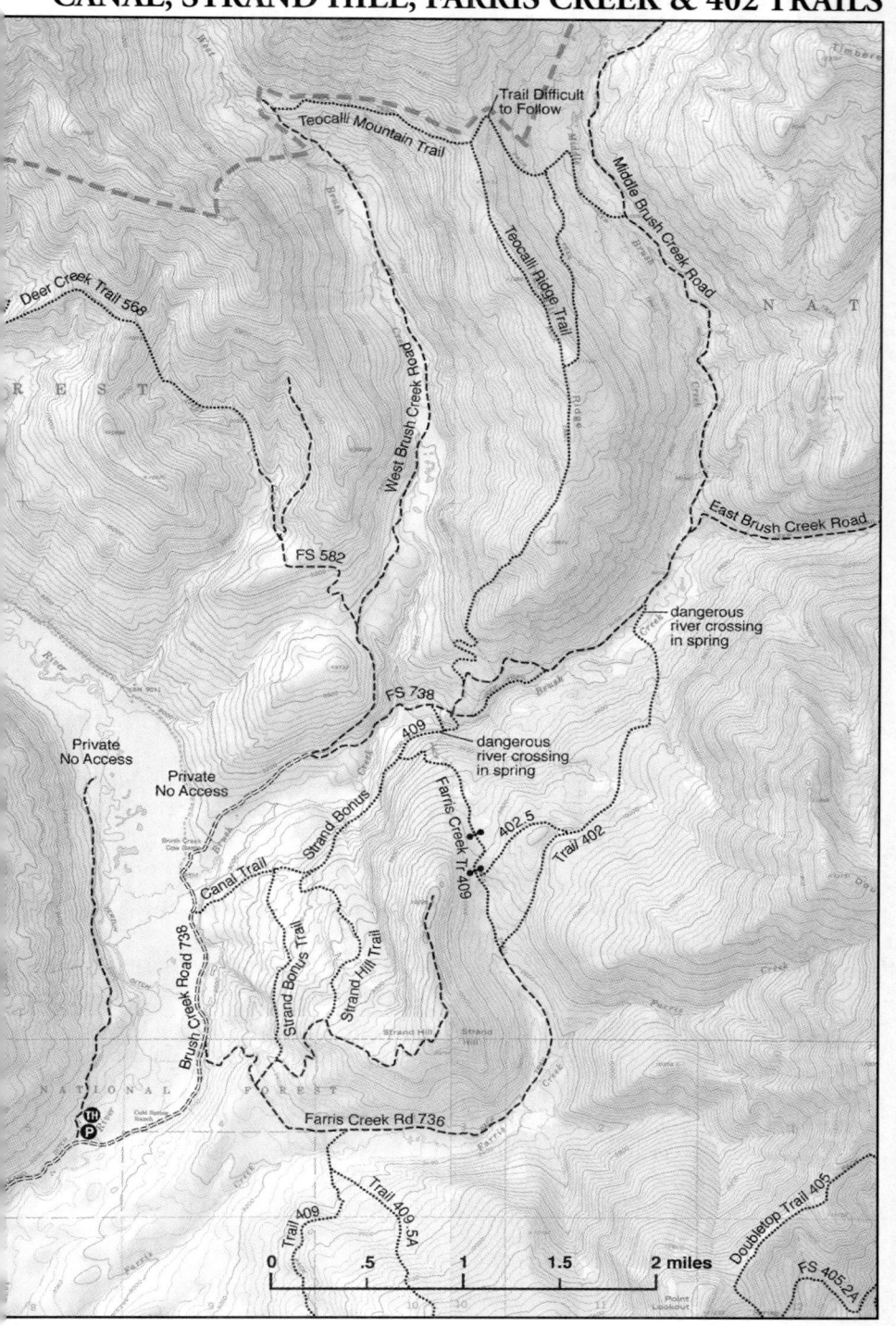

SNODGRASS TRAIL
Ride Information

Description: The Snodgrass Trail is a very beautiful intermediate ride through the aspens and high altitude meadows, right out of Mount Crested Butte. It is quite popular. The trail is a great short ride by itself, or link it up with the Upper Loop, the ski area, Trail 403, Trail 401 or Deer Creek for a longer day. Mid-summer the lupine and other wildflowers crowd the trail as you swoop along the smooth, winding singletrack. Shorten the ride from Crested Butte by taking the Mountain Express public bus up to Mount Crested Butte (for information call 349-7318 or check the bus stop at the four-way stop for pickup times.) Snodgrass is just as much fun and about the same exertion ridden in reverse (Enjoy it both directions for a nice out and back.) Some sections of the trail have some tree roots, the first climb is steep but quite short, and a couple short sections of the trail are sloping and tricky.

Distance: 13 mile loop: 3.5 miles of singletrack, 4.2 miles of dirt road, 7.3 miles of pavement and cement bike path.

Time: 1½-2½ hours

Difficulty: Intermediate

Technical Skill: Intermediate

Aerobic Effort: Moderate

Elevation: Top: 10,000' **Gain:** 1,300'

Season: The Snodgrass Trail is usually open mid-May or when the trail dries out, and closes around mid-August. It is closed seasonally due to private access. Please respect the closure so we can continue to ride the trail.

Finding Route: Easy. All junctions are marked.

Maps: Latitude 40 Crested Butte/Taylor Park Trails or the 5th edition Latitude 40 Aspen/ Crested Butte/Gunnison or the Alpineer Bike Trail Map.

Location: Start at the four-way stop in Crested Butte at the corner of Elk Avenue and Highway 135 (6th Street.) There is a large public parking lot here behind the visitor center.

Mileage Log:

0.0   Start riding north toward the ski area on 6th Street (6th Street becomes Gothic Road.) Stay on the shoulder.

0.2   Turn right on Teocalli Avenue. Ride 2/10ths of a mile and turn left onto the signed dirt bike path. Follow this along the Slate River.

0.6   Turn left and ride over the Slate River on a large wooden bridge. Cross a marsh on a long wooden bridge and continue toward the ski area on the concrete path.

1.2   Cross a private road and continue straight ahead on the bike path.

2.7   The bike path crosses Gothic Road. Cross carefully and continue up the bike path through the town of Mount Crested Butte. Cross the road again near the ski area to continue on the path, then ride up the road when the path ends.

4.8   End of pavement. Continue riding on Gothic Road.

5.2   The Snodgrass Trail is on the left just before crossing the forest service boundary. It will be posted here if it is open or closed. Cross the stair/fence if open, and start riding up the steep dirt doubletrack.

5.3   Unmarked singletrack to the right, by an old shelter. Stay with the road or see option, below, for information on this trail that leads up to the start of the Snodgrass singletrack.

5.5   Take the unmarked singletrack shortcut on the left or stay on the road.

5.9   Cross a stair/fence and ride straight ahead onto the signed Snodgrass singletrack as the road turns right. Some short, steep climbs lead to the next intersection and a nice view spot.

6.4   End the most difficult section of climbing on the trail at this intersection. Stay left and descend and cross a creek. Roll through the meadows and aspens. Caution, once you start a short, steep downhill section less than 1/2 mile past this intersection, be alert for a gate that is occasionally CLOSED. The trail continues to wind around Snodgrass Mountain through the aspens.

7.3   Stay right on the main trail, passing a spur on the left.

8.4   Cross over a fence, then head left along the fenceline.

8.8   The singletrack ends. Turn left on Washington Gulch Road and ride back toward town.

12.0   Cross Gothic Road and ride left briefly on the road to intersect a faint trail that leads to the bike path. Turn right on the path and return to Crested Butte.

14.5   Back to the four-way stop.

Option: When you begin the dirt road climb toward the Snodgrass Trail, about 1/10th of a mile up there is a singletrack to the right, at mile 5.3. There is an old cabin at the turn. This leads to a collection of singletracks, with one of them leading back to the Snodgrass singletrack at the top. If you have a good sense of where you are going and decide to take this trail, follow it as it contours around the hillside, cross a small creek, and take the second left up through the meadow. (If you end up on the lower trail heading down and toward Gothic Mountain, go back up and left for the correct trail.) Once the trail enters the aspens it goes to the right, and then switchbacks to the left. Follow this up steeply, stay left at a split and ride parallel to the fenceline and dirt road. This trail ends just across the road from the signed Snodgrass singletrack. It is easier to follow in reverse on the way down if you ride the Snodgrass Trail from the other direction. Look for it just after the trail ends and you cross the fence. It is across the road in the aspens on the left. ᠔ᢙ

THE CANAL TRAIL
Ride Information

See map pages 36-37

Description: The Canal Trail is a smooth, mostly easy introduction to singletrack near Crested Butte. It rolls through grassy meadows, wildflowers, and sagebrush and has nice views of the East River Valley. Riders can go as far as they like and return the same way, or continue on to do a loop that returns via Brush Creek Road. The loop is not safe to do when Brush Creek is high (typically until mid to late June.) The loop is fun in reverse.

Distance: Up to 7.8 miles, out and back or loop. 3-6 miles of road, 2-4 miles of singletrack.

Time: 1-2 hours.

Difficulty: Beginner-Intermediate, depending on how far you go on the singletrack.

Technical Skill: Beginner-Intermediate

Aerobic Effort: Low

Elevation: Top: 9,150'-9,190' **Gain:** 450'-600'

Season: June through October

Finding Route: Easy

Maps: Latitude 40 Crested Butte/Taylor Park or Latitude 40 Aspen/Crested Butte/Gunnison or Alpineer Trails map.

Location: Park at the Brush Creek Trailhead. To get here, ride or drive two miles south of Crested Butte on Highway 135 and turn left onto Brush Creek Road 738, just after crossing the Slate River. Continue 2.5 more miles to the Brush Creek Trailhead, on the left, just before crossing the East River.

Mileage Log:

0.0   Turn left out of the parking area onto Brush Creek Road. Descend to cross the East River.

1.1   Stay on Brush Creek Road, passing Farris Creek Road that turns off fairly steeply to the right. Descend a short hill.

1.6   In an open meadow, turn right onto the unmarked Canal Trail. The trail is a little hard to see because of tall grass. Immediately cross a big canal. The first hill is short and steep, but after this the trail is gradual and rolls along sagebrush hillsides.

2.6   Stay left, passing the Strand Bonus Trail coming in on the right. (The Strand Bonus Trail is a fun way to climb up to Strand Hill, but it is more advanced as a climb.)

2.7   Stay left, passing the Strand Hill Trail coming in on the right. This is a good place for beginners to turn around as the trail becomes more technical, unless you don't mind walking a few short sections. If you continue, descend a couple hills and swing right in meadow and climb.

3.1   Ride through a gate, and close it behind you.

3.5   Stay left, passing the Farris Creek Trail coming in on the right.

3.7   Drop down a rocky hill and cross Brush Creek. Please keep your shoes on when crossing. Do not attempt to cross when the water is high, it can be very dangerous. After crossing, walk up the hill and turn left at the top. Follow this singletrack briefly to Brush Creek Road.

3.8 Turn left on Brush Creek Road and descend.

4.0 Cross West Brush Creek and climb. This crossing is also dangerous at high water.

4.6 Stay left at the road fork and descend.

6.1 Pass the start of the Canal Trail. Retrace your route back to your car.

7.8 Back to the Brush Creek Trailhead. 🚲

See map pages 36-37

STRAND HILL TRAIL
Ride Information

Description: The Strand Hill loop is a popular loop with locals and visitors alike. It is fairly short in comparison to many of the Crested Butte rides, but has one of the best downhills around. The classic loop starts with a nice warm-up spin out Brush Creek Road followed by a fairly steep doubletrack climb (or see option 3, below, to ride the Strand Bonus Trail up, adding more singletrack.) The top has beautiful views of surrounding mountains and the East River Valley. The singletrack descent is long, fast and smooth as it winds through the aspens. The loop is finished with the fast and smooth Canal Trail. The trail rides well in reverse, challenging as a climb but all rideable. This isn't recommended on busy days because of high speed downhill traffic. To shorten the ride by 9.4 miles of dirt and paved roads, drive to the Brush Creek Trailhead at mile 4.7 of the description below, and start there. The mileage points for this option are in parenthesis starting at mile 4.7. To add more singletrack on to the end of the ride, see options 1 and 2, below.

Distance: 16.3 mile loop from town: 3 miles of singletrack, 2 miles of pavement, 11.3 miles of dirt road and forest doubletrack. From the Brush Creek Trailhead: 6.9 mile loop: 2.7 miles of singletrack, 7.2 miles of dirt road. See options, below to ride more singletrack.

Time: 2-3 hour loop from town

Difficulty: Intermediate

Technical Skill: Intermediate. Most of this ride is smooth, but there a few short sections of the singletrack descent that are loose, steep, or rocky.

Aerobic Effort: Moderate with the exception of 1.5 miles of steep climbing (high effort.)

Elevation: Top: 9,750' **Gain:** 1,550'
    Gain from the Brush Creek Trailhead: 1,050'

Season: June through October

Finding Route: Easy

Maps: Latitude 40 Crested Butte/Taylor Park Trails or the 5th edition Latitude 40 Aspen/Crested Butte/Gunnison

Location: Start at the four-way stop in Crested Butte at the corner of Highway 135 (6th Street) and Elk Avenue. There is a large public parking area here behind the visitor center.

STRAND HILL TRAIL
Ride Information

Mileage Log: *Note: The mileage points in parenthesis starting at mile point 4.7 are for riders starting at the Brush Creek Trailhead.*

0.0   Ride east on Elk Avenue away from the main downtown area. Turn right on 9th Street and follow it several blocks past Red Lady Avenue and behind the school, where it turns to dirt. This dirt road eventually narrows to a singletrack that parallels the highway. Follow the singletrack over a private paved road and continue to the end.

2.0   Turn left on Highway 135 at the end of the bike trail, and cross the Slate River.

2.2   Turn left on Brush Creek Road (County Road 738, marked by the Crested Butte Country Club sign.) Follow this road out past Skyland and on to where the road turns to dirt. Climb a long gradual hill, and then descend toward the East River.

4.7   (0.0) Pass the Brush Creek Trailhead and descend to cross the East River. One mile past the East River crossing, Farris Creek Road takes off to the right.

5.8   (1.1) Turn right and start climbing signed Farris Creek Road 736. This is private property, so please stay on the road and close the gate behind you.

6.5   (1.8) Turn left onto Strand Hill Road 736.1A at the signed intersection. Pass the signed Strand Bonus Trail on the left in 2/10ths of a mile on the left. Continue up the road switchbacks through the aspens. After a steep, rocky climb go through a gate. Please close the gate.

7.2   (2.5) High Point in the loop in an open meadow. The road continues up, but the signed Strand Hill singletrack is straight across the meadow. Enjoy views of Teocalli, Castle, and White Mountains, and Mount Crested Butte. From here, begin the rolling, fast descent of the Strand Hill Trail 556.

8.5   (3.8) Turn hard left onto the signed Strand Bonus Trail. This turn is after a rocky drop, a tight, fast corner and a short, steep climb.

8.6   (3.9) Ride straight ahead through the next intersection and onto the Canal Trail. (The Strand Bonus Trail turns left and climbs.)

9.9   (5.2) Cross the canal and arrive at the end of the singletrack. Turn left on Brush Creek Road and ride back toward Crested Butte.

11.6 (6.9) Pass the Brush Creek Trailhead.

16.3 Back to the four-way stop in Crested Butte.

Option 1: (Expert) To get a bit more singletrack riding in, try riding the Upper Upper Loop on the way back to Crested Butte. After turning left onto Brush Creek Road at mile 9.9, spin through the valley, cross the East River, and climb up a long gradual hill. The Upper Upper Trail takes off right at the top of this hill just before the cattleguard, 2.4 miles after the end of the Canal Trail. This technical singletrack starts with a steep 6/10ths of a mile climb. After reaching the top, ride down this rocky, switchbacking trail. Stay right past the signed Whetstone Vista Trail to the intersection with the signed Upper Loop Trail. Turn right and continue ¼ mile to the intersection with Tony's Trail and turn left. Follow Tony's smooth switchbacks down, through a gate and to the end of the trail. Turn right on this dirt road and ride back to town. This option adds about ¾ of a mile and about ½ hour to your ride, and bumps the rating up to Expert. This is a good option to ride in reverse, before Strand Hill, see Tony's Trail, The Upper Upper Loop, Whetstone Vista.

Option 2: (Intermediate) After finishing the Canal Trail, ride back toward Crested Butte for 3.6 miles to Skyland Drive. Turn right and follow this 4/10ths of a mile to Country Club Drive, turn left and ride for 6/10ths of a mile to the dead-end and the Upper Loop trailhead. Follow the Upper Loop up ½ mile, turn left and continue on the Upper Loop to Tony's Trail. Turn left and follow Tony's Trail down the smooth switchbacks, through a gate, and to the end. Turn right and ride back to town. This is one mile longer will add 30 minutes to your ride. This is also a good option to ride on the way to Strand Hill.

Option 3: (Hard Intermediate) Riding up the Strand Bonus Trail instead of Strand Hill Road is a little more difficult climb but adds a lot of great singletrack to the loop. Instead of turning up Strand Hill Road at mile 5.8, continue ½ mile on Brush Creek Road to the unmarked Canal Trail. Turn right and cross the canal and continue on the trail 1 mile to the Strand Bonus Trail. Turn right and climb and contour 1.4 miles up to Strand Hill Road. Turn left and climb ½ mile to the Strand Hill Trail and continue the loop as described above from here. 🚲

Description: The Strand Bonus Trail is a smooth singletrack that traverses Strand Hill. It is an awesome trail, with beautiful views of the East River drainage and lots of wildflowers in the summer. This fairly easy loop starts with a short but steep climb up Farris Creek and Strand Hill Roads, followed by a smooth, rolling traverse and descent through the aspens. Riders end this loop with a wonderful, fast cruise on the Canal Trail. There are many options to link it to surrounding trails, as it is a good trail in either direction. Riding up the Strand Bonus Trail (the reverse of the loop described here) is a good climb, a great alternative to riding Farris Creek and Strand Hill Roads up to the Strand Hill Trail (See Strand Hill, options, and The Canal Trail for access and more information.) It is slightly more challenging in this direction.

Distance: 6 mile loop, 2.3 miles of singletrack, 3.7 miles of dirt road and forest doubletrack. Add 9.4 miles if ridden from town.

Time: 1-1½ hour

Difficulty: Intermediate

Technical Skill: Intermediate

Aerobic Effort: Moderate

Elevation: Top: 9,450' **Gain:** 650'

Season: June through October

Finding Route: Easy

Maps: Latitude 40 Crested Butte/Taylor Park Trails or Latitude 40 Aspen/Crested Butte/Gunnison or Alpineer Trails Map

Location: Ride or drive south of Crested Butte 2.2 miles and turn left on Brush Creek Road. Drive 2.5 miles and park at the Brush Creek Trailhead on the left.

STRAND BONUS TRAIL
Ride Information

This is right before the road crosses the East River. If you ride from town, a good alternative to riding out Brush Creek Road is to take Tony's Trail to the Upper Loop to Skyland to Brush Creek Road, or Tony's to the Upper Loop to the Upper Upper Loop to Brush Creek Road.

Mileage Log:

0.0   From the Brush Creek Trailhead, turn left onto Brush Creek Road and ride down and cross the East River. Continue past the barn on the left and out the road.

1.1   Turn right and ride up the signed Farris Creek Road that starts out fairly steeply.

1.8   Turn left onto the signed Strand Hill Road at the next intersection.

2.0   Turn left on the signed Strand Bonus Trail and enjoy the roll through the aspens and meadows!

3.4   T-intersection with the Canal Trail. Turn left on this fast, smooth, rolling singletrack.

4.3   Cross the canal and turn left onto Brush Creek Road.

6.0   Back to the Brush Creek Trailhead. 🚲

FARRIS CREEK TRAIL
Ride Information
See map pages 36-37

Description: Farris Creek is a beautiful medium length ride in the Brush Creek drainage, in the same area as Strand Hill. After spinning out Brush Creek Road, riders climb a short, steep section of Farris Creek Road and then meander through open meadows and aspen groves below Doubletop Mountain on doubletrack. There are great views of Teocalli Mountain and the climb narrows to singletrack in the upper meadows. The descent is very rocky and rutted. (An alternate return route on Trail 402 avoids this descent, see option, below.) After riding the technical section of the descent, the Canal Trail is a smooth, fun and fast spin through the sage. To shorten the ride by 9.4 miles of dirt and paved roads, park at the Brush Creek Trailhead, at mile 4.7 of the description below.

Distance: 21 mile loop from town: 5 miles of singletrack, 2 miles pavement, 14 miles of dirt road and forest doubletrack.

Time: 2-4 hours

Difficulty: Intermediate, with the exception of 8/10ths of a mile of expert singletrack descent.

Technical Skill: Intermediate, with an expert descent.

Aerobic Effort: Moderate

Elevation: Top: 9,850' **Gain:** 1,650'
     Gain from the Brush Creek Trailhead: 1,150'

Season: June through October

Finding Route: Easy, all turns are marked.

Maps: Latitude 40 Crested Butte/Taylor Park or National Geographic/Trails Illustrated Crested Butte/Pearl Pass or the 5th edition Latitude 40 Aspen/Crested Butte/Gunnison or the 2002 Alpineer Bike Trails Map

Location: Start at the four-way stop at the corner of Highway 135 (6th Street) and Elk Avenue in Crested Butte. There is a large public parking lot here behind the visitor center.

Mileage Log:

0.0   Ride east on Elk Avenue away from the main downtown area. Turn right on 9th Street and follow it past Red Lady Avenue and behind the school, where it turns to dirt. This dirt road eventually narrows to a singletrack that parallels the highway. Follow the singletrack over a private paved road and continue to the end. Turn left onto Highway 135 and cross the Slate River.

2.2   Turn left on Brush Creek Road (County Road 738.) This turn is marked by a Crested Butte Country Club sign. Ride out the road passing Skyland Road and the golf course on the left. The road turns to dirt. Climb a gradual hill.

4.7   Pass the Brush Creek Trailhead on the left and then descend to cross the East River. Ride past an old ranch house and barns on your left. About one mile after crossing the East River look for Farris Creek Road on the right.

5.8   Turn right and start up the Farris Creek Road. Close the gate behind you.

6.5   Continue straight on Farris Creek Road, passing Strand Hill Road that climbs left.

7.0   Ride through the gate and down a short hill. Stay left with the road, passing the signed Farris Creek Trail 409 on the right. (Do not take this turn, this loop is on the north end of the Farris Creek Trail.)

7.9   Shortcut trail on the left. Take this or stick with the road, both end in the same place.

8.2   Farris Creek crossing.

8.3   Pass an unmarked singletrack on the left. Take the singletrack or stay with the doubletrack. If you take the doubletrack, pass two doubletrack spurs on the right as you ride through the aspens. Descend into open meadows again.

8.8   The singletrack rejoins the road back out in the open meadows.

9.0   Stay left on the Farris Creek Road, passing Trail 402 that is marked only by three large rocks. Teocalli Mountain is straight ahead. Climb through meadows and into the aspens.

9.7   The unmarked Trail 402 ½ is on the left. (See option, below.)

9.8   Top of the ride. Ride straight ahead on the singletrack and start downhill. There is a better rest stop just 2/10ths of a mile ahead with a nice view.

10.0   This is a great spot for a break before starting the descent! Stay left and ride through the old fence where the singletrack reappears.

10.8   Arrive at a signed T-intersection. Turn left onto the Strand Bonus Trail. Be careful of a technical drop coming up in less than ¼ mile.

FARRIS CREEK TRAIL
Ride Information

11.2 Ride through a gate and close it behind you. Roll through a meadow, swing left and head uphill.

11.6 Stay right on the Strand Bonus Trail, passing the Strand Hill Trail on the left.

11.7 Stay to the right through the next intersection, riding onto the Canal Trail. The Strand Bonus Trail turns left and climbs to Strand Hill Road. (This is a great climb to link up to the Strand Hill Trail to add on more great trail to your loop.)

12.7 Cross the canal and reach the end of the singletrack. Turn left on Brush Creek Road and head back to Highway 135, turn right and return to Crested Butte.

21.2 Back to the four-way stop.

Option: To avoid the technical descent on the Farris Creek Trail, turn right onto the unmarked Trail 402 ½ at mile 9.7. This is a non-system trail, it is not well maintained but is a fun climb and link to Trail 402. In 7/10ths of a mile (mile 10.5) Trail 402½ crosses a meadow and disappears, go straight across to intersect Trail 402. Turn right and descend this nice section of trail. At mile 11.5 you will rejoin Farris Creek Road, turn left and retrace your tracks back to Crested Butte. ⚲

TRAIL 402
Ride Information

See map pages 36-37

Description: Trail 402 is a little known trail that takes off from Farris Creek Road. It is a beautiful ride through aspen groves and high altitude meadows, with great views of Teocalli Mountain. It is a nice alternative to the Farris Creek Trail, with a slightly more strenuous climb and a little more primitive feel. Trail 402 is one of the few moderate-length rides in the area, not as long and difficult as Teocalli Ridge or Deer Creek. It rolls up Farris Creek Road through grassy high altitude meadows next to big beaver ponds, and zooms down through dark forest and aspen groves on rugged singletrack. It is a nice fall ride because of the many aspen groves it rolls through. The last part of the descent is in very rough shape; many riders will walk. The creek crossing is dangerous in the early summer, better to wait to ride Trail 402 until the spring runoff is slowing down.

Distance: 22 mile loop from town: 7 miles of singletrack, 2 miles of pavement, 13 miles of dirt road and forest doubletrack. Shorten the ride by 9.4 miles by driving to the Brush Creek Trailhead at mile 4.7.

Time: 2½-4 hours

Difficulty: Advanced intermediate with and expert descent.

Technical Skill: Intermediate, with an expert one mile descent

Aerobic Effort: Moderate

Elevation: Top: 10,000' **Gain:** 1,700'

Gain from the Brush Creek Trailhead: 1,200'

Season: Late June through October

Finding Route: Fairly easy, most turns are marked. The turn at the beginning of the singletrack off Farris Creek Road is marked only with large rocks.

Maps: Latitude 40 Crested Butte/Taylor Park Trails or 5th edition Latitude 40 Aspen/ Crested Butte/Gunnison or the 2002 Alpineer Bike Trails Map.

Location: Start at the four-way stop in Crested Butte at the corner of Elk Avenue and Highway 135 (6th Street.) There is a large public parking area behind the visitor center here.

Mileage Log:

0.0 Ride east on Elk Avenue away from the main downtown area. Turn right on 9th Street and follow it past Red Lady Avenue and behind the school, where it turns to dirt. This dirt road eventually narrows to a singletrack that parallels the highway. Follow the singletrack over a private paved road and continue to the end. Turn left on the Highway 135 and cross the Slate River.

2.2 Turn left on Brush Creek Road (County Road 738.) This turn is marked by the Crested Butte Country Club sign. Follow Brush Creek Road past Skyland and on to where the road turns to dirt. Ride up and then down a long, gradual hill.

4.7 Pass the Brush Creek Trailhead on the left. Descend to cross the East River. Continue out the valley one mile to Farris Creek Road.

5.8 Turn right on signed Farris Creek Road 736. If the gate is closed when you arrive, close it behind you. Start climbing this steep doubletrack.

6.5 Stay right on Farris Creek Road, passing Strand Hill Road.

7.0 Ride through a gate and down a short steep hill. Stay left on Farris Creek Road, passing Farris Creek Trail 409 on the right.

7.8 A singletrack heads left. Take this or the road, they end up in the same place.

8.2 Cross Farris Creek.

8.3 On the left just a little past the crossing is a singletrack. Take this or the road. If you continue on the road, ride uphill, passing two doubletracks on the right in the aspens, and ride down and into open meadows.

8.9 The singletrack rejoins the road. If you took the singletrack, turn left on the road.

9.0 Turn right at the unsigned intersection of Trail 402. This intersection is marked only by three large boulders. Follow this trail up through the aspens, into a meadow, and straight ahead, just right of a small pond. This trail has been illegally ridden by ATV's. Please report any of this activity you see to the forest service. See listing of services in the back of this book for information.

10.0 Top of the climb. Ride into the dark woods, and head downhill! Watch for technical sections.

11.3 Very technical section. I suggest walking unless you are very confident.

11.5 Brush Creek crossing. Keep your shoes on! Veer right and upstream after crossing to follow this overgrown section of trail. It is often quite boggy here.

TRAIL 402
Ride Information ————————————————————

11.7 Turn left on Brush Creek Road at the end of the trail.

12.2 Reach the top of a hill and a cattleguard, start downhill briefly.

12.4 Ride straight ahead onto a singletrack as the road climbs and turns right. Follow this shortcut around the hillside, above the creek. Be careful as this trail is eroding into the steep sided creek. Some riders may want to walk. Near the end of the shortcut the singletrack widens to doubletrack.

13.0 Intersect Brush Creek Road. Turn left at this junction on the signed Farris Creek 409 singletrack. Descend briefly on this trail, then turn left at the split and ride steeply down to cross Brush Creek. (An option would be to stay on Brush Creek Road all the way back to Highway 135, then turn right and ride back to town. This is nine easy miles back.)

13.2 Carry your bike across Brush Creek and ride up the trail on the other side. Keep your shoes one! Caution, this creek crossing can be swift and dangerous early in the summer. Turn around and return to Crested Butte on Brush Creek Road if it is high.

13.4 Stay right and ride straight ahead through the next intersection and onto the Strand Bonus Trail, as the Farris Creek 409 Trail turns left and up.

13.6 Caution, technical but rideable rock section. Continue down the trail and through a gate. Please close the gate. Ride through the meadow and then left and up.

14.2 Stay right passing the Strand Hill Trail.

14.3 Ride straight ahead through the next intersection and onto the fast and smooth Canal Trail. The Strand Bonus Trail climbs left and up.

15.3 Cross the canal and finish the singletrack on Brush Creek Road. Turn left and ride back to Highway 135, turn right and ride back to Crested Butte.

21.8 Back to the four-way stop. 🚲

DEER CREEK
See map pages 36-37
Ride Information ————————————————————

Description: This classic cross-country ride completely circumvents Mount Crested Butte on the flanks of White Mountain on a wonderful singletrack. It has a wilderness feel to it and riders can occasionally spot elk grazing in high meadows above the trail in the spring. In early summer, the higher meadows of Deer Creek become solid purple with immense fields of Larkspur! Deer Creek starts with a nice long spin on Brush Creek Road, a steep road climb, and a very strenuous singletrack climb to beautiful views at the top. It rolls along high alpine meadows and through aspen forests and down a long and fast descent to Gothic Road. A final road spin leads back to Mount Crested Butte and Crested Butte. Riders still wanting a little more singletrack riding can add on the Snodgrass Trail, or ride the Upper Loop and Tony's Trail back to Crested Butte. An option to riding out on Highway 135 at the beginning of the ride is to take Tony's Trail and The Upper Loop or The Upper Upper Loop to Brush Creek Road and heading out from here. Deer Creek tends to dry out a little quicker in the spring than the other long rides around town due to its' south and west facing slopes. Later in the summer it can get really messy with cow tracks, especially after rain. Check with a bike shop on the trail condition prior to riding it. Deer Creek is quite fun ridden from Gothic Road to Brush Creek Road as well. See option, below, to add on Teocalli Ridge and turn the ride into an epic after riding it this direction.

Distance: 29 mile loop from town: 9 miles of singletrack, 5 miles of pavement and cement bike path, 15 miles of dirt road and forest doubletrack.

Time: 3-5 hours

Difficulty: Expert

Technical Skill: Expert

Aerobic Effort: High

Elevation: Top: 10,650' **Gain:** 3,300'

Season: Mid-June through early or mid-October

Finding Route: Easy to Moderate. The route is well-signed and easy to follow early in the summer, but numerous cow trails can make it confusing late in the summer. Always look for the main trail.

Maps: 5th edition Latitude 40 for Aspen/Crested Butte/Gunnison or Latitude 40 Crested Butte/Taylor Park or 2001 National Geographic/Trails Illustrated Crested Butte and Pearl Pass.

Location: Start at the four-way stop at the corner of Elk Avenue and Highway 135 (6th Street) in Crested Butte. There is a large public parking lot behind the visitor center here.

Mileage Log:

0.0 Ride east on Elk Avenue away from the main downtown area. Turn right on 9th Street and follow this several blocks and past Red Lady Avenue and behind the school, where it turns to dirt. This dirt road eventually narrows to a singletrack that parallels the highway. Follow the singletrack over a private paved road and continue to the end.

2.0 The singletrack ends. Turn left on Highway 135 and cross the Slate River.

2.2 Take the next left on Brush Creek Road (County Road 738) marked by the Crested Butte Country Club sign. Follow this road out past Skyland, and on to where the road turns to dirt. Climb gradually, and then drop down to cross the East River and ride out the valley past Farris Creek Road.

6.5 Begin climbing more steeply after crossing Brush Creek.

8.0 At the fork in the road, turn left on West Brush Creek Road. The road climbs steeply at first, and then levels. Cross a cattleguard.

8.9 At the next fork in the road, turn left on Deer Creek Road and climb several long switchbacks.

9.5 Top out on the road, Teocalli Mountain in view straight ahead. Ride through the gate and close it behind you if you found it closed. Follow the road a short distance down and cross a gully.

9.7 Turn left and downhill immediately after crossing the gully. This turn is marked with a small "Deer Creek" sign. Follow this steep road down and around the corner to the dead-end.

DEER CREEK
Ride Information

10.1 The Deer Creek Trail begins at the road's end. Climb steadily up Deer Creek, crossing two forks of the creek, and then climb steeply. This is a very challenging climb and most will have to walk part of it.

11.6 Top of biggest climb in the ride! This is a nice spot for a break with wonderful views. From here ride through the aspens and above a steep earth flow, where a fast descent into Dry Basin begins. Next, cross a creek and climb through aspen groves.

13.2 Ride through big, open meadows with views of Gothic and Baldy Mountains straight ahead. Pass two ponds, ride through a gate and descend to cross Perry Creek.

14.1 After crossing the wide Perry Creek, head left and climb just out into the meadow where the trail switchbacks to the right. Often there is a cow trail heading straight ahead, be sure to go right and up. Next there is a difficult switchback to the left and then contour around the hill, heading northwest. Enjoy the rolling terrain!

15.1 Start down some steep switchbacks.

15.6 After entering the aspens and riding down steeply for a short distance, the trail turns sharp left. There are often plenty of cow trails here to confuse the route, but follow the main trail back out into the meadow below the switchbacks. Next the trail turns right and crosses a creek, and descends a short, steep hill. Head right again with Gothic and Baldy Mountains straight ahead, ride through wonderful rolling meadows, and then descend through the aspens.

17.8 Turn left for a quick uphill at the signed private property.

18.5 Veer right in lower meadows, the main trail is marked by poles.

18.6 Turn right on a dirt two-track at the end of the trail.

20.4 Turn left on Gothic Road, and ride down and cross the East River. Ride gradually up Gothic Road a little less than three miles, passing the Snodgrass Trail on the right at the summit of your climb.

23.5 From the summit of the climb, descend through Mount Crested Butte or ride the Snodgrass Trail, on the right, for a little more singletrack.

26.5 Turn left off the pavement onto the bike path, or continue on the shoulder of Gothic Road back to town. (The bike path takes off left at the bottom of a long downhill, right before a sharp right turn in the road. Careful, this is a dangerous corner crossing.)

29.2 Back to the four-way stop.

Option: The Deer Creek Trail is a nice ride in the opposite direction as well, from Gothic Road to Brush Creek Road. For an epic day, ride it this direction, and when you get to the junction of Deer Creek Road and West Brush Creek Road, turn left and ride the Teocalli Ridge Trail. This is a big day of climbing (4,800') and adds 9 miles and about 2 hours to your ride.

Description: Teocalli Ridge is a very challenging ride with great singletrack and rewarding views of Castle Peak and the surrounding mountains at the top. The flowers on this ride in July are truly unbelievable, waving over your head as you climb and descend high altitude meadows. The ride begins with a long road approach through beautiful meadows along Brush and West Brush Creeks. The road narrows to a steep, primitive doubletrack up higher. The singletrack begins with sustained, grueling climbs that challenge even the strongest riders. Luckily there are small breaks in the climb and awesome views of the West Brush Creek Valley. The descent will delight those who love difficult and moderately technical, but still fast, downhills. Early in the summer the crossing of Brush Creek can be very dangerous on the return trip, but usually it is lower by the time the trail is dry and rideable as a loop. Before the trail is open as a loop, ride it as an out and back to about mile 13. To shorten the ride by 9.4 miles, park at the Brush Creek Trailhead, at mile 4.7 of the description below.

Distance: 27 mile loop: 6 miles of singletrack, 2 miles of pavement, 19 miles of dirt road and primitive forest doubletrack. 17.4 mile loop from the Brush Creek Trailhead: 6 miles of singletrack, 11.4 miles of dirt road and primitive doubletrack.

Time: 3½-5½ hours

Difficulty: Expert

Technical Skill: Expert. Continuous climbing on steep, narrow singletrack, and a steep and rutted descent.

Aerobic Effort: Strenuous

Elevation: Top: 11,286' **Gain:** 3,300'

Season: July-early October.

Finding Route: Easy. All junctions are marked.

Maps: Latitude 40 Crested Butte/Taylor Park Trails or the 5th edition Latitude 40 Aspen/Crested Butte/Gunnison map or the National Geographic Trails Illustrated Pearl Pass.

Location: Start at the four-way stop in Crested Butte at the corner of Elk Avenue and Highway 135 (6th Street.) There is a large public parking area here behind the visitor center. Shorten the ride by 9.4 miles by driving to the Brush Creek Trailhead at mile 4.7 of this description. The mileage points if you start at the Brush Creek Trailhead are in parenthesis, starting at mile 4.7.

Mileage Log:

0.0 Ride east on Elk Avenue away from the main downtown area. Turn right on 9th Street and follow it several blocks and past Red Lady Avenue and behind the school, where it turns to dirt. This dirt road eventually narrows to a singletrack that parallels the highway. Follow the singletrack over a private paved road and continue to the end.

2.0 Turn left on Highway 135 and cross the Slate River.

2.2 Turn left on Brush Creek Road 748, marked by the Crested Butte Country Club sign. Follow this road out past Skyland Road and the golf course on the left. The road turns to dirt. Climb up a long, gradual hill, and then ride down to cross the East River.

4.7 (0.0) Pass the Brush Creek Trailhead on the left. Ride up the valley and pass Farris Creek Road on the right.

6.5   (1.8) After crossing Brush Creek, begin climbing more steeply through open meadows that boast Lupine, Delphinium and Mule's Ears in late June and early July, and lots of other wildflowers throughout the summer.

8.0   (3.3) Turn left at the fork, taking the West Brush Creek Trail, which is also a road, more steeply up.

8.9   (4.2) Stay right at the junction with Deer Creek Road, riding toward the Teocalli Ridge Trail. Descend gradually.

10.1   (5.4) Arrive at West Brush Creek, which can be quite swift and deep early in the summer. Go upstream through the campsite a short distance to a log bridge to cross the creek. After crossing, wind around left and rejoin the road, following West Brush Creek up toward Teocalli Mountain. Soon White and Whiterock Mountains come into view.

12.4   (7.7) The road levels out for a moment. Turn right on the signed Teocalli Mountain Trail to the right, riding toward the Teocalli Ridge Trail. (West Brush Creek Trail dead-ends shortly at the Maroon Bells Wilderness boundary.)

13.6   (8.9) Once again the trail levels out for a moment at an old broken down fence. Turn right on the signed Teocalli Ridge Trail and climb more gradually, descend a short distance, and then climb steeply to reach the summit of the ride. (The Teocalli Mountain Trail continues down to Middle Brush Creek but is very hard to follow and not recommended.)

14.4   (9.7) Relax and enjoy the view of Castle Peak off the left side of the trail. From here ride straight ahead and down.

15.0   (10.3) Stay right on the Teocalli Ridge Trail and pass a trail to the left heads down to Middle Brush Creek. (This trail is not shown on the Latitude 40 map, and is not recommended for biking.)

17.6   (12.9) End of the Teocalli Ridge Trail. Turn right on Brush Creek Road, and ride down a steep doubletrack hill.

17.9   (13.2) Turn sharp right and continue downhill on the road. Cross Brush Creek and climb up, then again downhill on Brush Creek Road. Follow this back to town the way you came. Or, see option below for a singletrack extension.

22.1   (17.4) Pass the Brush Creek Trailhead.

26.8   Back to the four-way stop.

Option: Want to add a bit more singletrack on to the end of the ride? At mile 17.9, take the signed Farris Creek Trail 409 straight ahead. Ride downhill to a fork in less than 2/10ths of a mile. Turn left at the fork and descend steeply to cross Brush Creek. This crossing can be swift and dangerous in early summer, so be sure you are confident to cross it and keep your shoes on! Continue up the other bank and roll through the open meadows. Ride straight ahead at the corner of Farris Creek Trail 409 and onto the Strand Bonus Trail. Stay to the right at the junction with Strand Hill Trail and again stay to the right when the Strand Bonus Trail goes uphill and left. You are now riding on the Canal Trail. Follow this all the way back to Brush Creek Road, turn left and ride back to town. This is actually shorter than the road but will take just a bit longer. ᚛

Strand Hill Trail

DYKE TRAIL, CARBON & GREEN LAKE TRAILS

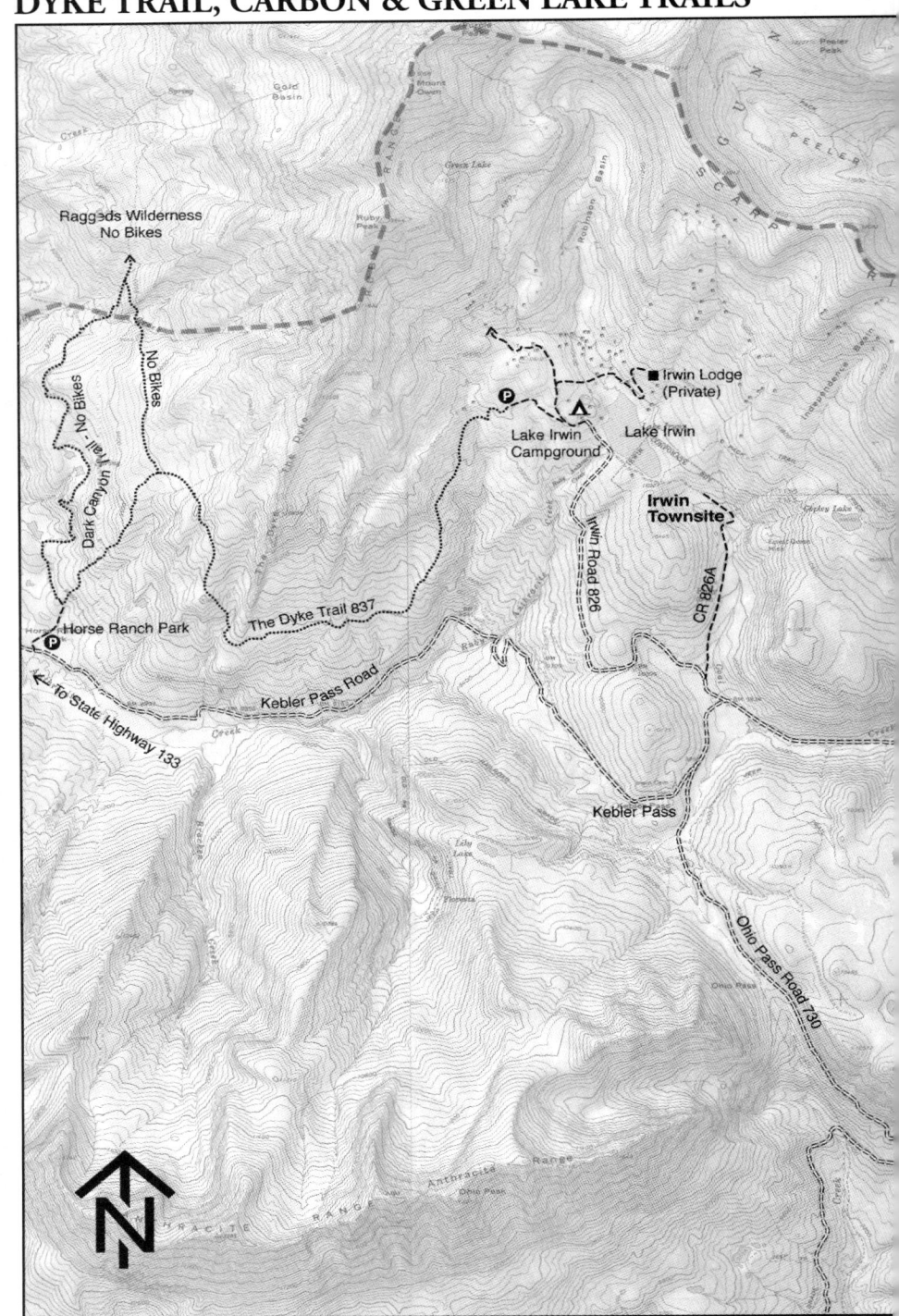

DYKE TRAIL, CARBON & GREEN LAKE TRAILS

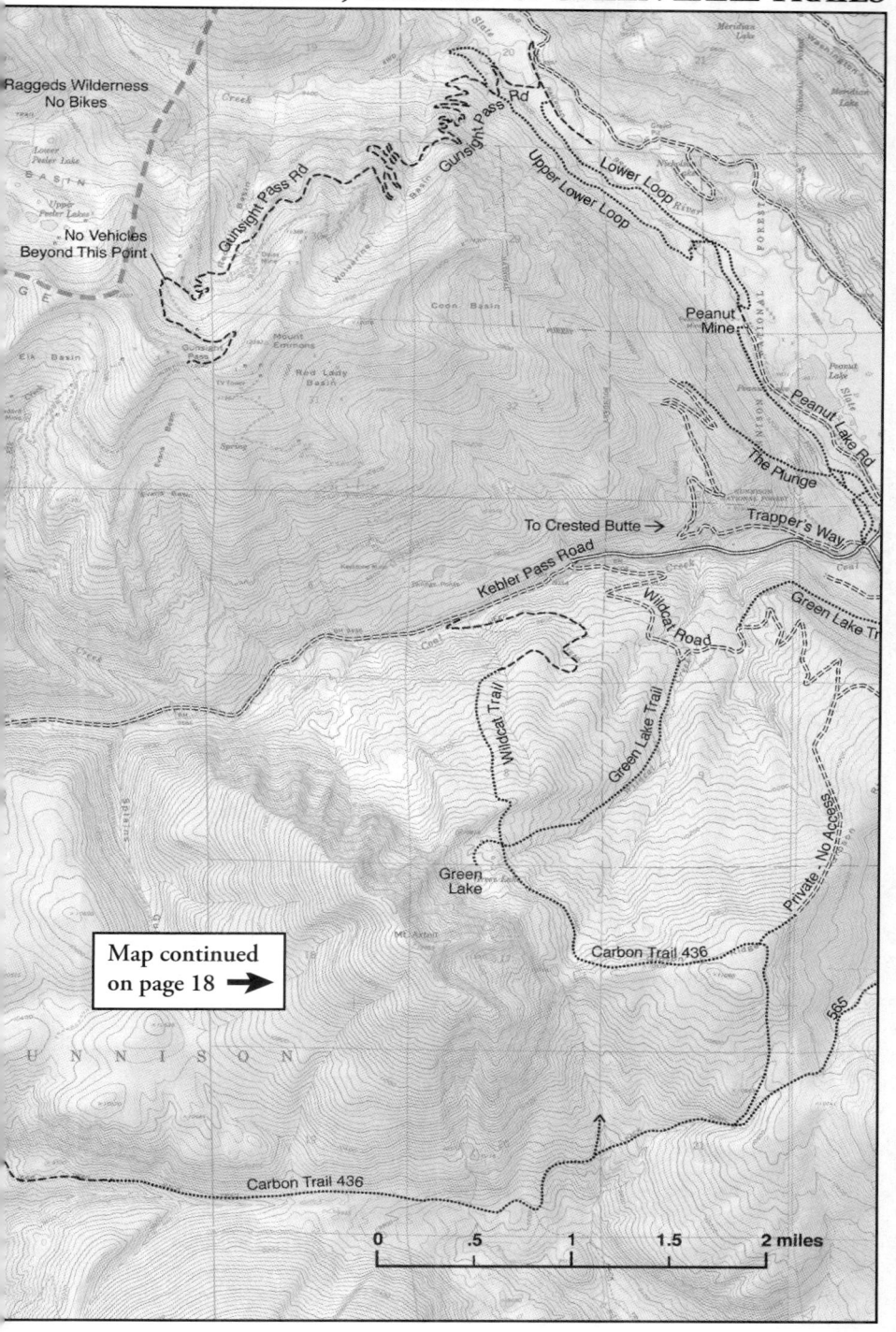

Raggeds Wilderness
No Bikes

No Vehicles
Beyond This Point

Gunsight Pass Rd

Gunsight Pass Rd

Upper Lower Loop

Lower Loop

Peanut
Mine

Peanut Lake Rd

The Plunge

To Crested Butte →

Trapper's Way

Green Lake Tr

Kebler Pass Road

Wildcat Road

Wildcat Trail

Green Lake Trail

Green
Lake

Private - No Access

Map continued
on page 18 ➡

Carbon Trail 436

565

UNNISON

Carbon Trail 436

| 0 | .5 | 1 | 1.5 | 2 miles |

THE DYKE TRAIL
Ride Information

Description: The Dyke Trail is a moderate length ride through beautiful aspen groves. It is an awesome fall ride, and also great any time in the summer. There are beautiful views of the Ruby Range on the road to the trail. The descents are fast and very fun as you swoop through the aspens on this narrow and winding singletrack. There are several short technical ditch crossings to test your skills, and a lung busting set of climbs leading to the summit of the ride. A hike-a-bike section of the climb has been recently re-routed by CBMBA volunteers, and is now all rideable. Beware of deadfall on the descents. The loop includes a fair amount of road spinning at the beginning and end, especially if ridden from town. Because of the amount of traffic on busy summer weekends on Kebler Pass and Irwin Lake roads, it is better to ride the Dyke Trail mid-week or on less busy weekends, or early morning. This ride can become very slick if it rains, so save it for a dry day! Intermediate riders do fine on this trail as long as they are willing to walk a few short expert sections. This is one of the classic Crested Butte trails, don't miss it!

Distance: 14 mile loop from the junction of Kebler Pass Road and the Forest Road 826: 5 miles of singletrack and 9 miles of dirt road. Add 14 miles of paved and dirt roads if you ride from Crested Butte.

Time: 2-4 hour loop from the junction of Kebler Pass Road and Forest Road 826, 4-6 hours from town.

Difficulty: Advanced intermediate to expert.

Technical Skill: Advanced intermediate with some expert sections.

Aerobic Effort: High

Elevation: Top: 10,500' **Gain:** 1,930' **Gain from town:** 3,450'

Season: June through September

Finding Route: Moderate. It is easy to miss the turn at mile 7.4 even though it is marked.

Maps: Latitude 40 Crested Butte/Taylor Park Trails or the 5th edition Latitude 40 Aspen/ Crested Butte/Gunnison.

Location: Start at the corner of Kebler Pass Road (County Road 12) and Forest Road 826 (to Lake Irwin.) To get here, drive or ride west up Elk Avenue from the four-way stop at the corner of Elk Avenue and Highway 135 to First Street. Go left and continue 2 blocks to Whiterock Avenue, and turn right. Whiterock turns into Kebler Pass Road. Follow this 6.5 miles to Forest Road 826, on the right, and park here.

Mileage Log:

0.0 Begin (or continue) riding toward Lake Irwin on Forest Road 826. In 2/10ths of a mile the road splits, stay left. (If you take the right hand turn through the historic townsite of Irwin, just continue past the houses and left to the lake, then follow the road around the bottom of the lake. This will reconnect with Forest Road 826.)

2.5 Continue past Lake Irwin and stay left past the Lake Irwin Campground. The road switches back and climbs steeply for a short distance.

3.1 The road forks, stay left following signs for the Dyke Trail. Ruby and Owen Mountains are straight ahead. Ride down and around a gradual and fast corner, up a short incline, and straight ahead to the signed Dyke Trail.

3.3   Begin the signed Dyke Trail. Ride downhill and right to the first steep creek crossing. Stay alert for technical areas along the mostly descending trail.

6.1   Begin climbing some switchbacks and a challenging set of climbs with very little break in between.

7.0   When the Dyke (a rocky volcanic outcropping) and Ruby Mountain come into view and you've gained an open meadow, you are at the summit of the singletrack section of the ride. There is a nice view and lunch spot a short walk up to the left of this meadow. When ready to continue, head straight through the meadow and again downhill.

7.4   Turn sharp left on the Dyke Trail. Straight ahead leads into the Dark Canyon and the Raggeds Wilderness, where no bikes are allowed. This turn is shortly after a flat creek crossing in the dark timber. Don't miss it! There is a small sign pointing left to the Dyke Trail. Continue down the next fast section of trail through the aspens, watching out for downed logs, one technical rocky area, and horses.

8.7   Arrive at the end of the Dyke Trail. Turn left on the dirt Horse Ranch Park Road and ride down to Kebler Pass Road.

9.1   Turn left onto Kebler Pass Road and follow this gradually up to Kebler Pass.

13.9   From Kebler Pass, ride left and down. Pass the Ohio Pass Road on your right.

14.5   Back to your car. If you rode from town, enjoy the easy and mostly downhill spin back to Crested Butte on Kebler Pass Road. 🚲

CARBON AND GREEN LAKE TRAILS

See map pages 54-55, 18-19   **Ride Information**

Description: The Carbon Trail is a beautiful, isolated ride that traverses around Mount Axtell. The high point in the ride, the saddle between Mount Axtell and Whetstone Mountain, rewards riders with amazing views of the Elk Mountains and Crested Butte. It is and adventurous and difficult ride. Much of trail is rough, and the descent to the Green Lake Trail is quite rocky and very rutted from heavy motorcycle use. A short side trip to Green Lake is worth the effort and a great place to swim on a hot summer day. The descent on the Green Lake Trail is fast and fun, it is the one section of this loop that is well maintained. This loop is fun and quite challenging in reverse, the climb in this direction is technically and aerobically difficult.

Distance: 23 mile loop from town: 12 miles of singletrack, 3 miles of pavement, 10.8 miles of dirt road.

Time: 3-5 hours

Difficulty: Expert

Technical Skill: Expert.

Aerobic Effort: High

Elevation: Top: 10,950' **Gain:** 2,700'

Season: Late June through mid-October

CARBON AND GREEN LAKE TRAILS
Ride Information

Finding Route: Moderate to difficult. None of the turns are marked except on the Green Lake Trail, but there are only a few turns.

Maps: Latitude 40 Crested Butte/Taylor Park Trails

Location: Start in Crested Butte at the four-way stop at the corner of Elk Avenue and Highway 135, by the visitor center. There is a large public parking lot here.

Mileage Log:

0.0   Ride west up Elk Avenue to First Street, and turn left. Follow First Street two blocks to Whiterock Avenue.

0.5   Turn right on Whiterock Avenue, which becomes Kebler Pass Road as it leaves town and begins to climb. Follow this road for the next several miles.

7.1   Stay left past the turn to Irwin, continuing on Kebler Pass Road.

7.5   Turn left on County Road 730 toward Ohio Pass.

8.6   Once over the pass, ride down and past big views into the top of the Ohio Creek Valley. When you come to the first switchback with a big talus slope to the left of the road, you are almost to the turn for the Carbon Trail.

10.4   Turn sharp left on the unmarked road cutback, just after the switchback. Ride back past the many parking spots, and over a large talus field. Continue on this singletrack for several miles. (The ATV's are turning this into a four-wheeler trail.)

13.0   Pass more talus and climb more steeply. Nice views of Whetstone Mountain straight ahead.

14.5   Stay right and pass an ATV spur to the left that climbs, and descend briefly to cross a creek. Ride left and up through some willows that are crowding the narrow ATV track. Next the trail climbs up the side hill on the left side of the creek.

15.1   Stay left at the second fork in the four-wheeler track and climb up a big meadow with two small creeks to your right. As you near the top of the meadow, swing left and stay with the water eroded trail. The trail levels out somewhat near the top, enters the forest, and swings gradually left away from Whetstone Mountain.

16.0   Reach the summit of the trail, which is now singletrack, on the meadowed flank of Mount Axtell. Views of Mount Crested Butte, the Maroon Bells, and the town of Crested Butte open in front of you. Nice spot for a break! From here head left on the trail and contour, rolling gradually downhill. Pass an inviting trail off to the right, but don't take it! All the area below the trail is private property! This trail is long and very rocky, and has some badly eroded spots.

18.4   Intersect the Green Lake Trail. Turn right and descend to Crested Butte on the Green Lake Trail. This is fast and fun, somewhat technical. (Straight ahead is a singletrack, the Wildcat Trail, climbing up a moraine hillside. This trail descends to Kebler Pass Road via a very rocky and rough route down Splains Gulch. Left leads up to Green Lake in less than ½ mile.)

20.2 Intersection with the private Trapper's Crossing Road. Turn right on this road and ride gradually down around a corner, then uphill.

20.6 Turn left and descend on the signed Green Lake Trail.

21.0 The trail funnels onto an old road, turn left and down.

21.3 Turn right off the road onto the continuation of the Green Lake Trail. The road is blocked with sticks at this point. This beautiful section of singletrack winds gradually down through the aspens.

22.3 End of the singletrack at the signed Green Lake Trailhead. Turn right onto the neighborhood dirt road. Just past several houses look for an old dirt road that is your next turn.

22.6 Turn left on the unmarked doubletrack and ride down to the Nordic Center. Follow the street at the bottom straight ahead. Turn right on Whiterock and ride to 6th Street, turn left and ride back to the four-way stop.

23.3 Back to the four-way stop.

Option: For an epic day, ride the Dyke Trail from town. Climb up to Kebler Pass from Horse Ranch Park after the Dyke Trail descent. Turn right on Ohio Pass Road as you begin the descent toward town. Ride Carbon and Green Lake Trails, as described above from mile 7.5. Add 14.5 miles and 2 hours to your ride. ᚛ᚗ

Cement Mountain Trail
(Reno-Flag-Bear-Deadman Gulch Loop, Rosebud option)

CEMENT CREEK TRAILS

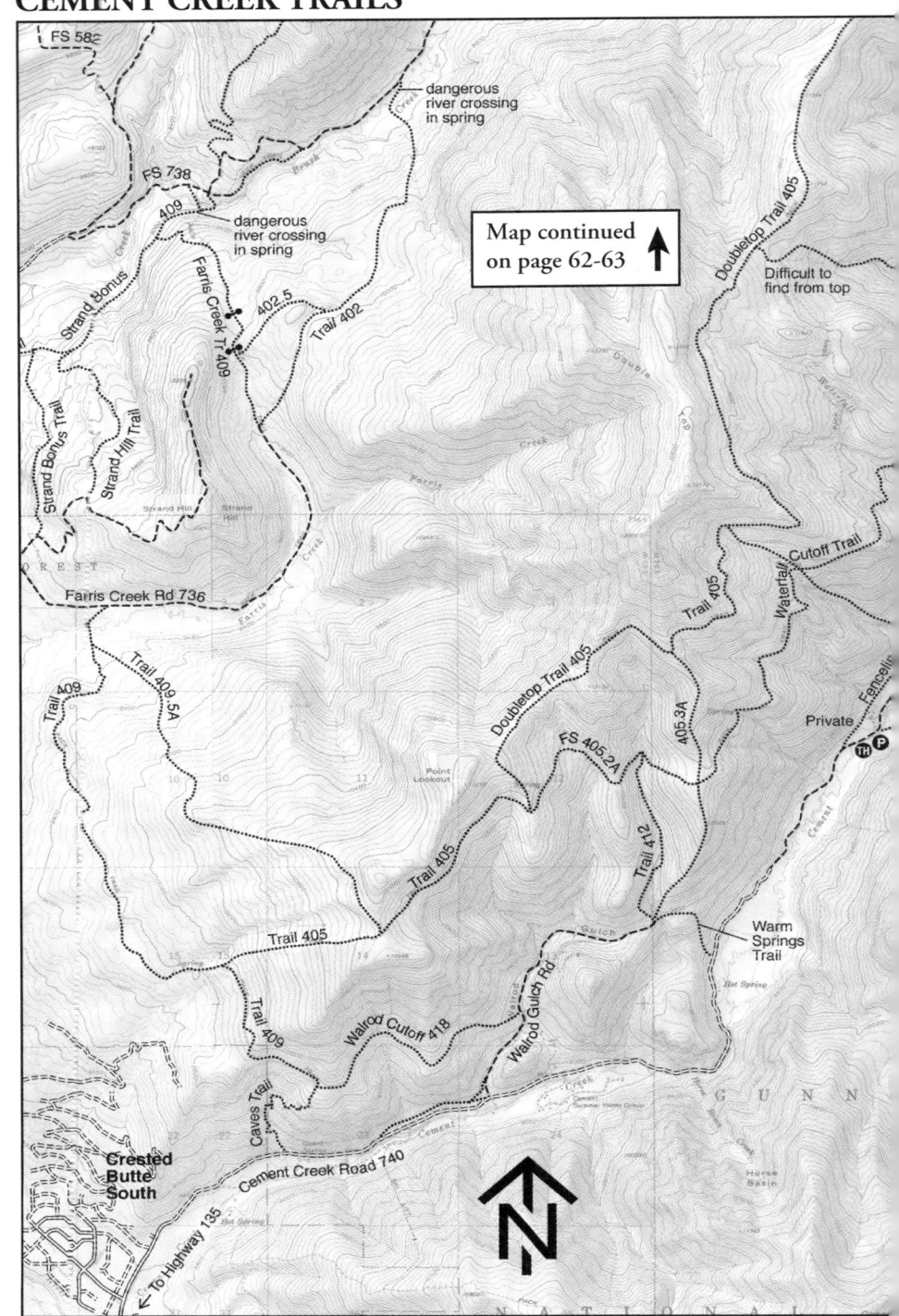

FS 582

dangerous
river crossing
in spring

FS 738

409

dangerous
river crossing
in spring

Strand Bonus Trail

Strand Bonus Trail

Strand Hill Trail

Farris Creek Tr 409

402.5

Trail 402

Map continued
on page 62-63

Doubletop Trail 405

Difficult to
find from top

Strand Hill

Waterfall Cutoff Trail

Farris Creek Rd 736

Trail 405

Trail 409

Trail 409.5A

Doubletop Trail 405

405.3A

Fenceline

Private

TH P

FS 405.2A

Point
Lookout

Trail 412

Trail 405

Warm
Springs
Trail

Trail 405

Gulch

Walrod Cutoff 418

Walrod Gulch Rd

Trail 409

Caves Trail

Hot Spring

Crested
Butte
South

G U N N

Cement Creek Road 740

Horse
Basin

to Highway 135

Hot Spring

N

N A T I O N A L

UPPER BRUSH & CEMENT CREEK TRAILS

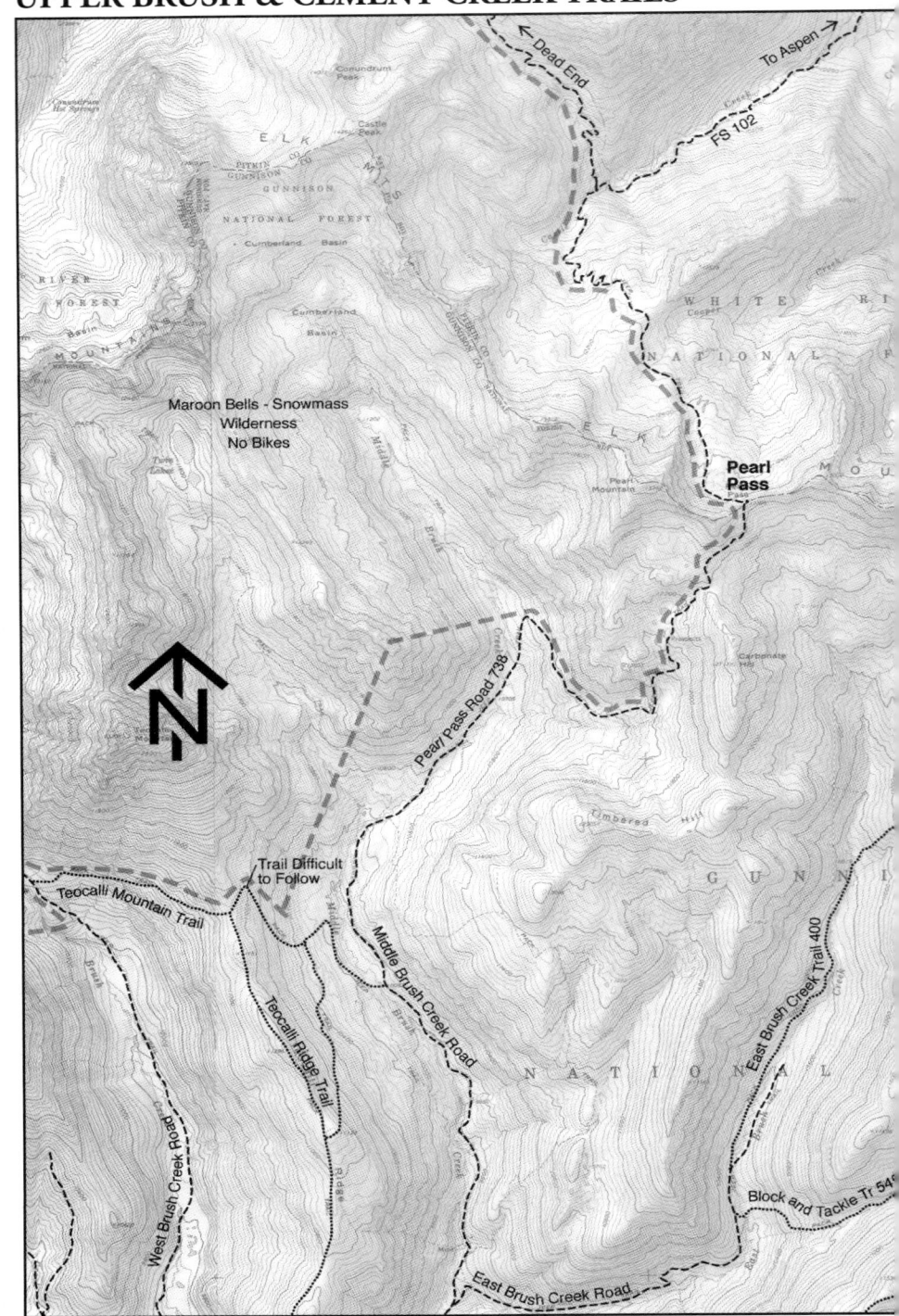

To Aspen
Dead End
FS 102

Conundrum Pass

Castle Peak

ELK MTNS

PITKIN CO
GUNNISON CO

GUNNISON NATIONAL FOREST

Cumberland Basin

RIVER FOREST MOUNTAINS

Cumberland Basin

WHITE RI

NATIONAL

Maroon Bells - Snowmass
Wilderness
No Bikes

Middle Brush

ELK MOU

Pearl Mountain

Pearl Pass

Carbonate Hill

Pearl Pass Road 738

Timbered Hill

GUNNI

Trail Difficult to Follow

Teocalli Mountain Trail

Teocalli Ridge Trail

Middle Brush Creek Road

East Brush Creek Trail 400

NATIONAL

West Brush Creek Road

Block and Tackle Tr 54

East Brush Creek Road

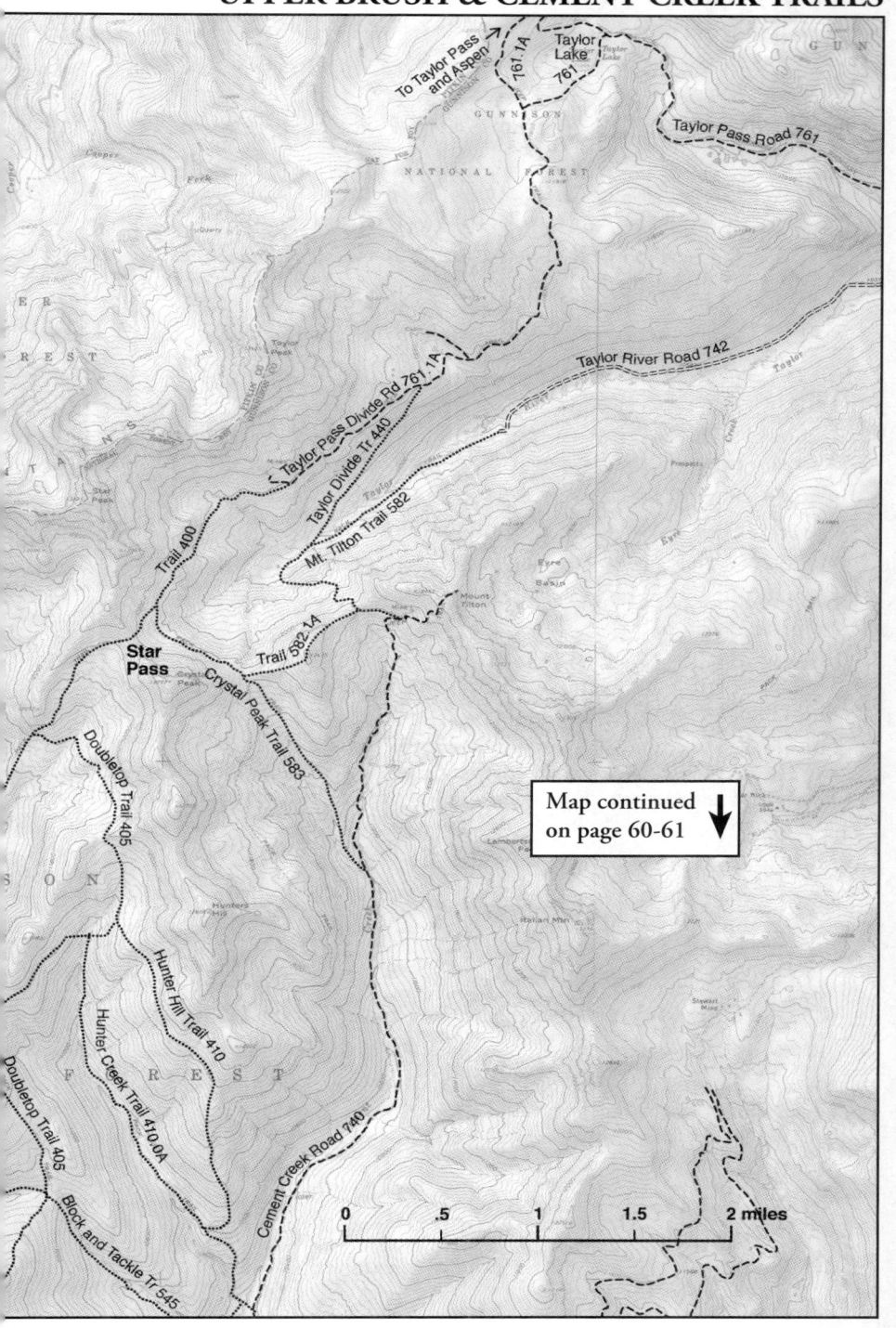

To Taylor Pass and Aspen

761.1A

Taylor Lake 761

Taylor Pass Road 761

GUNNISON

NATIONAL FOREST

Taylor River Road 742

Taylor Pass Divide Rd 761.1A

Taylor Divide Tr 440

Mt. Tilton Trail 582

Trail 400

Trail 582.1A

Eyre Basin

Mount Tilton

Star Pass

Crystal Peak Trail 583

Map continued
on page 60-61 ↓

Doubletop Trail 405

Hunter Hill Trail 410

Hunter Creek Trail 410.0A

Doubletop Trail 405

Block and Tackle Tr 545

Cement Creek Road 740

0   .5   1   1.5   2 miles

THE CAVES LOOP
Ride Information

See map pages 60-61

Description: The Caves Loop is a short, but challenging singletrack ride in Cement Creek. It tends to melt out sooner than a lot of the rides around Crested Butte, making it a popular early season ride or a quick loop in the summer. Sustained singletrack climbs on this ride will challenge early season lungs! Once the ridge is gained, the trail rolls pleasantly around sage and wildflower hillsides on excellent singletrack, with wonderful views into Cement Creek. Ride the trail from Crested Butte to get a good road spin in before and after, or drive to Cement Creek for a short ride.

Distance: 4.6 mile loop:1.8 miles of dirt road and 2.8 miles of singletrack. If you ride to the trailhead and back from Crested Butte, add 14 miles of paved road and 3 miles dirt road.

Time: From the Farris Creek Trail 409 Trailhead: 1-1½ hours. From town: 2½ -4 hours.

Difficulty: Expert

Technical Skill: Expert. Steep singletrack climbs and steep, loose switchbacks on the descent. The upper trail is exposed over steep hillsides.

Aerobic Effort: Moderate with sections of high on the trail.

Elevation: Top: 9,650' **Gain:** 1,050' **Gain from town:** 1,550'

Season: Late May through October

Finding Route: Fairly easy. Walrod Gulch Road and the singletrack shortcut to it are not marked.

Maps: Latitude 40 Crested Butte/Taylor Park or the 5th edition Latitude 40 for Aspen/ Crested Butte/Gunnison, or National Geographic/Trails Illustrated Crested Butte/Pearl Pass.

Location: Start at the four-way stop in Crested Butte at the corner of Highway 135 and Elk Avenue. Drive (or ride) 6.8 miles south on Highway 135 to Cement Creek Road. Turn left and continue 1.8 miles farther to a parking lot on the right, directly across from the Farris Creek Trail 409 trailhead. Begin (or continue) the ride here.

Mileage Log:

0.0 Begin (or continue) riding up Cement Creek Road from the Farris Creek Trailhead.

0.5 Take the unsigned singletrack on the left in the flat sage meadow. Stay low here on the singletrack and parallel the road.

0.7 Ride straight across the campsite road and continue on the singletrack.

1.0 Turn left and up at the fork in the singletrack, and cross a creek.

1.1 Turn left onto the Walrod Gulch Road and begin climbing. (If you missed the singletrack at mile 0.5, Walrod Gulch Road is the next road on the left past the campsite with a large boulder in it.)

1.5 Continue straight past an unmarked dirt road on right.

1.8 Turn left on signed Walrod Cutoff Trail 418. Begin to climb and contour through the open hillside meadows.

3.5 Junction of Farris Creek Trail 409. Turn left and begin the challenging switchback descent.

4.6 Back to your car on Cement Creek Road. If you rode from town, turn right onto Cement Creek Road and head back to Crested Butte. 🚲

WALROD GULCH TO TRAIL 409.5A

See map pages 60-61, 36-37 ——————————— **Ride Information**

Description: This is a great ride in the Cement Creek drainage south of Crested Butte. The loop is popular with locals, but otherwise little known. It is a moderate length ride on excellent singletrack! The loop combines both moderate and challenging climbs, smooth contouring singletrack through hillside meadows loaded with wildflowers, and a fast, and in sections fairly steep and rutted descent through big meadows and aspen forest. This loop is great from town, but it can be shortened by 18 miles by parking at the Farris Creek Trail 409 Trailhead on Cement Creek Road, see option 2, below. The mileage for this loop is in parenthesis in the description below starting at 6.6 and in option 2. Trail 409.5A can be ridden in the opposite direction to connect up with other trails in the area, but it is grueling as a climb. Most riders like it best as described below, from town. Locally this ride is known as "410," although it is not signed as this on any part of the trail. Parts of the trail have recently been re-routed by CBMBA volunteers and are now rideable. Add on The Strand Bonus Trail at the end for more singletrack and not much more climbing, see option 1.

Distance: 25.2 mile loop from town: 8 miles of singletrack, 8 miles of pavement, 9.5 miles of dirt road. From the Farris Creek Trail 409 Trailhead: 7.9 miles of singletrack and 1.7 miles of forest doubletrack.

Time: From town: 3 ½-5 ½ hours. From the Farris Creek Trail 409 Trailhead: 2 ½ -4 hours.

Difficulty: Expert

Technical Skill: Expert

Aerobic Effort: High

Elevation: Top: 10,900' **Gain:** 3,000'

Season: June through September

Finding Route: Moderate. Walrod Gulch and the shortcut trail leading to it are not marked. There are many turns on this loop.

Maps: Latitude 40 Crested Butte/Taylor Park Trails or National Geographic/ Trails Illustrated Crested Butte/Pearl Pass (note that the trail numbers for Walrod Gulch and Walrod Cutoff are switched on the Trails Illustrated map) or the 5th Edition Latitude 40 Aspen/Crested Butte/Gunnison

Location: Start at the four-way stop in Crested Butte at the corner of Elk Avenue and Highway 135. There is a large public parking lot here behind the visitor center.

Mileage Log:

0.0 Ride 6.8 miles south on Highway 135 to Cement Creek Road (County Road 740.) Turn left and ride across the East River and past Crested Butte South. The road turns to dirt. Begin climbing gradually.

8.6 (0.0) Pass the Farris Creek Trail 409 Trailhead on the left and parking lot on the right.

9.4 (0.8) An unsigned singletrack takes off to your left. Take this and parallel the road.

9.6 (1.0) Cross a dirt road to a campsite and continue on the singletrack.

9.8 (1.2) The singletrack splits, turn left and up, and cross a creek.

9.9 (1.3) Turn left and ride up the Walrod Gulch Road at the end of the singletrack. (If you missed the singletrack or ended up back to Cement Creek Road, just turn left on the Walrod Gulch Road. It is the next road on the left after the campsite with a large boulder in it.)

10.3 (1.7) Continue straight past an unmarked dirt road on the right.

10.6 (2.0) Continue straight past the signed Walrod Cutoff Trail on the left. Stay with the road and follow the creek up, then cross it and begin climbing more steeply.

11.5 (2.9) Continue up and left, passing two unmarked trails to the right. The climb steepens again as the trail narrows to singletrack.

11.6 (3.0) Begin the signed Walrod Gulch Trail with a 2/10ths of a mile hike-a-bike section, then continue riding up the trail. Soon cross the creek and climb up the opposite bank.

12.6 (4.0) Cross the creek again, and climb a short distance to an intersection.

12.7 (4.1) Take a sharp left on the Walrod Spur Trail 405.2A and ride steeply up through the aspens.

13.7 (5.1) Ride straight ahead through the next signed intersection and onto the Doubletop Trail 405, which comes in from the right. (Don't go right up the steep hill!) This is the end of the Walrod Spur Trail. Continue contouring and climbing on this beautiful section of singletrack, first through hillside meadows and aspens, and then into the dark forest.

15.0 (6.4) High Point! Nice spot for a snack and to enjoy the view. Turn right here on the signed Farris Creek Bypass Trail 409.5A. Ride up a short distance, and then across an open meadow with great views of Mount Crested Butte, the town of Crested Butte, and Whetstone Mountain. Begin a steep, fast descent. Once the trail turns sharply to the right at the edge of an aspen grove, watch out for muddy, heavily eroded areas. (There is a faint, closed off doubletrack trail to the left of this right turn, be sure not to take it. Stick with the more defined trail.)

18.0 The Farris Creek Trail 409 merges in from the left at the bottom of a meadow. Ride across a small earthen damn and continue a short distance to Farris Creek Road 736.

18.1 Turn left on Farris Creek Road, ride up a short, steep hill and through a gate. This is a fun, fast road descent.

18.6 Ride straight ahead passing Strand Hill Road to the right, and continue downhill. (Or turn right and ride uphill 2/10ths of a mile to the Strand Bonus Trail to finish off the loop with more singletrack, see option 1, below.)

19.3   Turn left on Brush Creek Road and spin back toward Crested Butte.

23.0   Turn right on Highway 135, cross the Slate River, and turn right onto the singletrack that parallels the highway back to Crested Butte.

25.2   Back to the four-way stop.

Option 1: To finish the loop from town with The Strand Bonus Trail, ride as described in the main description to mile 18.6.

18.6   Turn right and climb up to the Strand Bonus Trail.

18.8   Turn left on the signed Strand Bonus Trail.

20.2   Turn left on the Canal Trail.

21.1   Turn left on Brush Creek Road.

27.6   Back to Crested Butte.

Option 2: (Expert) To make this a shorter ride, drive to mile 8.6 and park at the Farris Creek Trail 409 Trailhead. Ride from here as described until the high point in the above description, mile 15.0 (6.4). The mileage for this option is in parenthesis, above, starting at the Farris Creek Trail 409 Trailhead.

(6.4)   Instead of turning right onto Trail 409.5A here, ride straight ahead, staying on Trail 405. Descend this rutted, very steep hill to Farris Creek Trail 409.

(7.3)   Turn left on Trail 409 and ride through more aspen forests, then out into the open hillside meadows.

(8.4)   Intersect the Walrod Cutoff Trail 418. Turn right and ride down the steep, loose switchbacks on Trail 409. (Or turn left on the Walfod Cutoff Trail for a traversing, gentler descent to Walrod Gulch Road, turn right and descend to Cement Creek Road. Turn right on Cement Creek Road and head back to your car.)

(9.5)   Back to your car. (Or 12.0 miles if you take the Walrod Cutoff Trail.) 🚴

Trail 409.5A

by Rob Mahedy

TRAIL 409
Ride Information

Description: Trail 409 is a hard ride that connects The Cement Creek drainage to The Brush Creek drainage. It has many short, steep climbs that challenge most riders aerobically and about one mile of very technical descent. It rolls through many beautiful aspen groves and mountain meadows, and has great views of Whetstone Mountain and Cement Creek. The ride starts with a quick spin down Highway 135 and a moderate climb up Cement Creek and Walrod Gulch, next the route follows the Walrod Cutoff Trail to Trail 409. Walrod Cutoff is an awesome trail with short, steep climbs and contouring singletrack across open hillside meadows. Trail 409 begins as a moderately technical climb, and then rolls along through the aspens and meadows. All riders will probably walk up the short re-route of the trail around private property. After some moderate descents and climbs through the aspens, the trail becomes increasingly technical as it crosses a talus field and muddy areas. Plan to walk some unless you are a very good technical rider. This ride opens earlier than many of the longer Crested Butte area rides.

Distance: 24 mile loop from town: 7 miles of singletrack, 8 miles of pavement, 9 miles of dirt road.

Time: 2½-4 hours

Difficulty: Expert

Technical Skill: Expert. Narrow, sustained singletrack climbs, and extremely rocky terrain on the traverse toward Brush Creek. The trail can be muddy and boggy in sections.

Aerobic Effort: High

Elevation: Top: 10,200' **Gain:** 2,300'

Season: June to mid-October

Finding Route: Fairly easy, most junctions are marked.

Maps: Latitude 40 Crested Butte/Taylor Park Trails or the 5th edition Latitude 40 Aspen/Crested Butte/Gunnison or the Alpineer Bike Trails Map or National Geographic/Trails Illustrated Crested Butte, Pearl Pass.

Location: Start at the four-way stop in Crested Butte at the corner of Highway 135 and Elk Avenue. There is a large public parking area here.

Mileage Log:

0.0 Ride south on Highway 135. This is a mostly downhill spin to Cement Creek Road.

6.8 Turn left and ride up Cement Creek Road 740. Pass Crested Butte South.

8.6 Pass the Farris Creek Trail 409 Trailhead. Continue up Cement Creek Road.

9.1 Take the unmarked singletrack on the left that parallels Cement Creek Road. Stay low on this trail and parallel the road.

9.4 Ride straight across the road to a campsite and continue on the singletrack.

9.6 The singletrack splits. Turn left and up and cross a creek.

9.8 Turn left and ride up Walrod Gulch Road. (If you missed the singletrack at mile 9.1, Walrod Gulch is the next road on the left past the campsite and just over a creek.)

10.4   Turn left on the signed Walrod Cutoff Trail 418 and begin a challenging set of climbs.

12.0   Turn right at the junction with the Farris Creek Trail 409. Climb up and then roll along through a beautiful aspen forest. Enjoy views of Whetstone Mountain across the valley on the left.

12.3   Begin a short, steep re-route around private property.

13.3   Stay left, passing Doubletop Trail 405. Ride through meadows, then into the aspens.

14.8   Ride through a gate. The trail becomes more technical.

16.6   Trail 409 merges with Trail 409.5A and crosses a small earthen damn.

16.7   Turn left on Farris Creek Road, and ride up a short hill. Ride through a gate and continue on the road. (Or turn right and ride Farris Creek or Trail 402 for a longer loop. See Option1.)

17.2   Stay left past the intersection of Strand Hill road and head downhill. (Or turn right and climb up to ride The Strand Bonus or The Strand Hill Trail for more singletrack with very little climbing see Option2.)

17.9   Turn left on Brush Creek Road. Follow this across the East River, up a long gradual hill, past the Skyland Country Club, and on to Highway 135.

21.6   Turn right on Highway 135. Just after crossing the Slate River look for the singletrack on the right that will take you back to town.

23.8   Back to the four-way stop.

Option 1: At mile 16.7, turn right on Farris Creek Road and continue on to ride the north section of the Farris Creek Trail. This will add six miles and one hour to the ride.

Option 2: At mile 17.2, turn right and ride Strand Bonus or Strand Hill. This will add up to three miles and ½ hour to the ride.

Lower Loop Trail

CEMENT CREEK TRAIL
Ride Information

See map pages 60-63

Description: The Cement Creek Trail is a gradual intermediate loop located in the Cement Creek Valley, 7 miles south of Crested Butte. There is little elevation gain on the loop unless The Warm Springs and Walrod Cutoff Trails (The Caves Loop) are added at the end. The beginning of the loop winds up the beautiful canyon and upper valley of Cement Creek on smooth dirt road. There are great views of Italian and surrounding mountains here, and lots of wildflowers in the big meadows. After wading Cement Creek, parallel the creek and road back down the valley on The Cement Creek Trail. The trail is easy except for several boggy areas that require carrying your bike. Cement Creek and the boggy areas can be deep in the spring, better to wait until after spring runoff has slowed. Continue on The Fenceline Trail to finish off the loop, or add on a climb up the Warm Springs Trail and down Walrod Gulch to The Walrod Cutoff Trail for more singletrack. (These are expert trails.)

Distance: 20 mile loop, 10.7 -15 miles of dirt road, 5-10.3 miles of singletrack.

Time: 2 ½-4 hours

Difficulty: Intermediate, expert if you add on the Warm Springs and Walrod Cutoff Trails.

Technical Skill: Intermediate, expert if you add on the Warm Springs and Walrod Cutoff Trails.

Aerobic Effort: Moderate, high if Warm Springs and Walrod Cutoff Trails are added.

Elevation: Top: 10,200' **Gain:** 700' **Gain if Warm Spring and Walrod Cutoff Trails are added to loop:** 2,000'

Season: Late-May to late October

Finding Route: Easy to moderate

Maps: Latitude 40 Crested Butte/Taylor Park or National Geographic/Trails Illustrated Crested Butte/Pearl Pass

Location: The beginning of the ride is at the Farris Creek Trail 409 Trailhead. To get here, drive 6.8 miles south of the four-way stop in Crested Butte to Cement Creek Road 740. Turn left and drive 1.8 miles to the Farris Creek Trailhead and park on the right.

Mileage Log:

0.0 Turn right out of the parking area and begin riding up Cement Creek Road.

1.0 Pass an unmarked singletrack. Take this or the road. If you take the singletrack, stay low and parallel the road. When the trail splits, turn right and return to Cement Creek Road.

5.3 Pass the Deadman Gulch Trailhead on the right. Continue up Cement Creek Road.

6.6 Cross Cement Creek and switchback up, continuing on the road. In early spring when Cement Creek is high, ride the single track as an out and back from here. It heads up Cement Creek on the left before the road crosses the creek.

7.0 Stay left and pass the shortcut trail to Reno Divide Road and Reno-Flag-Bear.

7.5 Stay left on Cement Creek Road and pass Reno Divide Road when the road forks.

8.5   Stay left on Cement Creek Road, passing the signed Grassy Trail on the right.

8.6   Pass Trail 580 on the left, stay on the road.

9.6   Turn left onto the signed Block and Tackle Trail and wade Cement Creek. Keep your shoes on! Walk up a short hill out of the creek and turn left on the unmarked Cement Creek Trail.

10.7 Continue straight ahead, crossing the unmarked Trail 580.

11.9 Cross a deep little creek and continue straight across the signed Waterfall Creek Trail.

12.4 The trail splits here. For an easier end to your loop, turn left and ride down Cement Creek Road. Intersect the road in 1/10th of a mile, turn right on the road and return to your car at mile 19. For more singletrack, turn right and climb. This section includes some short sections of advanced technical riding, but these can be easily walked.

13.5 Ride into an open meadow. Look for a spur trail to the left and take it. Even though the Fenceline continues another 1 ½ miles, it is closed up ahead because it crosses private property.

14.0 Back to Cement Creek Road. Turn right and descend to an aspen grove just before Cement Creek Ranch.

14.6 (approx. mileage) In the aspen grove just before Cement Creek Ranch is a trail heading right and up, The Warm Springs Trail. There is a sign here that says no uphill motorcycle traffic. Turn right on the trail and climb. (Or continue on Cement Creek Road down to your car. Be careful of traffic coming up.)

15.7 (approx. mileage) Top of the Warm Springs Trail on Walrod Gulch Road. Turn left and descend on the road.

17.1 Turn right on The Walrod Cutoff Trail. This turn is right by a telephone pole. Climb and contour on the trail through beautiful hillside meadows.

18.8 Turn left on Farris Creek Trail 409 and descend steep switchbacks to your car.

19.9 Back to your car. 🚲

RENO-FLAG-BEAR-DEADMAN GULCH

See map pages 60-61 ———————————————— **Ride Information**

Description: Reno-Flag-Bear-Deadman Gulch is an awesome ride just south of Crested Butte in the Cement Creek drainage. It has miles of great singletrack in just a 20 mile loop. This popular ride starts out with a long but mostly moderate climb on the Reno Divide Road. Riders are rewarded with great views at the top. From then on the loop is all singletrack: fast downhills, winding, creekside trail, and aerobically challenging climbs. The loop finishes with the famous 32 descending switchbacks on the Deadman Gulch Trail. For a little longer version of this loop, ride The Rosebud Trail up instead of the Deadman Gulch Trail. See Rosebid option, below. If you only have a few days to ride, make sure to include this loop!

Distance: 20 mile loop: 14 miles of singletrack and 6 miles of forest road. Add 30 miles of paved and dirt road if you ride from Crested Butte.

RENO-FLAG-BEAR-DEADMAN GULCH
Ride Information

Time: 3-5 hours from the Deadman Gulch Trailhead.

Difficulty: Expert

Technical Skill: Expert. The trails that make up this ride have recently been repaired so it is smooth and fast, but often they become very deeply rutted and eroded due to heavy motorcycle use. It also has some rocky and rutted sections alongside the creeks, and some deep creek crossings.

Aerobic Effort: High. This ride has three long, sustained climbs with several steep sections, two of which are narrow singletrack.

Elevation: Top: 11,150' **Gain:** 3,400'

Season: Mid-June through mid-October

Finding Route: Easy. There are several turns, but the trail is well marked. The turn at the top of the Bear Creek climb at mile 11.1 is a little confusing.

Maps: Latitude 40 Crested Butte/Taylor Park or the 5th edition Latitude 40 Aspen/Crested Butte/Gunnison

Location: From the four-way stop in Crested Butte at the corner of Elk Avenue and Highway 135, drive (or ride) 6.8 miles south to Cement Creek Road and turn left. Continue 6.8 miles up Cement Creek Road to the parking lot for the Deadmans Gulch Trail on the right. (After driving past Cement Creek Ranch and through a long, open meadow, this parking lot is just after you climb a short, steep hill into the aspens.)

Mileage Log:

0.0   Turn right out of the parking area and begin riding up Cement Creek Road.

1.3   Pass a singletrack that heads left up the creek. Switchback to the right and cross Cement Creek, staying on Cement Creek Road. Ride up a couple switchbacks.

1.7   Take the well established but unsigned shortcut trail leading off to the right, just before a small downhill on Cement Creek Road. (If you miss this turn, just turn right at the signed Reno Divide Road 759, ½ mile past the shortcut, and ride up from there. This is slightly longer than the shortcut.)

2.1   After taking the shortcut, turn right on Reno Divide Road, and continue uphill. Climb on this road for a few miles, passing an old cabin and reaching wonderful views at the top.

5.7   Top of the road climb! Go through a gate and close it, and ride straight ahead to the signed singletrack for Flag Creek Trail 422. This is a rippin' downhill, but be aware of technical areas and creeks. The creek crossings are deep, I suggest walking them.

8.8   Turn right onto the signed Bear Creek Trail 415. (This turn is 1/10th of a mile after the trail crosses a compacted gravel bridge. It is just after the trail enters the dark woods. If you end up on a forest road, you've gone too far.) Cross Flag Creek and begin riding up one of its' tributaries. The trail climbs up the creek, sometimes steeply, and then heads out into a large meadow. After riding around the top of the meadow, swing right and pass a closed trail on the left. Continue up a short steep hill to Forest Road 744.

11.2   Turn left on the road and follow it gradually uphill. Do not cross the road, the singletrack leading up the other side leads up to Reno Divide.

11.9   Ride straight ahead through the fork in the forest road, over a dirt berm and between the trees, onto the continuation of the signed Bear Creek Trail. Ride through a big meadow, and cross a wooden bridge. Continue down and cross Bear Creek. The trail steepens, following the left bank of Bear Creek.

13.2   Re-cross Bear Creek, and descend along the right bank. Lower down the creek, the trail curves to the right away from the creek and around the hillside, and then flattens out just before it joins the Deadman Gulch Trail.

15.3   Turn right and begin climbing up the signed Deadman Gulch Trail 420. This is a beautiful creek and the climb is mostly gradual, but continuous, with a couple steep and challenging sections. (Or see the Rosebud Option, below, for a little longer ride.)

17.6   Near the top, pass Cement Mountain Trail 553 on the left. Continue up the switchbacks to the summit of Reno Ridge.

17.8   Continue straight ahead, passing the Reno Divide Trail to the right, and ride through the gate. Start down the Deadman Gulch Trail's switchbacks. When you reach the bottom, follow Cement Creek upstream a short distance, then cross it on a big log bridge. Follow the trail up to the parking lot.

20.2   Back to your car!

Rosebud Option: For a slightly longer and different version of this ride, continue down the Bear Creek Trail one mile past the Deadman Gulch turn at mile 15.3.

16.3   Cross Rosebud Creek, and turn right on the signed Rosebud Trail 423. Again cross the creek, climbing up high on the right bank. Settle in for a long and scenic climb, which becomes quite steep at the top.

19.2   In the dark forest, arrive at a T-intersection. Turn right on the signed Cement Mountain Trail 553. This trail has wonderful views! Roll through the big open meadows, and descend quickly through the dark forest to rejoin the Deadman Gulch Trail.

23.0   Turn left and climb a short distance up the switchbacks to the summit of Reno Divide.

23.2   Ride straight ahead, passing the unmarked Reno Divide Trail to the left, and through the gate. Descend the switchbacks to your car.

25.6   Back to your car. This adds about 45 minutes-1 hour to the ride. 🚲

RENO RIDGE
Ride Information

Description: Reno Ridge is a shorter option to the more popular Reno-Flag-Bear-Deadman Gulch ride that is just south of Crested Butte. It is still great riding but with less singletrack. It starts with the same gradual climb up Reno Divide Road to the summit of Reno Ridge, where riders are treated with great views. The route then follows the ridge up and down on a doubletrack with some short, challenging climbs. Some sweet singletrack leads to the Deadman Gulch Trail. The singletrack is eroded from heavy motorcycle use in a few spots, but most of it is in good shape. Finish off the loop by descending the famous 32 singletrack switchbacks on the Deadman Gulch Trail. If you have never ridden Reno Ridge or Reno-Flag-Bear-Deadman Gulch, the latter is a better ride, but Reno Ridge is a fun option for another day or as a link to the Cement Mountain and Rosebud Trails, or as a way to ride back after riding Reno-Flag- Bear-Deadman Gulch in reverse. (A challenging expert loop. Don't ride it in this direction during heavy use periods. You'll likely be in a collision with a high speed downhiller.)

Distance: 13.5 mile loop, 8.4 miles of dirt road and doubletrack, 5.1 miles of singletrack.

Time: 2-3 hours

Difficulty: Expert

Technical Skill: Expert

Aerobic Effort: Moderately high

Elevation: Top: 11,363' **Gain:** 2,400'

Season: Late June through mid October

Finding Route: Easy to moderate, the route is straightforward and most turns are signed.

Maps: Latitude 40 Crested Butte/Taylor Park Trails or Latitude 40 Aspen/Crested Butte/Gunnison

Location: From the four-way stop in Crested Butte at the corner of Elk Avenue and Highway 135, drive 6.8 miles south to Cement Creek Road and turn left. Drive 6.8 miles farther to the signed parking lot for the Deadman Gulch Trail 420 on the right.

Mileage Log:

0.0 Turn right out of the parking area, and begin riding up Cement Creek Road.

1.3 Cross Cement Creek to the right, passing the Homestead Trail heading left and up the creek. Ride up a couple switchbacks on the road.

1.8 Turn right and climb on the unmarked but very well established four-wheeler track shortcut to the Reno Divide Road.

2.3 Turn right on the road at the end of the shortcut and climb this road for several miles.

5.7 Top out on the road on a saddle. Turn right before the gate and start climbing on the doubletrack on top of the ridge. The road rolls up and down on the ridge.

7.4 Stay right on the road, passing a singletrack to the left. This singletrack heads down to the top of the Bear Creek climb on the Reno Flag Bear Deadman Gulch ride.

8.4   Turn right at a fork in the road and ride toward the signed Reno Ridge singletrack, which begins in a short distance.

11.3   End of the Reno Ridge singletrack and the top of the Deadman Gulch Trail switchbacks. Turn right, go through a gate and descend 32 switchbacks, cross a huge log bridge (some can ride this) and climb up a hill to the parking area.

13.5   End at your car. 🚲

CRESTED BUTTE TO ASPEN

See map pages 60-63, 36-37 ———— Ride Information

Description: Riding to Aspen from Crested Butte is a wonderful, challenging adventure through the Elk Mountains, and over Star and Taylor Passes is the singletrack way to go. East Brush Creek Road and Trail 400 are very beautiful and nearly all rideable on the way up. Star Pass offers amazing views before riders descend, still on Trail 400, through wildflowers and high altitude meadows. From here, a primitive doubletrack with great views of the Collegiate Peaks takes riders toward Taylor Pass, the entire way above 11,000 feet. The Elk Mountains tower above Taylor Pass and Express Creek Road, another great spot for a break. As you start down toward Aspen, look for the spectacular Malamute and Castle Peaks on the left. Descend on steep dirt road and fast pavement to Aspen. For an overnight adventure, plan on spending the night in Aspen and ride back over Pearl Pass. Or ride to Aspen by way of Pearl Pass and back to Crested Butte over Taylor and Star Passes to enjoy the singletrack Trail 400 as a fast, winding and narrow singletrack descent. Pearl Pass is also quite spectacular, but is quite rocky and involves some hike-a-bike in either direction. It is all four-wheel drive road. Be sure to start your ride early to avoid thunderstorms and lightning when you are up high.

Distance: 40 miles one way. Call Dolly's Mountain Shuttle at 970-349-2620 (local Crested Butte) or 970-948-9893 (local Aspen) or check visitcrestedbutte.com and click on shuttle for information on a one-way ride to or from Aspen, or spend the night and ride back!

Time: 5-7 hours

Difficulty: Expert-Epic

Technical Skill: Expert

Aerobic Effort: Strenuous

Elevation: Top: 12,200' **Gain:** 4,400'

Season: July through late September or early October

Finding Route: Easy

Maps: Latitude 40 Aspen/Crested Butte/Gunnison

Location: Begin the ride at the four way stop in Crested Butte. This is located at the corner of Highway 135 (6th Street) and Elk Avenue by the visitor center. There is plenty of public parking behind the visitor center.

Mileage Log:

0.0   Begin riding south toward Gunnison on Highway 135.

2.2   Turn left on Brush Creek Road, just after crossing the Slate River.

2.7   Roll past the entrance to Skyland on the left and continue on Brush Creek Road. Soon it turns to dirt. The route follows this road for several miles and riders may not need to consult the directions except at road junctions.

4.7   Pass Brush Creek Trailhead and descend to cross the East River.

5.9   Continue on Brush Creek Road, passing Farris Creek Road on the right.

7.2   The road starts to climb.

8.0   Stay right on Brush Creek Road when the road forks. Left is West Brush Creek Road and leads to Teocalli Ridge and Deer Creek.

8.4   Descend to cross West Brush Creek and climb out of the drainage.

8.9   As Brush Creek Road veers left and climbs steeply, ride straight ahead onto a primitive doubletrack. Pass the signed Farris Creek Trail 409 singletrack on the right. The doubletrack soon narrows to singletrack and is a nice shortcut. It is a steep dropoff to the side of the trail in spots, you may have to walk short sections.

9.6   Reach the end of the shortcut and rejoin Brush Creek Road. Continue straight ahead, riding downhill into a beautiful valley.

10.7   Cross Middle Brush Creek and continue on the road, now climbing.

11.0   Stay right on East Brush Creek as the road forks. Middle Brush Creek Road turns left and climbs to Pearl Pass.

12.8   Continue on the road, passing Block and Tackle Trail on the right.

13.2   Turn left onto the signed Trail 400. This is a wonderful section of singletrack.

15.2   Cross East Brush Creek and begin climbing more steeply.

16.3   Stay left on East Brush Creek Trail 400, passing the turn to the Doubletop Trail on the right. The climbing here is quite steep and challenging.

17.5   Reach the top of Star Pass at 12,200', and enjoy amazing views before starting the descent.

17.7   Stay left on Trail 400, passing the Crystal Peak Trail (a fun trail leading into the Cement Creek drainage, for another day) to the right. Continue down on Trail 400 through high alpine meadows, then climb to the end of the trail.

19.0   Turn right at the end of the trail and descend on Taylor Pass Divide Road, a rough doubletrack.

20.2   Stay left, passing Taylor Divide Trail 440 on the right.

20.5   Stay on the main road, passing a spur road that heads left.

22.5   Pass a small lake and stay left, passing Taylor Pass Road 761 on the right.

23.3   Enjoy the views on Taylor Pass! Ride ahead and left to the signed Express Creek Road 122 to Ashcroft, and begin descending. (Right is Taylor River Road and Taylor Lake is below, and straight ahead and up leads to Richmond Ridge.)

26.3   Stay on the main road, passing a turn to Markley Hut to the left.

28.3 Turn right onto the paved County Road 102 at the T-intersection. Stay on the shoulder, there is fast traffic on this road.

38.9 Reach the hospital, just before the intersection with Highway 82. Turn right at the hospital onto the bike path and follow the signs back to Aspen. 🚲

TRAIL 400 TO THE HUNTER CREEK TRAIL

See map pages 60-63, 36-37 ——————————— **Ride Information**

Description: This is a long and adventurous ride with wonderful views and great singletrack. It connects the Brush Creek and Cement Creek drainages by way of several rugged, high altitude singletracks. The loop starts with a long and steady road climb up the Brush Creek drainage from Crested Butte, winding through sage and wildflower meadows and aspen groves. The climb becomes more adventurous once riders start up East Brush Creek Trail 400 toward Star Peak. It starts with a gradual roll through high altitude meadows and becomes steep and challenging as it climbs into the forest. Back out in the open, a short hike-a-bike stint on the Doubletop Trail leads to a steep and rutted, then smooth and fun descent on The Hunter Creek Trail that ends in the Cement Creek drainage. Unfortunately the lower half of this trail has been opened to four-wheelers, and is often loose and rutted due to motorized traffic on the steep lower section. The Cement Creek Trail takes riders through the beautiful upper meadows of Cement Creek where a road spin or more singletrack (Walrod Gulch and Trail 409.5) take you back to Crested Butte. Don't attempt this ride if thunderstorms are lurking on the horizon because of the length and high altitude. Get an early start and be prepared for a long day. This loop is also good in reverse.

Distance: 29.8 miles, 12 or more miles of singletrack, 8 miles of pavement, 10 miles of dirt road.

Time: 5-7 hours

Difficulty: Expert to Epic

Technical Skill: Expert

Aerobic Effort: Strenuous

Elevation: Top: 12,200' **Gain:** 3,725'

Season: July through September

Finding Route: Easy to moderate

Maps: Latitude 40 Crested Butte/Taylor Park or 5th edition Latitude 40 Aspen/Crested Butte/Gunnison

Location: Begin at the four-way stop in Crested Butte at the intersection of Elk Avenue and Highway 135 (6th Street.)

Mileage Log:

0.0 Ride east on Elk Avenue away from the main downtown area. Turn right on 9th Street and follow it past Red Lady Avenue and behind the school, where it turns to dirt. This dirt road eventually narrows to a singletrack that parallels the highway. Follow the trail over a paved road and continue to the end. Turn left on Highway 135 and cross the Slate River.

TRAIL 400 TO THE HUNTER CREEK TRAIL
Ride Information

2.2 Turn left on Brush Creek Road (County Road 738) marked with the Crested Butte Country Club sign. Follow this mostly gradual road for several miles. It winds through the beautiful East River Valley and up into the Brush Creek drainage.

2.8 Pass Skyland Drive, staying with the main road. The road turns to dirt. Climb a gradual hill, then descend to cross the East River.

5.9 Pass Farris Creek Road to the right.

7.2 The road begins to climb more steeply after crossing Brush Creek.

8.0 The forest road splits. Stay right on Brush Creek Road. Descend to cross Brush Creek and then begin climbing again. (Left is West Brush Creek Road and leads to the Teocalli Ridge and Deer Creek trails.)

8.9 As you climb into the aspens and Brush Creek Road veers left and climbs, ride straight ahead onto a primitive two-track. Signed Trail 409 heads right from this intersection also. The two-track will narrow to a singletrack. Be careful of eroded drop-offs on this shortcut trail.

9.6 Reach the end of the shortcut, continue straight ahead on Brush Creek Road and through the valley.

10.7 Cross Middle Brush Creek and begin climbing again.

11.0 Stay to the right when the road to Pearl Pass splits off to the left. Continue climbing, now on East Brush Creek Road.

12.8 Continue straight ahead on East Brush Creek Road, passing the Block and Tackle Trail on the right.

13.2 At a high point in the road, turn left on the signed Trail 400. (The road descends to the creek and dead-ends.)

15.2 Cross East Brush Creek and a marshy meadow, and begin climbing steeply into the dark timber. This is a big lung buster to clean!

16.3 Out in the meadows right below the high mountain ridges, turn right on the signed Doubletop 405 Trail. Soon you will be hiking your bike up to the saddle.

17.2 Reach the saddle. Descend steeply straight ahead.

17.6 Pass the Hunter Hill Trail on the left.

17.8 Ride straight ahead and down on the Hunter Creek Trail at the next intersection. (Right is the continuation of the Doubletop Trail.)

19.7 Stay right and continue down on the Hunter Creek Trail, passing the bottom of the Hunter Hill Trail on the left.

20.3 Turn right just before crossing Cement Creek, and cross Hunter Creek. This junction is unmarked and fairly easy to miss, but you can return to it if you arrive at Cement Creek. After crossing Hunter Creek, parallel Cement Creek on the singletrack, riding straight ahead at all junctions for the next few miles. This trail is in bad shape in some spots, with deep motorcycle ruts that fill with water. It is better after a dry spell. I suggest walking across the creeks and muddy areas.

20.6 Cross the Block and Tackle Trail.

21.6 Cross the unmarked Trail 580.

22.8 Ride past the signed Waterfall Creek Trail that climbs to the right, just after crossing a small creek.

23.3 Stay left as the trail forks at some big rocks. (Straight ahead, The Fenceline Trail, is now closed in 1.6 miles because of a section of private property. You can ride the first 1.1 miles of it and turn left on an unmarked singletrack in a meadow. This will take you down to Cement Creek Road.)

23.5 Turn right onto Cement Creek Road. From here, take Cement Creek Road all the way to Highway 135, turn right and ride back to Crested Butte. (Or ride Walrod Gulch to 409.5A back to town. This turn is 5.3 miles down Cement Creek Road on the right, and involves quite a bit of climbing.)

29.8 Back to Crested Butte. 🚲

CRYSTAL PEAK TRAIL TO TRAIL 400
See map pages 60-63, 36-37 ————————— **Ride Information**

Description: This is a beautiful, very high alpine ride, a little known Crested Butte loop for the adventurous rider! In July and August, ride through huge fields of wildflowers on nearly the whole loop. The ride begins with a fast spin south down Highway 135 and a long and beautiful spin up Cement Creek Road. From here, the short but steep and high altitude climb on the Crystal Peak Trail leads to Crystal Pass, where riders are rewarded with great views of Star and Taylor Peaks. One more climb to Star Pass puts you at the top of Trail 400 for a fast and beautiful singletrack descent. The ride continues to descend East Brush Creek Road, a narrow two-track that winds through the aspens. Finish the loop with a little more smooth singletrack on Trail 409 and the Canal Trail. Add the Upper Upper Loop and Tony's Trail on at the end, if desired. Expect to walk some on the ascents, the trail is steep and deeply rutted by motorcycles in spots. Start early to avoid thunderstorms and lightning while at high altitude.

Distance: 41 mile loop, 8 miles of pavement, 10 miles of singletrack, 13 miles of graded dirt road and 10 miles of forest road.

Time: 5-7 hours

Difficulty: Expert

Technical Skill: Expert to Epic

Aerobic Effort: Strenuous

Elevation: Top: 12,200' **Gain:** 4,300'

Season: July through late September. Wear orange on this ride during hunting season.

Finding Route: Easy

Maps: 5th Edition Latitude 40 Aspen/Crested Butte/Gunnison or Latitude 40 Crested Butte/Taylor Park Trails.

CRYSTAL PEAK TRAIL TO TRAIL 400
Ride Information

Location: Begin at the four-way stop in Crested Butte at the corner of Elk Avenue and Highway 135 (6th Street), by the visitor center. There is a large public parking lot here.

Mileage Log:

0.0 From the four-way stop in Crested Butte, ride south on Highway 135.

6.8 Turn left onto Cement Creek Road, Forest Service 740. Continue on this road for nearly 15 miles. The road is straightforward and riders probably do not need to look at the mile-by-mile directions until reaching the Crystal Peak Trail.

7.2 Stay right, passing the Crested Butte South subdivision. Begin climbing gradually.

13.8 Pass the Deadman's Trailhead on the right.

15.1 Cross Cement Creek on a switchback.

15.5 Stay left on the road, passing the shortcut trail to Reno Divide Road.

16.0 Stay left on Cement Creek Road, passing signed Reno Divide Road on the right.

17.0 Stay left on the road, passing the signed Grassy Trail on the right.

17.2 Stay on the road, passing the unmarked Trail 580 on the left that eventually leads to the Doubletop Trail.

18.1 Pass the Block and Tackle Trail on the left, continue on Cement Creek Road.

18.3 Pass the Hunter Hill Trail on the left. Some sections on the road climb more steeply after this. This part of the road usually boasts lots of flowers in the summer!

21.3 Turn left on the signed Crystal Peak Trail on the left. Ride into the dark woods. Enjoy amazing meadows of wildflowers on this challenging climb.

22.7 Arrive at a saddle with awesome views of Star and Taylor Peaks, straight ahead, and the junction of the Mt. Tilton Spur. Turn left and ride down briefly into the very top basin of the headwaters of the Taylor River, then climb up to Trail 400.

23.5 Turn left on East Brush Creek Trail 400, and climb steeply to the pass.

23.7 Arrive at Star Pass, 12,200'. From here follow the contouring trail to the right, then plunge into the East Brush Creek drainage.

24.8 Stay right, passing Trail 405, Doubletop, on the left.

28.0 End of Trail 400, ride straight ahead onto East Brush Creek Road. Continue descending.

28.2 Pass the Block and Tackle Trail.

30.2 Stay left and continue downhill, passing Middle Brush Creek Road on the right.

30.4 Cross the Middle Fork of Brush Creek.

31.6 After a short climb and a cattleguard, turn left onto an unmarked singletrack to the left. This shortcut avoids a couple steep climbs on Brush Creek Road. Be aware of the steep drop to the left on eroding sections of the trail. Sometimes walking is necessary here.

32.2 The shortcut trail ends on Brush Creek Road at the intersection with Farris Creek Trail 409. Turn left on Trail 409 to finish the loop with singletrack. (Or follow Brush Creek Road all the way back to Highway 135, turn right and continue back to Crested Butte. This is 9 easy miles back to town.) Descend on Trail 409 to a fork on the edge of a hill.

32.4 Turn left at the fork, ride down a short, steep hill, and cross Brush Creek. Be careful, there is a gate at the bottom of the hill just before the creek that is often closed.

32.9 Ride straight ahead onto the Strand Bonus Trail, passing the Farris Creek Trail descent coming in on the left.

33.4 Stay right at the fork, passing the Strand Hill Trail coming in on the left.

33.5 Ride straight ahead onto the Canal Trail, as the Strand Bonus Trail climbs to the left.

34.5 Cross the canal and turn left on Brush Creek Road. Ride back to town.

38.6 Turn right on Highway 135. There is a singletrack that takes you back to town on the right, just after crossing the East River.

40.9 Back to the four-way! 🚲

Photo by Xavier Fane

Trail 400

DOUBLETOP TRAIL
Ride Information

See map pages 60-63, 36-37

Description: The Doubletop Trail makes for quite an adventurous day! Doubletop is not for the weak of leg, lung, heart, or attitude. This is a very strenuous and difficult trail with many steep climbs and rough descents, but the remote location and wonderful 360 degree views from the top make it worth the effort. The first loop option, described below, begins with a long, gradual ride up the Cement Creek drainage and a steep singletrack climb to the ridge on Doubletop Mountain. The trail then follows the exposed Doubletop ridge, so it is not a good ride to do if thunderstorms are lurking on the horizon. The trail climbs and descends several times along the ridge, and traverses high altitude meadows. Finally it descends steeply to intersect Trail 409 and rolls through aspens to either a smooth, contouring descent of Trail 412 or a steep descent of the switchbacks on Trail 409, back to Cement Creek Road. Another loop option starts from Crested Butte and follows Brush Creek Road, East Brush Creek Road, and the beautiful Trail 400 up to Doubletop (See Trail 400 to Hunter Hill.) It next follows the same route along Doubletop Ridge as the loop described below, but descends on Trail 409.5 to Farris Creek. From here, roll back to town on Brush Creek Road. This option is longer, but doesn't involve driving or that much more effort. There are many other options to climb up to or descend from Doubletop, check out the Latitude 40 maps for exploration ideas. All of these trails are steep in spots and involve carrying your bike up, and all are eroded in parts from heavy motorcycle use. Don't ride the Doubletop Trail after rain, it is a total mud-fest.

Distance: 27 mile loop from the Farris Creek Trail 409 trailhead: 21 miles of singletrack and 6 miles of dirt road

Time: 5-8 hours

Difficulty: Expert to Epic

Technical Skill: Expert. This trail is heavily used by dirt bikers, so much of the trail on the upper sections is deeply rutted and stays muddy for a long time. Steep, loose, and rocky descents and very strenuous singletrack climbing are the norm on this ride.

Aerobic Effort: Strenuous.

Elevation: Top: 11,742' **Gain:** 4,800'

Season: Mid-July through September to mid October. Usually done with the first snow in the fall.

Finding Route: Moderate to difficult in certain areas. There are faint unmarked side trails on the ridge. The main trail is more prominent and mostly well signed.

Maps: Latitude 40 Crested Butte/Taylor Park or the Latitude 40 Aspen/Crested Butte/Gunnison or the National Geographic/Trails Illustrated Crested Butte/Pearl Pass.

Location: Drive 6.8 miles south from the four-way stop in Crested Butte (at the corner of Elk Avenue and Highway 135) on Highway 135 to Cement Creek Road 740. Turn left and drive 1.8 miles farther to a parking lot on the right, directly across from the Farris Creek Trail 409, and park here.

Mileage Log:

0.0   Turn right out of the parking area and ride up Cement Creek Road. Stay on this road for 6.6 miles, passing the Cement Creek Campground, Cement Creek Ranch, and the Deadman Gulch Trailhead. When the road enters a second narrow and steep gulch, you are nearing the first turn off the road.

6.6 Turn left onto a singletrack just before the road switchbacks and crosses Cement Creek, and head up the creek. This singletrack is marked only with a carsonite user sign and can be marshy in spots. This singletrack spur leads to the Cement Creek Trail. (Or continue up Cement Creek Road 3.2 miles to the turn for the Hunter Creek Trail, turn left and cross Cement Creek to intersect this description at mile 9.8.)

6.8 Keep riding straight ahead along the creek, passing the sharp left to the Fenceline Trail.

7.3 Continue straight and ride past the Waterfall Creek Trail on the left. Carry your bike across a small creek, it is deep and muddy. (This trail intersection is inaccurately represented on the Latitude 40 and Trails Illustrated maps, as the Waterfall Creek Trail does not continue down and cross Cement Creek to join the road on the other side. It ends here on the Cement Creek Trail.)

8.5 Continue straight ahead, crossing the unmarked Trail 580 (which does continue down to cross Cement Creek.)

9.5 Continue straight ahead, crossing the unsigned Block and Tackle Trail 545. Nice views of Italian Mountain straight ahead.

9.8 Cross Hunter's Creek, climb up the bank on the other side, and turn left immediately onto the steep Hunter's Creek Trail 410.

10.3 Ride straight ahead, passing the Hunters Hill Trail on the right. Continue climbing, sometimes very steeply.

12.2 Intersect Doubletop Trail 405. Turn left and climb and contour, then descend through the dark woods where it is quite rutted. There are many trails here due to motorcycles trying to avoid the mud and deadfall, pick your way through to the other side of the woods and the continuation of the main trail.

14.3 Ride straight ahead passing the signed Block and Tackle Trail on the right. This trail drops down to meet East Brush Creek Road.

14.4 Continue riding straight, passing the continuation of the Block and Tackle Trail that drops back down to Cement Creek. Begin a very challenging climb.

15.0 Ride into open meadows and pass Trail 580 on the left, marked only with a carsonite sign. Continue through beautiful meadows, enjoying the nearly 360 degree views. Italian Mountain is to the northeast, Cement Mountain is to the south, Gothic and Teocalli Mountains are to the west, Castle and Star Peaks are to the north. Ride a short downhill, and then climb up to next summit.

16.3 Highest summit of the day at 11,742 feet! Begin a fun downhill.

16.7 Pass a small lake on the right. The Waterfall Trail takes off left here, but the intersection is indistinct as is the beginning of the trail. Continue straight ahead and uphill again, then down across a meadow that parallels Doubletop Mountain on your right. The descending trail becomes rutted and wide and rolls over big slabs of rock.

17.6 At the bottom of this hill cross a creek that has been widened by many ruts, and go left to stay with the creek, riding downhill. Do not follow the less used trail going off to the right and up! Cross two side creeks, then roll up another short climb. Now the trail becomes a smooth, fun descent through the aspens and then crosses an open hillside meadow.

DOUBLETOP TRAIL
Ride Information

19.8 Stay to the right, passing the unmarked Hank Barlow Trail that heads left and down. (This trail is not on most maps. It quickly and steeply descends to the Fenceline Trail if a quick exit is needed.) Begin climbing again.

20.3 Arrive at a T-intersection at the summit of a tough little climb, next to two big trees on the left. Awesome views here! Stay right. (Left leads down to Walrod Gulch, but is confusing and braided. Not the best option for descent.)

20.6 Ride straight ahead, and pass a faint trail on the left. Big, rutted downhill coming up.

22.1 Descend to the junction with the Walrod Spur Trail 405.2A. Turn right and begin a beautiful, gradual climb across open hillside meadows and through the aspen groves. This section of the trail is in great shape.

23.5 Continue straight, passing the Farris Creek Bypass Trail 409.5A to the right. Still on the Doubletop Trail, descend another steep rutted hill.

24.4 Turn left at the intersection with Farris Creek Trail 409. Ride through aspen forest, and out into open hillside meadows.

25.6 Junction with the Walrod Cutoff Trail 418. Stay right and ride down the steep, loose switchbacks to Cement Creek Road. (Or, for a longer, smooth and contouring descent, turn left and follow Trail 412 back to Walroad Gulch. Turn right and descend to Cement Creek Road, again turn right and ride back to your car. This option is just a little longer.)

26.7 Back to your car! 🚲

WATERFALL CREEK CUTOFF TRAIL
Ride Information ─────────────── *See map pages 60-63*

Description: The Waterfall Creek Cutoff is a little ridden alternative to the Doubletop Trail, located in the Cement Creek drainage south of Crested Butte. Lower and shorter than Doubletop, it is characterized by narrow, challenging singletrack that contours above the Cement Creek Valley. The Cement Creek drainage is quite beautiful and this is an adventurous loop for those who've tried it all or like thin trails. The Waterfall Creek Cutoff is unmaintained by the forest service (a non-system trail) and much of it is in poor condition: expect deadfall, sections that are faint and difficult to follow, and some short sections of hike-a-bike. The trail is nice in the fall as it travels mostly through aspen forest. This is a good loop from town, see option, below

Distance: 17 miles: 9 miles of singletrack, 8 miles of dirt road and forest doubletrack; 32 miles if ridden from town as described in the option.

Time: 3-4½ hours, 5-6½ hours from town.

Difficulty: Expert

Technical Skill: Expert. Very narrow, primitive singletrack on steep hillsides, technical creek crossings, steep and rutted descents.

Aerobic Effort: High

Elevation: Top: 10,650' **Gain:** 2,800' **Gain from town:** 3,200'

Season: Mid-June through October

Finding Route: Difficult. Many turns are unmarked and one turn is unclear.

Maps: Trails Illustrated/National Geographic Crested Butte/Pearl Pass, or the 2002 Alpineer Bike Trails Map or Latitude 40 Crested Butte/Taylor Park Trails.

Location: Start at the four-way stop in Crested Butte at the corner of Elk Avenue and Highway 135(6th Street.) Drive (or ride) 6.8 miles south on Highway 135 to Cement Creek Road 740. Turn left and drive 1.8 miles to a parking lot on the right, directly across from the Farris Creek Trail 409 Trailhead. Park here.

Mileage Log:

0.0 Start (or continue) riding up Cement Creek Road. Continue past Cement Creek Campground, Cement Creek Ranch, the Deadman Gulch Trailhead, and climb up a narrow, steep section of road.

6.3 After the steep and narrow section of road, turn left on a singletrack that heads up Cement Creek as the road switchbacks and crosses Cement Creek. Do not cross Cement Creek! The trail is marked only with a carsonite user sign. This is the Cement Creek Trail. Ride (or walk to save your chain rings) over a couple technical sections.

6.5 Continue straight past a very sharp left. (This is the Fenceline Trail.) Ride straight up the creek.

7.0 At the end of a short meadow, turn left and ride up the signed Waterfall Creek Trail, just before a small creek. (The Waterfall Creek Trail is inaccurately represented on most maps, it does not continue down to the right to cross Cement Creek, it ends on the Cement Creek Trail.) The trail climbs along the creek for a short distance, descends left briefly, and then climbs steeply to the right and into the aspens. When the forest begins to open up to a meadow again, start looking for the next turn to the left, which is invisible near the intersection.

7.3 Turn left on the Waterfall Creek Cutoff Trail by three large pines and some downed logs just as the meadow opens up. Ride toward the pines and the trail will appear as it crosses a gully, then heads around and up the next hill. (The Waterfall Creek Trail that you just left continues up through the meadow, and is marked by posts. Don't continue up! It is continuously steep and difficult to follow in this direction.)

7.4 Cross a creek, and climb. There are great views of the upper Cement Creek Valley behind, and of Cement Mountain across the valley in front.

8.4 Steep, technical creek crossing.

8.9 Steep, loose climb and rocky dyke crossing. Most riders will walk this section.

9.7 The trail arrives at a T-intersection. Turn left and down this steep trail for just a few feet to where the continuation of the Waterfall Cutoff Trail turns right. Turn right and begin contouring again through open meadows and aspens, then cross a creek and ride into the dark forest. Climb more steeply. (Note: A right turn at the T-intersection leads to the Doubletop Trail, turning left descends steeply to the Fenceline Trail. This steep trail is not shown on most maps, it is locally known as the Hank Barlow Trail.)

11.1 Roll straight ahead through a four-way intersection. The trail disappears, but it becomes more visible as it descends straight ahead into the Walrod Gulch drainage. Descend to the creek and stay left. (Don't be tempted to go left on the more prominent trail in the flat meadow. This trail quickly becomes rutted and heads straight down the ridge. It's not a great option.)

11.4 Turn right at the signed intersection with the Walrod Gulch Trail 412, and climb on the Walrod Spur Trail 405.2A. (Left and down on the Walrod Gulch Trail leads back to Walrod Gulch Road and then down to Cement Creek Road. This is a very fun descent.)

12.3 Ride straight through the signed intersection with the Doubletop Trail. This becomes a beautiful, gradual climb through open meadows and aspens, then again into the dark forest.

13.7 Summit! Ride straight ahead on the Doubletop Trail, passing the signed Farris Creek Bypass Trail 409.5A to the right. Ride down a steep and rutted hill.

14.6 Turn left on the Farris Creek Trail 409. Climb just a bit more, then descend through the aspens and open meadows.

16.1 Stay to the right passing the signed Walrod Cutoff Trail 418, and head down the steep switchbacks to Cement Creek Road.

17.2 Back to your car!

Option: This is a great ride from town. Ride to the trailhead and follow directions to the summit (mile 13.7, above.) Turn right at this intersection on the Farris Creek Bypass Trail 409.5A and ride out across an open meadow, then descend 2.6 miles to the intersection with the Farris Creek Road. Turn left and follow this road. Stay left to pass Strand Hill Road in 6/10ths of a mile, and continue descending to Brush Creek Road. Turn left on Brush Creek Road. Follow this back to Highway 135, turn right and ride back to town. This option adds 15 miles and about 2 hours to your total riding time. 🚲

Deer Creek Trail

DOCTOR'S PARK

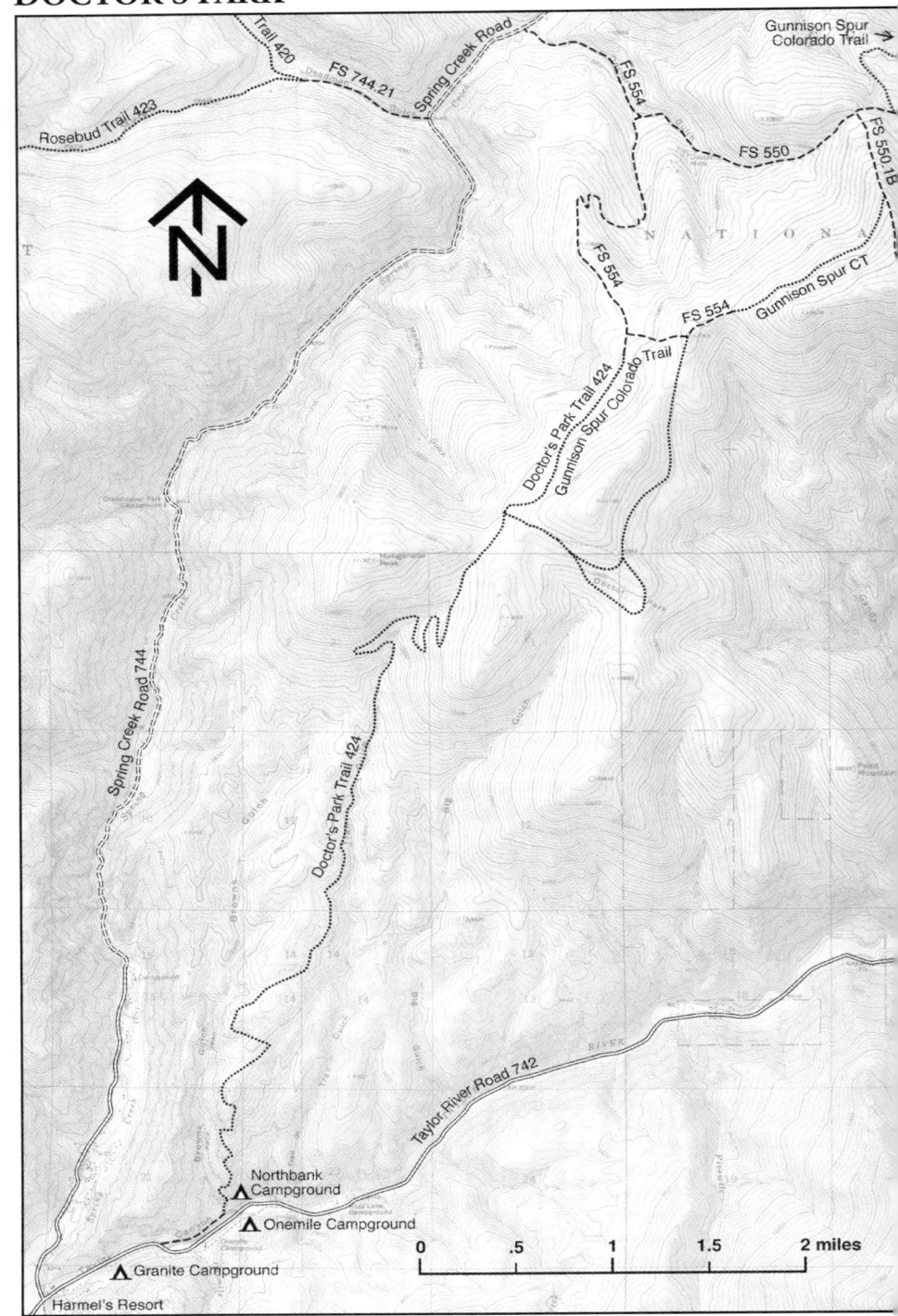

Description: Doctors Park is well known and loved by locals and visitors alike because of its long, smooth and fast descent through the aspens. Much of the climbing is moderate with just a few steep sections. The climb starts with a long gradual dirt road ride up Spring Creek that leads to a steeper forest road climb. The newly re-routed start of the descent has been tamed to a few short rocky sections and some long switchbacks. After this riders can open it up on an incredibly buff singletrack descent. The aspens speeding by will make you giggle! This is also a great fall ride. Be careful of a few rocky sections, deadfall on the trail in the spring and after storms, and the last mile of steep, sandy switchbacks. Doctors Park usually dries out a little sooner than many of the other longer rides around Crested Butte, but be aware that the crossing of Spring Creek at the beginning of the forest road climb may be quite deep and swift and unsafe early in the summer. Check with a local bike shop before riding it. The trail is also good as an out and back if the top has not dried out, riding it this way raises the difficulty rating to expert.

Distance: 20-22 mile loop: 7-9 miles of singletrack, 2 miles of pavement, 11-13 miles of gravel road and forest doubletrack.

Time: 3-5 hours

Difficulty: Advanced intermediate with short expert sections on the descent, mostly on the last mile of the trail.

Technical Skill: Advanced intermediate with short expert sections.

Aerobic Effort: High

Elevation: Top: 10,850' **Gain:** 2,750' **Option: Top:** 10,950' **Gain:** 3,150'

Season: Early to mid-June through early-October

Finding Route: Easy to moderate, most of the turns are clear but some are unmarked.

Maps: Latitude 40 Crested Butte/Taylor Park Trails or the 5th edition Latitude 40 Aspen/ Crested Butte/Gunnison

Location: 18 miles south of Crested Butte. From the four-way stop in Crested Butte at the corner of Elk Avenue and Highway 135, drive 11.6 miles south toward Gunnison on Highway 135. Turn left on the somewhat difficult to see Jack's Cabin Cutoff Road 813. There is a house and cottonwoods at the turn, and a small green sign. Follow this up and over a pass and down to the end on Taylor Canyon Road. Turn left and follow Taylor Canyon Road 1.4 miles, passing Harmels' Resort on the right, Spring Creek Road on the left, and crossing Spring Creek. Park on the left across from the Granite Campground, or somewhere near here. To get to the trail from Gunnison, drive north 9.2 miles on Highway 135 to Almont. Turn right on Taylor Canyon Road 742, and continue 7 miles to the Granite Campground.

Mileage Log:

0.0 Turn right out of the parking area onto Taylor Canyon Road 742, riding back toward Spring Creek.

0.6 Turn right on Spring Creek Road. Ride on this paved, then dirt road for the next 8.6 miles, crossing Spring Creek three times and winding up the narrow, forested canyon.

8.7 After riding around a large switchback, crossing a cattleguard, and passing

DOCTOR'S PARK TRAIL
Ride Information

Forest Road 744.21 on the left to the Rosebud Trail (marked only with a carsonite sign,) the valley begins to open a bit. It is less than one mile to the Doctor's Park turn. Continue past Forest Road 744.21 and up the hill.

9.5 At the top of the hill there is an unmarked right turn leading steeply down to Spring Creek, just before a roadside pullout. This turn is just before the valley opens up even more and before the remains of an old homestead cabin on the right. Take this turn, and cross the creek. Keep your shoes on because of the rocky bottom. After crossing, begin riding up the narrow gulch on Forest Road 554 until you reach a fork in the road.

10.4 Turn right at the road fork, staying with Forest Road 554, and climbing around and up to open views. The road is steep at first and then becomes more gradual, then enters the dark woods.

12.8 Turn right at the signed fork in the dark forest. (The sign points both ways for the Gunnison Spur of the Colorado Trail.) The road soon narrows to singletrack. (Or see option 1, below, for the longer and more scenic route to the left. This longer route dries out just a little quicker in the spring.)

13.9 Stay right and ride past a hunting camp.

14.0 Ride out into an open meadow to the top of the descent. This is a nice spot for a break. The beginning of the descent is fast, be careful of ruts, a few rocky sections and several sharp switchbacks. After crossing a small creek at the bottom of the technical section, zoom for miles through aspen groves on the smooth trail. After a short uphill section, begin the final section of descending switchbacks.

19.8 End of the Doctor's Park Trail at the Northgate Campground. Turn right on the dirt road and follow the river back to Taylor Canyon Road.

20.3 Turn right on Taylor Canyon Road.

20.6 Back to your car.

Option: For the longer and more scenic route, turn left at mile 12.8, above. Climb up a forest doubletrack and out to an open meadow on the Gunnison Spur of the Colorado Trail.

13.2 At the top of the ridge, enjoy a break and awesome views of the Fossil Ridge Wilderness. When ready to roll, continue straight ahead passing the trail sign and the continuation of the Forest Service 554 doubletrack to the left. Turn right on the unsigned contouring singletrack that becomes visible just below the top of the ridge. This trail climbs and descends along the hillside through meadows and forest.

14.7 Stay right when the singletrack splits out in the open meadow, and climb back toward the ridge. Stay right again when the spur singletrack rejoins the main trail from the left.

15.5 The trail forks just before entering the forest again. Turn left and skirt the woods.

15.6 Intersect the main Doctor's Park Trail (mile 14.0, above description) and begin the descent.

21.4 End of the Doctor's Park Trail. Turn right on the dirt road.

21.9 Turn right on Taylor Canyon Road.

22.2 Back to your car. 🚲

MATCHLESS

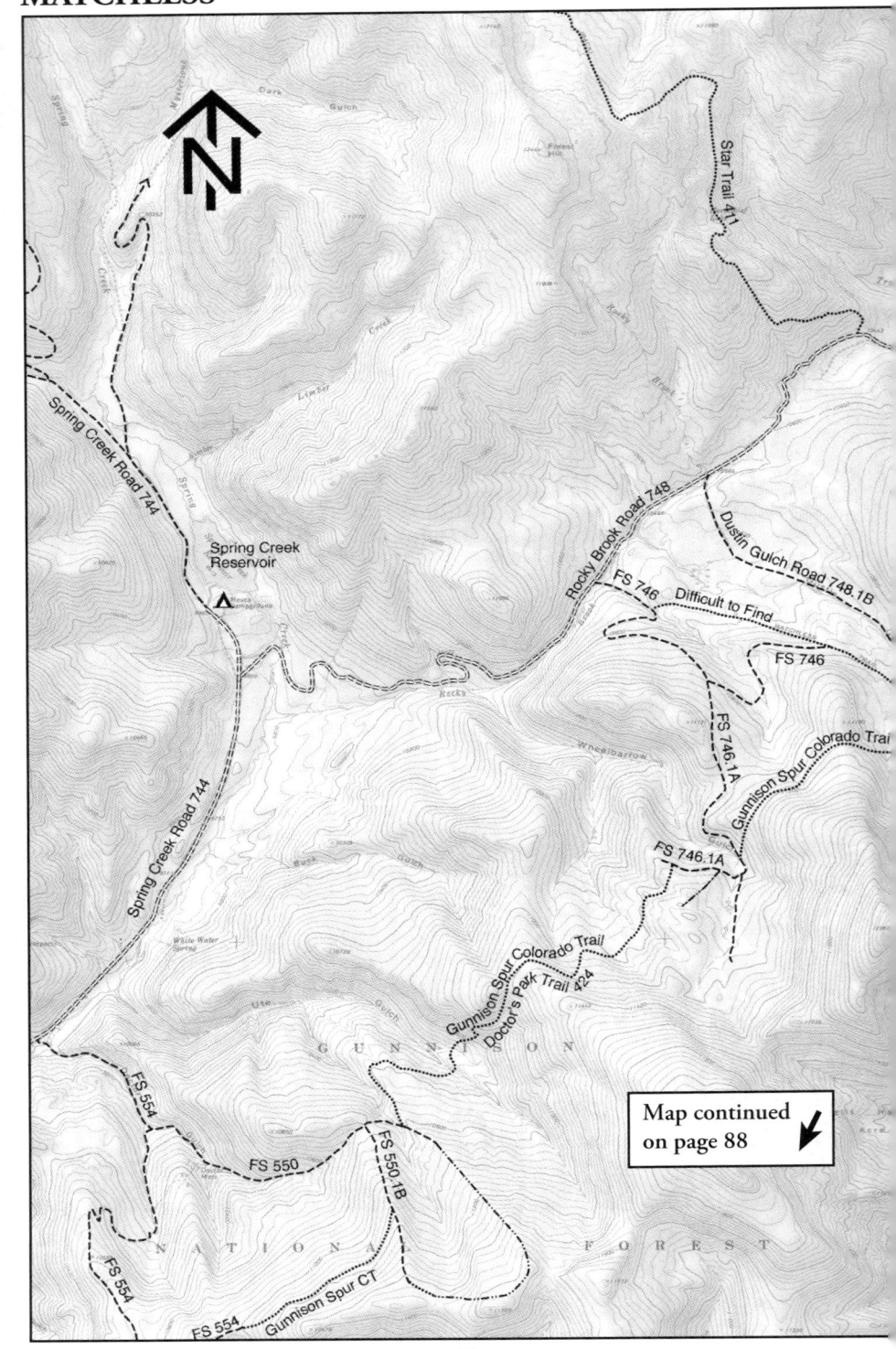

Spring Creek Road 744

Dark Gulch

Star Trail 411

Spring Creek Reservoir

Rocky Brook Road 748

Dustin Gulch Road 748.1B

FS 746

Difficult to Find

FS 746

FS 746.1A

Gunnison Spur Colorado Trail

FS 746.1A

Gunnison Spur Colorado Trail

Doctor's Park Trail 424

GUNNISON

FS 554

FS 550

FS 550.1B

Map continued on page 88

NATIONA

FOREST

FS 554

FS 554   Gunnison Spur CT

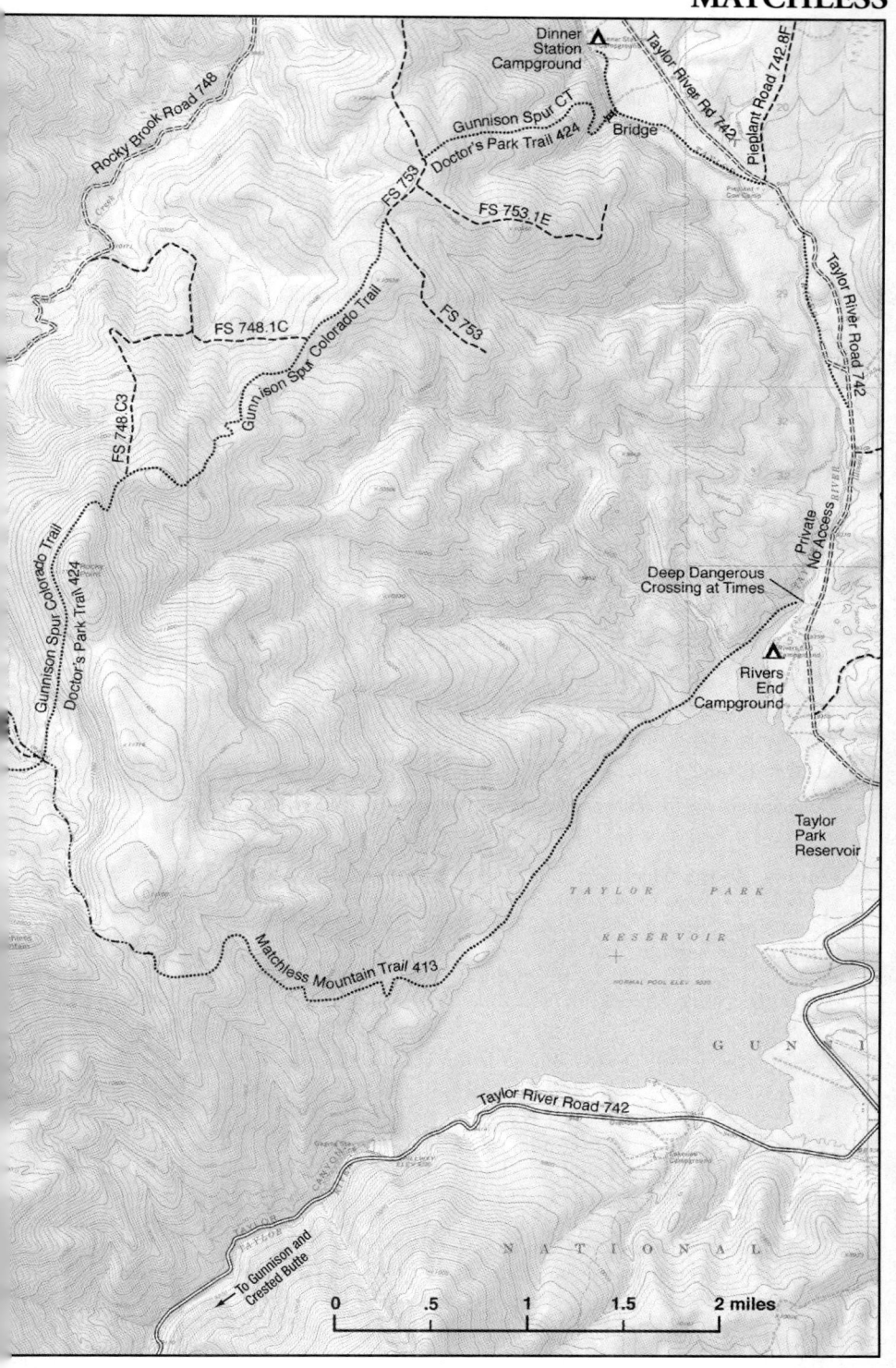

Dinner Station Campground

Rocky Brook Road 748

Taylor River Rd 742

Pieplant Road 742.8F

Gunnison Spur CT

Doctor's Park Trail 424

Bridge

FS 753

FS 753.1E

FS 748.1C

FS 753

Gunnison Spur Colorado Trail

Taylor River Road 742

FS 748.C3

Gunnison Spur Colorado Trail

Doctor's Park Trail 424

Deep Dangerous Crossing at Times

Private No Access

Rivers End Campground

Taylor Park Reservoir

TAYLOR PARK

RESERVOIR

NORMAL POOL ELEV. 9200

Matchless Mountain Trail 413

G U N I

Taylor River Road 742

N A T I O N A L

To Gunnison and Crested Butte

| 0 | .5 | 1 | 1.5 | 2 miles |

MATCHLESS
Ride Information

Description: The Matchless section of the Doctors Park Trail (also a part of the Gunnison Spur of the Colorado Trail,) is an adventure for those who like to spend all day on singletrack. It is also a great way to ride the awesome descent of the classic Doctor's Park loop, but on a much longer ride. Matchless, as it is locally called, starts in Taylor Park, about 36 miles from Crested Butte. Much of the trail is fast and smooth, but several sections are rocky and rutted from heavy motorcycle use. There are several lung busting climbs on the 23 miles of singletrack this ride covers. Most riders can plan on walking some short sections of the climbs. The singletrack ends with the awesome, fast and smooth Doctors Park downhill. The first half of the ride is mostly in dark forest, but has some excellent views from high points. The Doctor's Park descent rolls through mostly aspens and Douglas Fir forest for the last part of the ride. The beginning of this ride is isolated, chances are you may not see anyone until the last part of the ride. Do not ride it alone or without the recommended maps. This ride stays muddy and slick several days after significant rain because of the dark forest. It also climbs to many ridgetops, avoid the ride if there are thunderstorms and lightning in the forecast. Matchless is usually ridden with a shuttle, or connect it as a very long loop by riding up Spring Creek Road or Taylor River Road (Taylor River Road is narrow and has a lot of traffic at times.)

Distance: With a shuttle: 26 miles, 3 miles of forest doubletrack, 23 miles of singletrack. Add 20 miles of paved road if you ride it as a loop with Taylor Canyon Road and 25 miles of dirt road if you ride it as a loop with Spring Creek Road.

Time: 4 ½ -7 ½ hours, add 2 or more hours if you ride it as a loop.

Difficulty: Expert-Epic

Technical Skill: Expert-lots of sustained climbing and descending on narrow singletrack, many sections are rutted.

Aerobic Effort: Strenuous

Elevation: Top: 11,650' **Gain:** 4,450' Add 1,500' if you ride it as a loop.

Season: July through September.

Finding Route: Moderate. The trail is mostly well marked with Colorado Trail symbols and forest service signs, but there are many junctions and some of the signs are missing. The trail is signed as the Doctors Park Trail 424 and also the Gunnison Spur of the Colorado Trail. It is not marked as Matchless, this is just the local name for this section of trail. Don't confuse it with the Matchless Mountain Trail that climbs the saddle between the North and South Matchless Mountains and descends to Taylor Reservoir.

Maps: Latitude 40 Crested Butte/ Taylor Park Trails map is the best, Latitude 40 Aspen/Crested Butte/Gunnison is good also. The Gunnison Basin Public Lands map has the route, but not much detail.

Location: To get to the beginning of this trail, drive south on Highway 135 from Crested Butte 11.6 miles and turn left on the Jack's Cabin Cutoff Road 813. Follow this to its end and turn left on Taylor River Road 742. Drive 1.4 miles, passing Harmels Resort on the right and Spring Creek Road on the left, to the Granite Campground. (From Gunnison, drive 9.2 north on Highway 135 to Almont and turn right on Taylor River Road 742. Drive 7 miles to Granite Campground.) Leave a car across from the campground and continue 20 miles on County Road 742 with bikes and riders. Pass Taylor Reservoir, the road to Tincup and Cumberland Pass in

15 miles, Cottonwood Pass Road in 17 miles, and Texas and Illinois Creeks on the dirt section of Forest Service 742. The Gunnison Spur of the Colorado Trail is barely noticeable, but is just past the road to Pieplant and the Timberline Trail, which is marked with a big sign. Look for the Colorado Trail marker and singletrack on the left, just after the cattleguard. I suggest parking between Cottonwood Pass Road and Texas Creek Road to get a little warm-up before the first climb. If you can't find the trail near Pieplant Road, you can drive to the Dinner Station Campground, a little farther up Forest Service 742, and start here. Ride to the trails' start by heading southeast out of the campground on the singletrack.

Mileage Log:

0.0   Just past the road to Pieplant and the Timberline Trail and a cattleguard, turn left onto the Gunnison Spur of the Colorado Trail singletrack.

0.7   Turn left on the doubletrack toward the creek.

0.9   Turn left on the signed Doctors Park Trail 424. Cross a bridge over the Taylor River and begin a big climb.

2.5   Turn left on the unmarked doubletrack, Forest Service 753.

2.6   Turn right at the road split, staying with Forest Service Road 753. There are signs at this junction. (Forest Service 753.1E continues straight.) Roll gradually downhill.

3.3   Turn right on the signed singletrack, Doctors Park Trail 424.

4.0   Cross Forest Service Road 748.1C and continue on the singletrack. This section offers more challenging climbing.

5.9   Ride straight ahead on the singletrack. (Forest Service Road 548.C3 cuts off to the right. This road is listed as 748.C3 on the Latitude 40 Crested Butte/Taylor Park Trails map.)

7.1   Descend into Dustin Gulch. Enjoy views of Matchless Mountain straight ahead and a nice descent.

8.0   Pass the four-wheeler Matchless Mountain Trail on the right.

8.1   Cross the four-wheeler Matchless Mountain Trail and continue on signed Trail 424. (For another ride, The Matchless Mountain Trail climbs to a saddle and descends a challenging singletrack to Taylor Reservoir It turns left and follows the bank of the reservoir up to cross the Taylor River, which is deep and dangerous in the early summer. Do not continue north along the Taylor River, as this is private property with no access. Cross to the campground.)

9.0   Views of Boston Peak, Italian, and American Flag Mountains to the right.

9.9   Intersect Forest Service Road 746.1A. Ride uphill and left, then immediately right at split. South Matchless Mountain in view.

10.1   Stay right with main road, passing a grassy doubletrack spur to the left.

10.4   Turn left onto the signed wide singletrack, Trail 424.

11.6   Views of Spring Creek Resevoir and the Elk Mountains to the right.

12.1   Descend into Ute Gulch.

13.1   Stay left, passing a faint trail to the right in Ute Gulch. Cross the creek and climb out of the drainage.

13.9 Merge onto a trail that comes in from the right. Stay left and begin a continuous, steep climb on the four-wheeler track.

15.0 Summit of the climb! Enjoy great views here, look for all the fourteeners. Stay on the ridge and ride downhill on the Colorado Trail Spur, passing a closed trail on the left, and climb again. The trail narrows to a singletrack and heads into the woods.

16.1 The trail widens to a road and begins to descend a rocky hill. Descend this road briefly, then turn left and continue on signed Trail 424 singletrack. (Forest Service 550.1B continues down and straight ahead.)

17.3 The singletrack turns into a doubletrack in a little campsite. Continue on this road, Forest Service 554.

17.8 Junction with the climb from the classic Doctors Park loop. Signs here point right for the Gunnison Spur, but turn left onto the singletrack, which immediately swings right and contours and descends along the hillside. This trail then climbs through the woods. It rejoins the Gunnison Spur in two miles.

19.2 Out in the meadow the trail forks, turn right and climb toward the ridge. Stay right when this singletrack comes back in on the left.

20.0 The trail splits right before entering the forest. Turn left and ride around the edge of the trees.

20.1 Intersect the Doctors Park Trail. Turn left and begin a long, fast and mostly smooth descent. In the beginning there are some rocky sections and steep switchbacks, and toward the end are steep and loose, sandy switchbacks.

25.7 End of the trail at the Northgate Campground. Turn right on the road.

26.2 Turn right on Taylor River Road.

26.4 Granite campground and your car. Good riding! 🚲

A Fun Matchless Descent

Photo by Alison White

Trail 401

Photo by Alison White

Deer Creek Trail

TIMBERLINE TRAIL

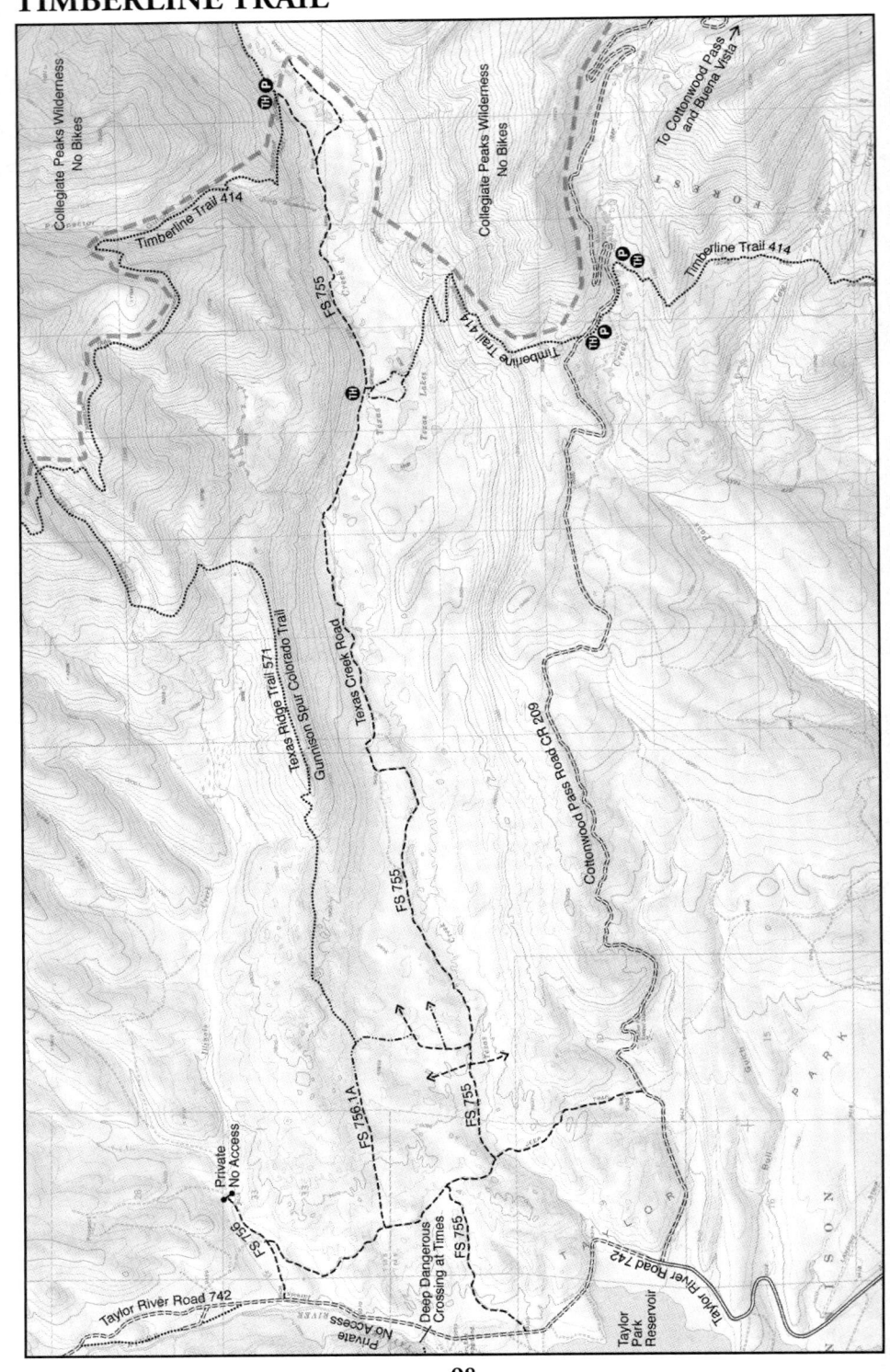

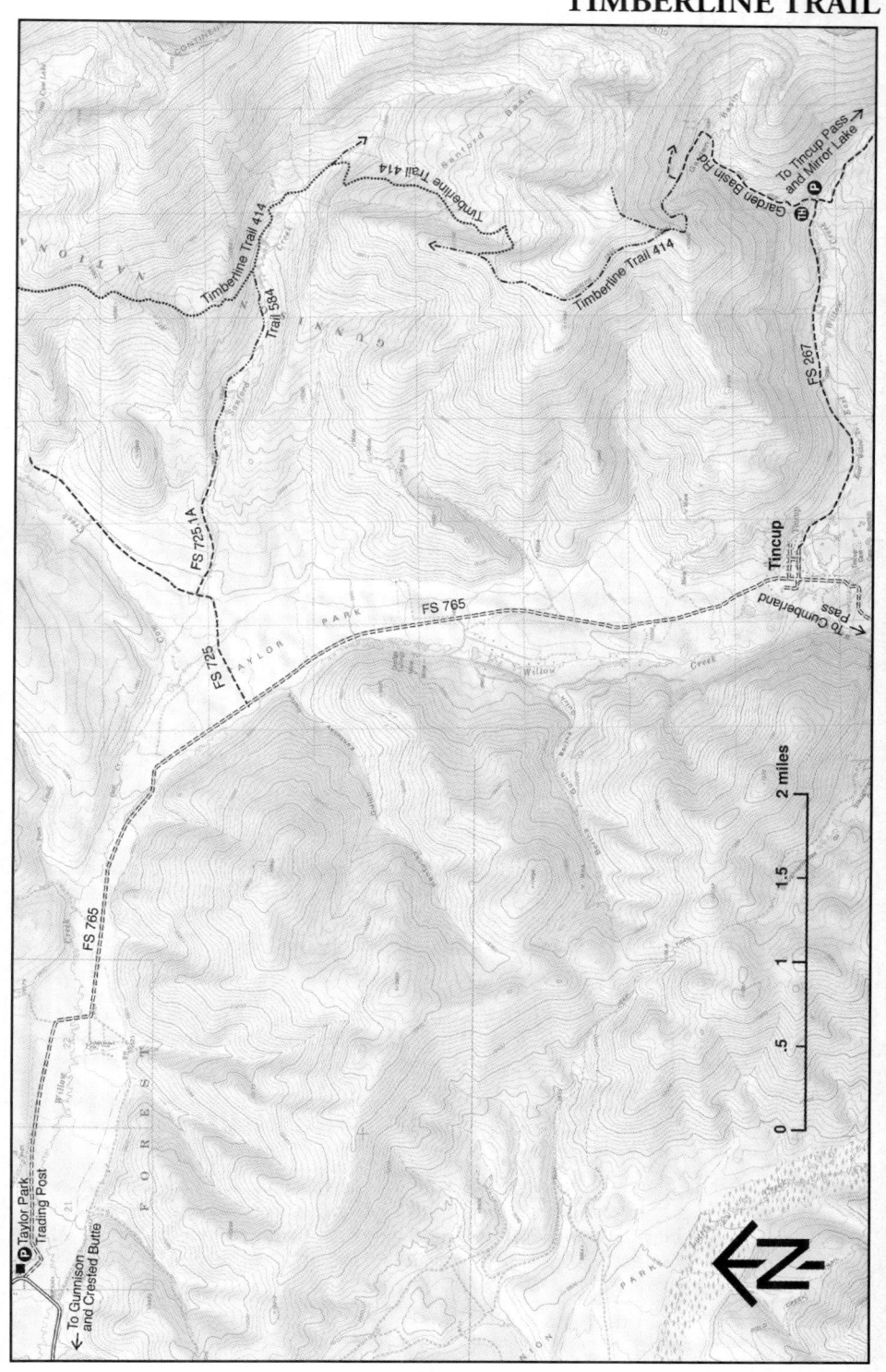

TIMBERLINE TRAIL
Gunnison Spur of the Colorado Trail
Ride Information
See map pages 98-99

Description: The Timberline Trail is another adventurous ride for those wanting a change of scenery. This section of the Timberline Trail is less difficult than the section starting near Tincup. It has miles of great singletrack. The descent on the Gunnison Spur of The Colorado Trail is very long and narrow, and non-motorized! This loop in the Taylor Park (about 1 hour from Crested Butte) combines a long, flat doubletrack ride up Texas Creek and a long and challenging singletrack climb on the Timberline Trail with a fast, rolling descent on the Gunnison Spur of the Colorado Trail. This section of the Timberline Trail mostly travels in dark pine forest with just a few views along the way. Sections of the trail are quite steep and rough, most can expect to walk some. The descent on the Gunnison Spur is cross-country, with a lot of up and down along Texas Ridge. It is rocky, but still quite fast. For an epic day of adventure, ride The Timberline Trail from Tincup, and continue on to this section. Wear orange on this ride during hunting season.

Distance: 23 miles, 12 miles of dirt road, 11 miles of singletrack.

Time: 3-5 hours

Difficulty: Expert

Technical Skill: Expert

Aerobic Effort: High

Elevation: Top: 11,550' **Gain:** 2,790'

Season: July through early October

Finding Route: Moderate

Maps: Latitude 40 Taylor Park Trails and National Geographic/Trails Illustrated Buena Vista Collegiate Peaks

Location: To get to the Timberline Trail from Crested Butte, drive 11.6 miles south of Crested Butte and turn left on Jacks Cabin Cutoff Road 813. This turn is difficult to see and is marked only with a small sign. Take Jack's Cabin Cutoff four miles to the end and turn left on Taylor River Road. Follow Taylor River Road 18.5 miles, 1.2 miles past Cottonwood Pass Road (where 742 turns to dirt.) Park on the right at the start of Texas Creek Road. From Gunnison, drive 9.2 miles to Almont and turn right on Taylor River Road. Continue 25.5 miles to Texas Creek Road.

Mileage Log:

0.0 Begin riding up Texas Creek Road. Right away pass a couple of spur roads to the right. Stay on this road for nine miles, passing many spurs. Always stay with the main road, and read the step by step directions at the main intersections.

1.1 Turn right and climb up a short hill as a spur heads left and across the open flats.

1.6 After descending the other side of the short hill, turn left and ride up Texas Creek, passing a spur to the right that crosses the creek. Stay on the main road for the next several miles, passing many spur roads. At one point the road becomes quite braided, just continue upstream. If you begin to climb away from the creek to the left, or cross the creek, you have taken a wrong turn.

2.2 Continue on the main road, crossing a spur road.

7.0   Stay left where the signed Continental Divide Trail, Timberline Trail, and Texas Lakes Trail (all one four-wheeler track) come in on the right. Continue up the road.

8.1   Stay left and continue up the road, passing an old section of the Timberline Trail.

8.6   Stay left when the road forks in a meadow.

9.1   The road ends at the trailhead. Turn left and begin a sustained climb on the signed Timberline singletrack. (Straight ahead is the Texas Creek Trail which heads into the wilderness. No bikes.)

10.2   Cross a creek.

11.1   Climb a steep loose switchback and then traverse a steep, open hillside on the narrow trail.

11.7   Top out in the pines. This is a nice break in the climb, but has no views.

12.4   Cross two forks of a creek in an open meadow and continue climbing. There is a view of Taylor Reservoir here.

14.0   Cross Illinois Creek and turn left on the southbound Gunnison Spur of the Colorado Trail and the Texas Ridge Trail at a four-way intersection. There is a sign just a few feet down the trail. (The Colorado Trail signs are a little confusing here.) The Timberline Trail to Pieplant and the northbound Gunnison Spur continue straight ahead, and a side trial heads up the creek.

15.4   Veer left, cross two forks of the Illinois Creek and contour left along the hillside. Climb gradually up to Texas Ridge, and then roll up and down along the ridge.

18.0   The trail begins to descend more than climb after this point.

20.2   End of the singletrack at a T-intersection on a four-wheeler track. Turn left and roll downhill.

20.5   Turn right on an unmarked doubletrack.

20.8   Stay right as a four-wheeler track comes in on the left.

20.9   Turn right on Texas Creek Road. Retrace your tracks back to your car.

21.1   Cross a doubletrack.

21.7   Turn right and climb a short hill away from the creek. Continue straight ahead and down the other side.

22.1   Turn left at the fork at the bottom of the hill.

23.3   Back to the car. 🚲

THE TIMBERLINE TRAIL
Tincup to Texas Creek
Ride Information ——————————————— *See map pages 98-99*

Description: This demanding, adventurous ride in the Taylor Park area (about one hour from Crested Butte) offers excellent views of the Collegiate Peaks and the Fossil Ridge area. It is a nice change of pace for strong riders who have done all the popular rides near Crested Butte. It is a popular motorcycle trail, but lightly used by mountain bikers. Much of the trail is rough, rocky, and quite steep; expect to walk some. The descents are long (4-6 miles!) making the grueling climbing worth it! The loop combines a long flat road approach, four-wheeler track, four-wheel drive road, rough singletrack, and fast, smooth singletrack! Here are two options, riding up to Tincup to start the Timberline Trail and exiting at Texas Creek, or the longer option, below, that ends with the very long and fast descent on the Gunnison Spur of the Colorado Trail. For a shorter version that involves riding up Texas Creek and down the Gunnison Spur, see Timberline Trail, Gunnison Spur of The Colorado Trail. Wear orange on this ride during hunting season.

Distance: 36 mile loop, 8 miles singletrack, 20 miles of dirt road, 2 miles of pavement, 6 miles of ATV track. **With the option:** 46 mile loop: 20 miles of singletrack, 18 miles of dirt road, 2 miles of pavement, and 6 miles of ATV track.

Time: 4 ½-6 hours. Add 2 hours if you continue on to ride the option.

Difficulty: Expert to Epic

Technical Skill: Expert

Aerobic Effort: Strenuous, very long and rocky climbs.

Elevation: Top: 12,060' **Gain:** 3,900' **Gain with option:** 6,100'

Season: July-September

Finding Route: Fairly easy, the route is mostly well signed.

Maps: National Geographic/Trails Illustrated Buena Vista/Collegiate Peaks or Latitude 40 Aspen/Crested Butte/Gunnison

Location: To get to the Timberline Trail from Crested Butte, drive 11.6 miles south of Crested Butte and turn left on Jacks Cabin Cutoff Road 813. This turn is difficult to see and is marked only with a small sign. It is near a farm house with large trees, right next to the road. Take Jack's Cabin Cutoff four miles to the end and turn left on Taylor River Road 742. Follow Taylor River Road 16.7 miles (three miles past Taylor Reservoir Dam) to Forest Road 765 and turn right. Park on the left in a large dirt area near the store and cabins. From Gunnison, drive 9.2 miles to Almont and take a right on Taylor River Road. Continue 22 miles to Forest Road 765 and turn right to the parking area.

Mileage Log:

0.0 Begin riding up Forest Road 765 toward Tincup. This road starts out flat, and then climbs gradually as it approaches the tiny town of Tincup.

1.8 Stay left on the main road toward Tincup when a county road spur turns right.

7.5 Enter the town of Tincup.

7.7 Turn left on Forest Road 267 to Mirror Lake, and climb.

10.5 Turn left at the trailhead and bathrooms. The trailhead is marked by a small sign once you enter the parking area. If you arrive at Mirror Lake, you have gone too far. From the trailhead, begin riding on Garden Basin Road toward the Timberline Trail. This road is challenging aerobically and is quite rocky in sections.

11.5 Cross a creek.

11.9 The road flattens out.

12.0 Ride straight ahead onto the Timberline Trail when the road turns hard right. Climb more ATV track toward the ridge.

13.0 Top out to great views! Ride straight ahead and pass a steep four-wheeler track to the right. Unfortunately, this section of trail was previously a singletrack, but has been turned into an ATV track. It traverses the hillside, giving you great views of the Collegiate Peaks.

14.0 (approx. mileage) Begin descending. This is a rough and rocky descent, and often wet and muddy in spots.

14.3 Stay right and traverse downhill, passing a user created fork.

14.5 Turn left and continue down, passing a faint fork up the drainage.

17.2 The trail splits at a signed intersection, stay right and climb on the Timberline Trail, now singletrack. (The Sanford Trail heads left and down.) This awesome section has short climbs and descents, smooth rolling singletrack, and a long and grueling, but smooth and rideable climb.

21.5 End at a gravel parking lot and trailhead. Stay left and ride a very short distance to the continuation of the trail.

21.6 Cross a campsite area.

21.9 Cross a doubletrack.

22.2 Carefully ride straight across Cottonwood Pass Road and onto the signed trail continuation. This next section is really fast and fun, mostly down with a few short uphills. It has recently been rerouted and is in great shape, and all rideable. (For emergency exit, take Cottonwood Pass Road left and down, but the trail from here isn't much more effort and is much safer and more fun. There is a lot of fast traffic on the road.)

25.5 Ride past a small lake on the right and arrive at a signed trail intersection. Turn left on the Timberline and Continental Divide Trail.

25.9 Pass another lake, then soon cross a bridge.

26.0 Turn left on Texas Creek Road. Stay on the main road as is meanders down Texas Creek, passing several spurs. Always stay with the creek until mile 31.4. (To continue on the Timberline Trail for an epic ride, turn right here. See option, below, for details.)

28.3 Stay right on main road.

28.7 Stay left on main road.

31.4 Turn right and climb a short hill away from the creek.

31.9 Turn hard left at a fork in the road.

33.0 Turn left on Forest Road 742.

THE TIMBERLINE TRAIL
Tincup to Texas Creek
Ride Information

34.2   Pass Cottonwood Pass Road on the left. Begin riding on pavement.

36.0   Take the shortcut doubletrack on the left back to the store and cabins. If you miss this, be sure to turn left on Forest Road 765.

36.5   Back to your car.

Option: To continue on the Timberline Trail and descend the Gunnison Spur of The Colorado Trail, turn right at mile 26, above. Continue up the road 2.1 miles, staying left when the road forks, to the continuation of the Timberline Trail, on the left. For detailed ride information, see Timberline Trail, Gunnison Spur of The Colorado Trail. 🚲

Taylor Park

Downtown Crested Butte-USA

The Alley Loop

Photo: Xavier Fane

Home of:

The Alley Loop

Thanksgiving Training Camp

Senior Winter Festival

CRESTED BUTTE

NORDIC

Crested Butte
Nordic Center

www.Cbnordic.org
(970)340_7047

THE RAGGEDS TRAIL

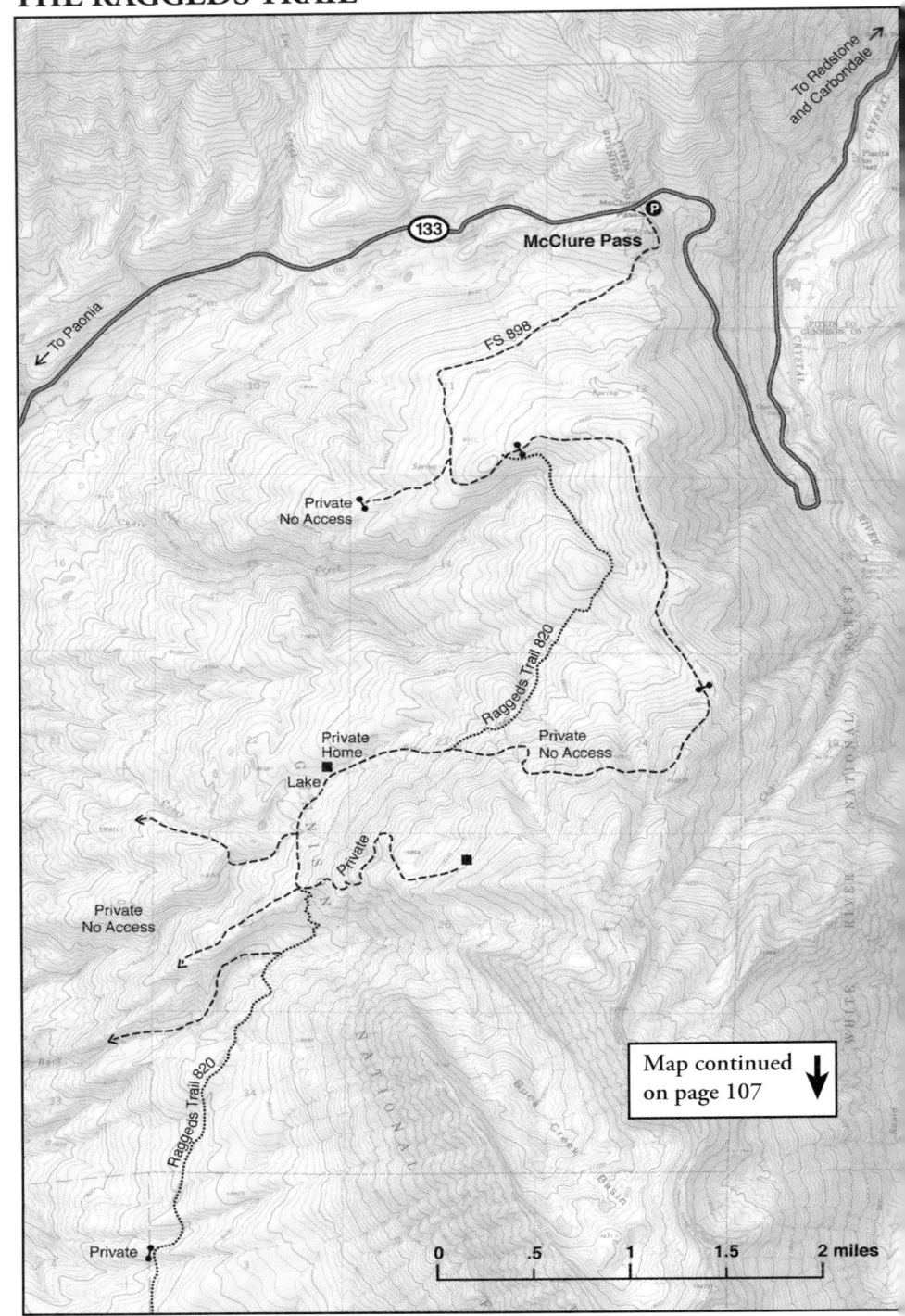

To Redstone
and Carbondale

133
McClure Pass
P

To Paonia

FS 898

Private
No Access

Raggeds Trail 820

Private
Home
Lake

Private
No Access

Private

Private
No Access

Raggeds Trail 820

Map continued
on page 107 ↓

Private

0   .5   1   1.5   2 miles

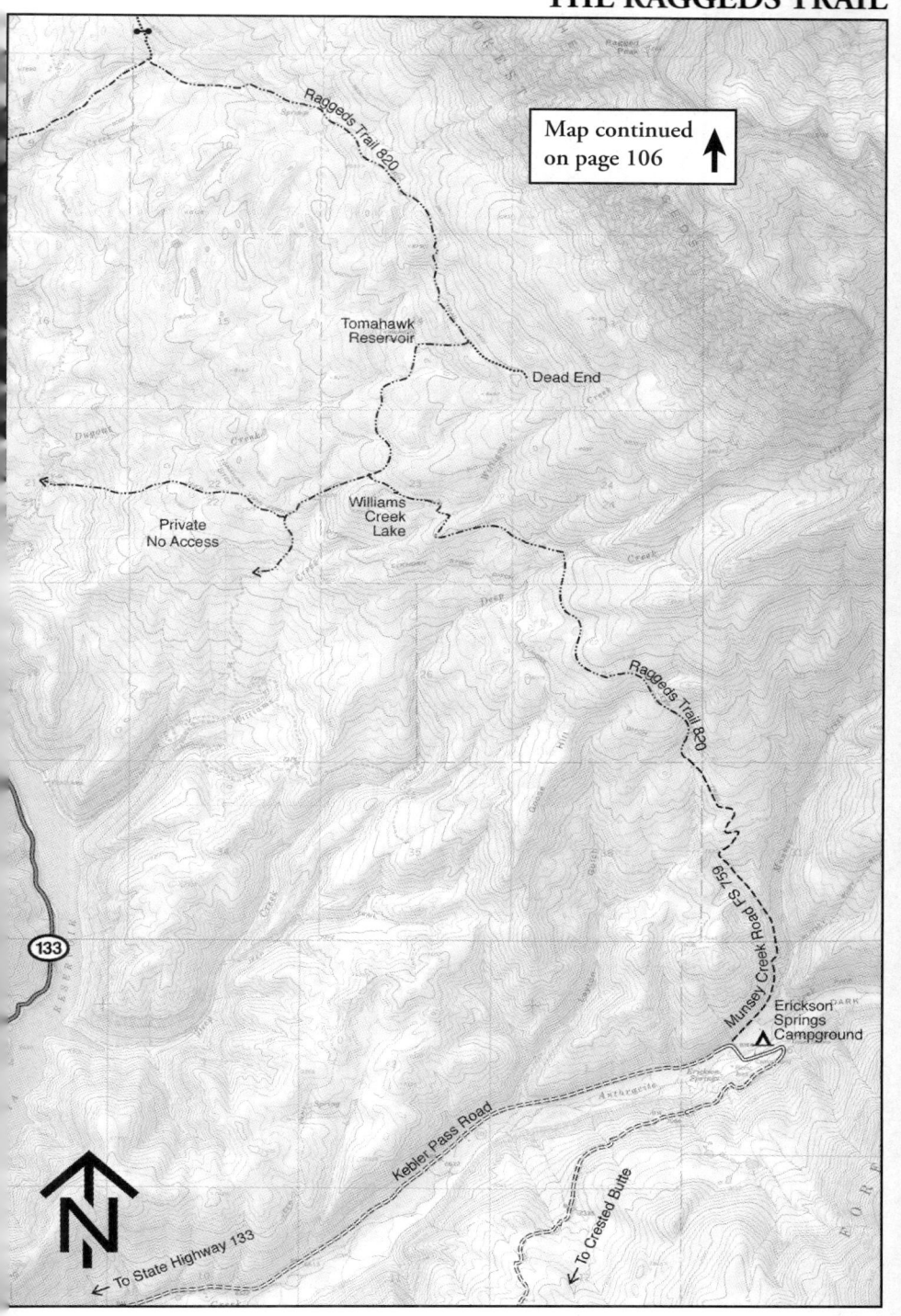

Map continued
on page 106

Raggeds Trail 820

Tomahawk
Reservoir

Dead End

Williams
Creek
Lake

Private
No Access

Raggeds Trail 820

Erickson
Springs
Campground

Munsey Creek Road FS 759

Kebler Pass Road

133

← To State Highway 133

To Crested Butte

N

THE RAGGEDS TRAIL
Ride Information ———————————— *See map pages 106-107*

Description: The Raggeds Trail is a great trail to ride in the Fall, as nearly the entire trail is in aspen forest. It follows along the base of the west side of the Raggeds Wilderness near Paonia Reservoir, and has beautiful views of the peaks in this wilderness. The ride starts on McClure Pass, between Carbondale and Paonia. It climbs a forest road to a wonderful singletrack that rolls through the aspens and conifers. The second half is all ATV trail through meadows and aspen groves. The trail is somewhat rough and often there are a lot of downed trees to carry over. Don't ride this trail after any amount of rain, it becomes very greasy and doesn't dry out quickly. The start of this remote and little known ride is 49 miles from Crested Butte and for most riders requires a shuttle. Local hard-cores ride The Raggeds as a loop that involves 6 miles of dirt road and 17 miles of pavement (the same route the shuttle vehicle would take) or as a very long loop from Crested Butte over Schofield and McClure Passes and returning by Kebler Pass (about 100 miles...) This ride is on your way to or from Crested Butte if you are coming from I-70 through Glenwood Springs or from Aspen.

Distance: 20.5 miles, 7 miles of singletrack, 7 miles of four-wheeler track, 6.5 miles of dirt road.

Time: 3 ½ –5 ½ hours with a shuttle.

Difficulty: Advanced intermediate to expert.

Technical Skill: Advanced intermediate to expert

Aerobic Effort: High-lots of short steep hills on loosely compacted road and trail.

Elevation: Top: 9,640' **Gain:** 2,800'

Season: June through early or mid-October

Finding Route: Moderate to difficult. Lots of turns, not all well marked. Riders must stay on the trail, as it is surrounded by private property and uses private easements.

Maps: There really is no great map for this trail. The newer Gunnison Basin Public Lands map and the National Geographic/Trails Illustrated Maroon Bells/Redstone/Marble and Kebler Pass/Paonia Reservoir show the route, but are lacking accurate details.

Location: To get to the Raggeds Trail from Crested Butte, drive 24 miles over Kebler Pass from the western end of Whiterock Avenue in Crested Butte to the Erickson Springs Campground. The campground is located on the right, off the short section of pavement at the bottom of some switchbacks, right on Anthracite Creek. Park one car here and continue with riders and bikes six miles farther to Highway 133, turn right and drive 17 miles to the top of McClure Pass. Park on the right (south) side of the highway and start the ride here.

Mileage Log:

0.0   Start riding east out of the parking lot at the top of McClure Pass and up the dirt road, Forest Service 898. The road is marked a little way up. Immediately pass a spur that heads down and left, continue climbing to the right. Stay on this road for 2.8 miles, mostly climbing. Pass several spurs on both sides on the way, none of which are signed.

2.4   Pass a spur that turns off right from a good view area.

2.8   Turn right on the signed Raggeds 820 singletrack. This is across from a pullout area and just before a locked gate on Forest Service 898. The first three miles of trail are easy to follow, most likely you may not have to look at the directions until you reach private land and a road.

3.6   Cross a small creek and climb.

3.9   Top out and descend.

4.1   Ride out to a wide flat area, the trail continues straight across and down from where you just came in. Next ride into a wide meadow with great views of Chair Mountain in the Raggeds Wilderness. Continue descending and cross several small creeks in the dark forest.

5.7   Ride by private land and forest service signs, then merge straight onto a dirt road and descend quite steeply. Stay on the route of The Raggeds Trail for several miles as it passes through private property on this road. This is an easement, please don't endanger it by trespassing.

6.6   Stay left, passing a lake and cabins on the right.

6.7   Pass a spur road on the right, continue left and climb steeply.

7.0   Top out on a ridge and cross a private road. Enjoy the great views of Buck Basin. Start down the steep signed Raggeds singletrack directly across the road. Be aware that in 6/10ths of a mile a left turn is coming up that is easy to miss.

7.4   The grade lessens and you are now riding on an old road grade turned singletrack. Pass a grassy spur on the left. It is faint, you may not notice it.

7.6   Arrive at a wide area and the start of a more prominent section of doubletrack. Turn left on the singletrack and contour. There is an old sign "Ragged Mountain" that is barely hanging in there marking the trail. Don't go down the road!! If you come to an open hillside on the right while on the road, a split in the road, or "no trespassing" signs, you have gone too far and are trespassing and getting lost!!

7.7   Cross the wide Buck Creek and then climb steeply on singletrack.

8.0   The trail levels out and then descends.

8.4   Pass a pond on the right and cross a creek. The trail is a bit hard to follow in this grassy cow trail area, it meanders to the right, and then to the left. Stick with the main trail. It does not gain or lose a lot of elevation through this area.

8.8   Ride through a large meadow with a pond on the left, then descend and cross a small creek. The trail levels again and rolls through the aspens.

9.4   Cross a small creek.

9.7   Cross a larger creek with steep sides.

10.0   Swing left at a gate to private property and descend briefly, then climb next to a fence.

10.5   Ride through a gate and close it, and stay on the signed Raggeds Trail.

10.8   Arrive at a signed T-intersection with a four-wheeler track. Turn left and start the longest climb of the ride, staying with the Raggeds Trail. (To the right is the only trail that has public access to the Highway 133 along the Raggeds

Trail route.) Cross two more small creeks early in the next climb.

11.5 Ride past a fenced spring on the right, then cross Spring Creek.

12.7 Start steeply down. Watch out for sharp turns in here!

13.1 Swing left on the four-wheeler track and cross a metal cattleguard.

13.2 Stay right on the four-wheeler track, passing a faint signed singletrack to the left. (This singletrack disappears and deadends shortly.)

13.7 Pass signed Tomahawk Reservoir access on the right as you ride along a small open ridge. Continue straight ahead and down.

14.0 Pass Tomahawk Reservoir and stay left, beginning another fast descent. Don't miss the sharp left in ¾ of a mile.

14.7 Turn sharp left on a signed corner, and climb on the more used track toward Williams Creek Lake and Munsey Creek Road. Right and down leads to private property.

15.0 Descend to Williams Creek Lake. This is a beautiful break spot with nice views of East and West Beckwith Mountains.

15.5 Cross Williams Creek.

16.3 Cross signed Deep Creek.

17.2 Pass Spud Pass Trail on the left and descend. The Spud Pass Trail heads into The Raggeds Wilderness, no bikes allowed.

18.0 Ride straight onto Munsey Creek Road, Forest Service 795. Descend this all the way to Kebler Pass Road, passing a couple much less used spurs on the way down. (This road is signed as both 795 and 759 within the first ½ mile. It is also inconsistently numbered on maps.)

20.4 End Forest Service 795 on Kebler Pass Road, turn left and ride 1/10th of a mile back to Erickson Springs and your car.

20.5 Back to your car! 🚲

Williams Creek Lake, The Raggeds Trail

The Raggeds Trail

View of Buck Basin, The Raggeds Trail

HARTMAN ROCKS

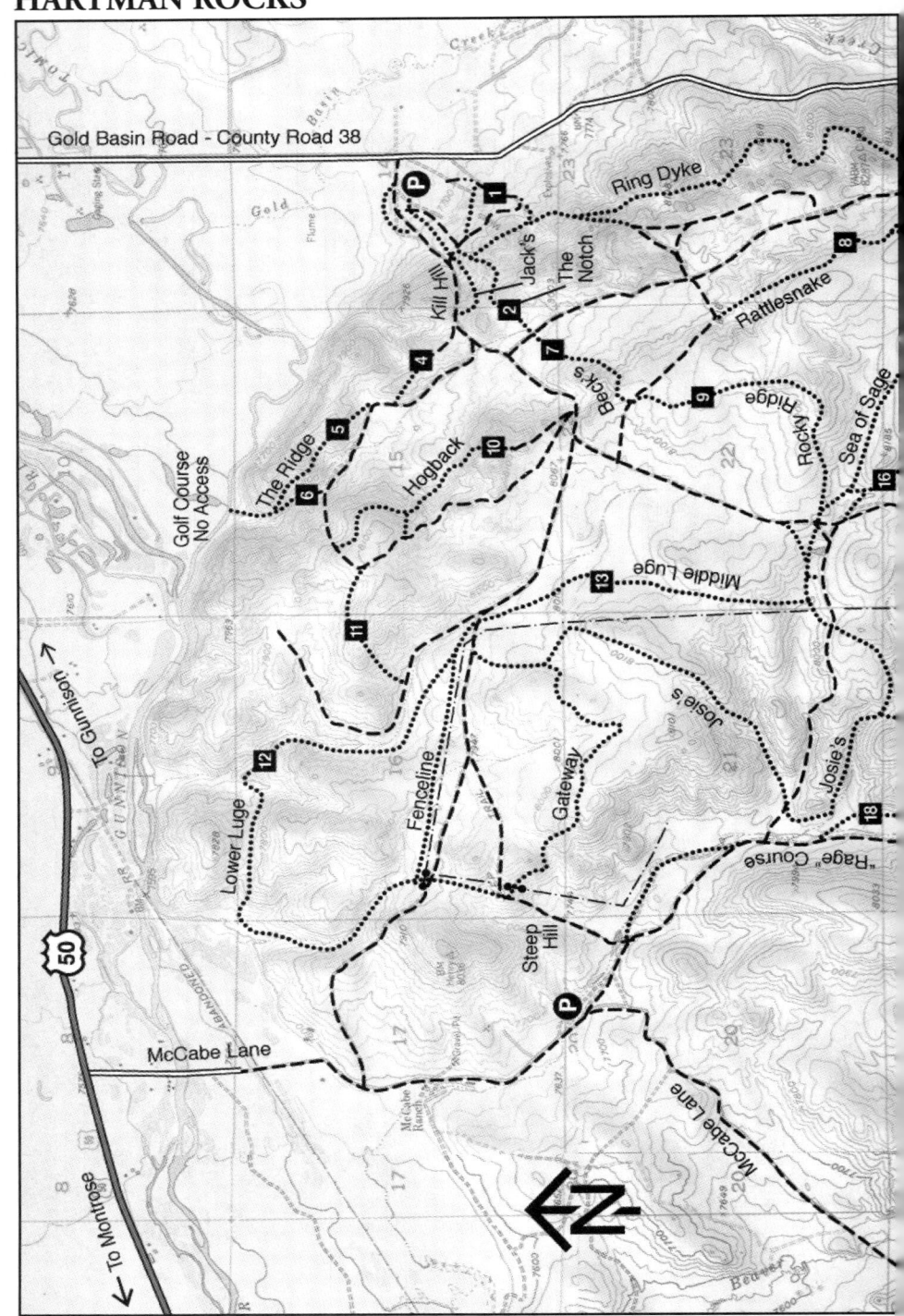

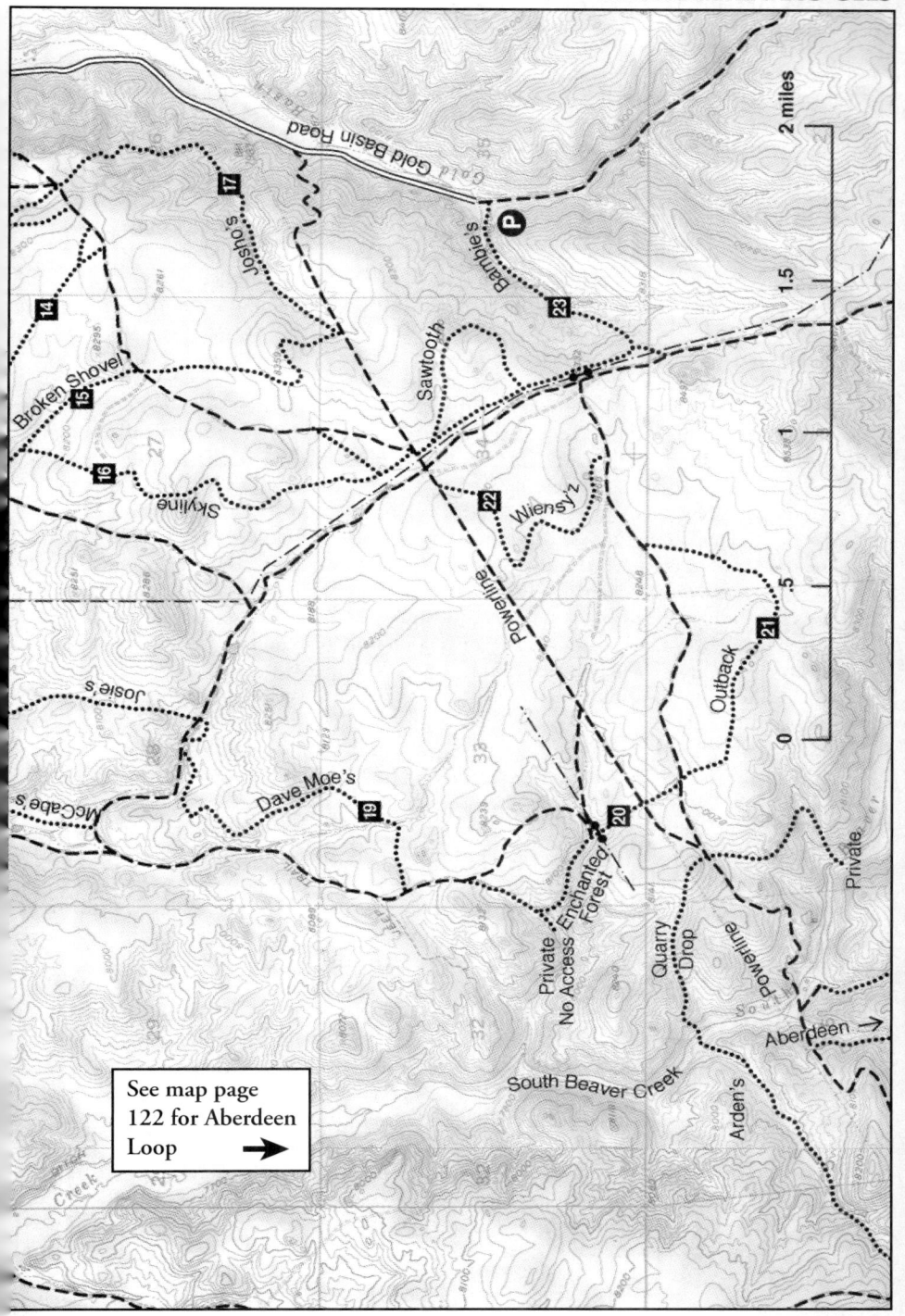

2 miles

Gold Basin Road

Bumbleseis

17

14

Joshot's

Broken Shovel

15

16

Skyline

Sawtooth

23

P

22

Wiensy'z

21

Outback

Josie's

Dave Moe's

19

McCabe's

20

Enchanted Forest

Private No Access

Quarry Drop

Powerline

Private

Aberdeen →

South Beaver Creek

Arden's

Powerline

See map page
122 for Aberdeen
Loop →

Creek

HARTMAN ROCKS INTRODUCTION
Ride Information

The Hartman Rocks Recreation Area is a maze of winding trails and doubletracks set amidst a most spectacular landscape in the high desert country of Gunnison. The narrow singletracks roll through sagebrush hills and granite rock formations, all with 360 degree views of the surrounding snow covered mountains. Hartman Rocks is a great place to ride, but is often overlooked because of the reputation of the riding in Crested Butte and on Monarch Pass (which is definitely great!) Hartmans has a much longer riding season than the surrounding mountains, often the trails are dry in April and I have often ridden there in November. It is good riding for beginners, intermediates, and experts alike. The climbs are moderate and nearly all the trails are good in both directions. It is lower in elevation than Crested Butte and Monarch Pass (the base area is 7,760',) and it is a good area to adjust to the altitude when visiting the area. The midsummer months can be hot here at Hartman's and there isn't much shade, so ride early and take extra water or ride here on a cool day. The trails here dry out more quickly after summer rainstorms due to the decomposed granite surface of the trails, so this is a great option after a big rainstorm. And very importantly, Hartman's has miles of singletrack in all directions: incredibly smooth, fast and winding, technical, and slickrock. It's all here! There are many ways to connect the loops at Hartman's, but it can be a bit confusing at first. Many of the trails are numbered and these correspond to a handout the BLM puts out. Find the handout map at the forest service office in Gunnison at 216 North Colorado. I recommend getting the Hartman Rocks Trail and Bouldering map, available at the bike shops in Gunnison. This map includes nearly all the trails in accurate locations. It has one drawback, it is a little hard to differentiate trail from road on some loops. Take along this book, a compass, the Hartman Rocks Trail and Bouldering map, and the handout to help find your way. Study the landmarks and have fun exploring. Keep track of the numbered trails to help you find out where you are. The powerlines are another good location marker. I often refer to the "main road" in the text, this is the road that starts in the main parking lot and climbs over the top of "Kill Hill," the steep road climbing out of the parking area. This road then descends into a valley behind the main ridge of rocks behind the parking lot, then climbs over another ridge. From here it is fairly level until it reaches an intersection with many trails, near a cottonwood grove. This road and cottonwood intersection can help you get your bearings, or get you back to the parking lot quickly. Please stay on the trails and roads, as you can see from the base area that the damage from off-road use lasts for years. Three loop options follow to get you started. To get to the main parking lot for Hartman Rocks, drive or ride 1.4 miles west on Highway 50 from its' junction with Highway 135. Turn left on County Road 38 (Gold Basin Road) just before the highway crosses the Gunnison River. There is a brown BLM "Hartman Rocks Recreation Area" sign on Highway 50 marking the turn. Continue 2.4 miles further and the signed lot for Hartmans is on the right. Another access to Hartmans is Bambie's Trail 23, 3.1 miles farther up County Road 38 past the main parking area, just after the pavement ends, on the right.

NOTE: Hartman Rocks Trails are not open until the main gate is open, when the trails are dry. The trails south of the power line are closed until May 15th for Sage Grouse protection. This area includes trails 21-23.

This is a quick description and length of the main trails at Hartman Rocks Recreation Area. Locate these on your Hartman Rocks map to link up trails for a great loop! Be aware that several changes are happening at Hartman Rocks, respect closures and private property that may not be posted at the time of this writing.

Trail 1: Doubletrack climb from base area. Intermediate. ½ mile.

Jack's Trail: A beautiful, switchbacking trail connecting Trail 1 to the top of the main ridge. An alternate to Kill Hill for a route up from the main parking area. Great descent also. Intermediate, ½ mile.

Trail 2, The Notch: A short technical trail that brings you over to the front side and parking lot. Lots of fun slickrock maneuvers. Expert. Challenging expert climb. ½ mile.

Trail 3, V-drop: Technical descent to front side, connects to Trail 1. Loose and rocky, hard to find from the top. Expert.

Trail 4: Very short, steep descent off the top of Kill Hill. Expert. Part of the Rage course. 1/3 mile.

Trail 5, Ridge Trail: Very technical with a big drop-off to the right. Beautiful views of the Gunnison River Valley. Starts near the bottom of Trail 4. Expert. 1 mile.

Trail 6, Golf Course: Smooth trail that descends to the golf course. Out and back only, no access through the golf course. Intermediate.

Trail 7, Becks: A winding, fast trail that leads down to The Notch Trail. Big air in the lower half. Good ascent as well. Intermediate. 3/10ths of a mile.

Trail 8, Rattlesnake: A very technical trail, lots of short slickrock obstacles. Easier to ride from south to north (start at Trail 17 end.) Excellent riding and good views. Expert. 1.8 miles.

Trail 9, Rocky Ridge: Combination of very smooth and technical riding along a small ridge. Great views and excellent singletrack. Hard Intermediate with a couple expert moves. Good both directions. 1.5 miles.

Trail 10, Hogback. This is a beautiful intermediate trail running right below a big granite rib. Some slickrock. A little hard to follow. 7/10ths of a mile.

Trail 11: A combination of rocky and smooth trail, on a ridge. Good views. Intermediate.

Trail 12, Middle Luge: An incredibly smooth and fun, winding trail. Excellent riding up or down. Beginner with short intermediate hill, but everyone loves this trail. 1.5 miles.

Trail 13, Lower Luge: Very fast and smooth for part of the trail, a few rocks and ruts. Short steep climbs and descents. Descends a long hill to the water treatment plant. Long climb out. Advanced intermediate with a short expert section or two. 1.8 miles.

Josie's: A fun smooth trail with plenty of short technical sections. Non-system trail, unmarked. First half: 1.9 miles, second half: 1.2-1.8 miles.

Fenceline: A short, fast intermediate connector trail between sections of the Luge. Cuts off the big hill to and from the water treatment plant.

HARTMAN ROCKS LIST OF TRAILS
Ride Information

Gateway: Fun mixed technical and smooth trail. Expert. Non-system trail. Closed until further notice by BLM.

Trail 14, Sea of Sage: Smooth as butter and fast! Good uphill spin or big chain ring downhill spin. Beginner, but everyone loves this trail. 1.2 miles.

Trail 15, Broken Shovel: Very smooth trail. Good both ways, also a nice middle chain ring spin uphill. Beginner. 1.7 miles.

Trail 16, Skyline: Very smooth, winding, and fast intermediate trail with a couple expert technical sections thrown in. 1.7 miles.

Trail 17, Joshos: Smooth, fast descent on either end. Some technical riding in the middle. Very fun trail. Advanced intermediate with short expert sections. 2.2 miles.

Trail 18, McCabes: A rollercoaster ride through a wash, starting near McCabes lane. Fun either way, but better descent starting near Trail 19. Braided trails. Intermediate, 1.2 miles.

Trail 19, Dave Moe's: Part of the Rage in the Sage Race Course. An awesome trail. Connects easily to 20 and 21 for an outer loop. Advanced intermediate with some fun expert technical sections. 1.2 miles.

Trail 20, Enchanted Forest: A smooth fast trail through tight aspens. Advanced intermediate. 8/10ths of a mile.

Trail 21, Outback: A beautiful trail through Ponderosas and big granite boulders. Lots of fun technical sections. Expert. 1.5 miles. Closed until May 15th.

Trail 22, Wiensy'z: A smooth, fast and winding trail. Intermediate. 1 mile.

Trail 23, Bambie's: A wonderful climb or descent down a granite boulder canyon. Beautiful! Mostly smooth with short technical sections. Advanced Intermediate. This trail offers access to Hartman Rocks, 3 miles past the main parking area on Gold Basin Road. 1.5 miles. Closed until May 15th.

Ring Dyke: Very technical and beautiful trail. Difficult to follow. Expert. 1.8 miles.

Sacrifice: A braided group of trails leading to the front side and parking lot. Loose technical sections mixed with smooth trail and switchbacks. Hard to find and follow. Expert.

Sawtooth: A very technical and fun short trail. Good either direction. Expert. 6/10ths of a mile. Closed until May 15.

Aberdeen: A longer, unmarked, non-system trail. It has beautiful views and longer stints of riding without intersections. Farther out toward McCabes Lane than the regular trails. 6 ½ mile loop including dirt roads. Closed 6/15 - 8/31 for Sage Grouse protection.

Skull Pass: Crosses private property.

HARTMAN ROCK EASY LOOP
Ride Information

Description: This is a short and easy loop at Hartman Rocks. It climbs up a beautiful granite boulder canyon and then follows smooth and gentle, winding trails through the sage. There are great views of the surrounding mountains from the Hartmans mesa, and often during the spring or late fall the weather is perfect at Hartmans while those surrounding mountains are socked in and raining. The descents on this loop are fast and smooth. A few technical sections are fun to maneuver on the Skyline Trail, but these are easily walked. There are many trails near or connecting to this loop, take your map and compass and explore to add on hours of fun! To avoid stopping at the many intersections at Hartmans, read ahead through the entire description and plot your route out ahead of time, then just ride!

Distance: 12.7 miles: 6 miles of pavement, 1.7 miles of doubletrack, 5 miles of singletrack. If you drive to Bambie's Trail trailhead it shortens the ride by six miles of pavement.

Time: 2-3 hours.

Difficulty: Easy Intermediate. Most of the trails are smooth and winding, with just a few short technical sections.

Technical Skill: Easy intermediate to intermediate.

Aerobic Effort: Moderate. Climbs in this loop are mostly smooth and gradual.

Elevation: Top: 8,340' **Gain:** 1,260' **Gain from Bambie's Trailhead:** 922'

Season: May 15 through October

Finding Route: Easy to moderate. Most turns are marked or obvious with this guide, but there are a lot of spur roads and trails at Hartman Rocks.

Maps: Hartman Rocks Trail and Bouldering Map, available at Gunnison bike shops. BLM handout map, available at 216 North Colorado in Gunnison.

Location: Start at the main parking lot at Hartman Rocks Recreation Area. To get here, drive or ride 1.4 miles west on Highway 50 from its' junction with Highway 135 in Gunnison. Turn left on County Road 38 (Gold Basin Road) just before the highway crosses the Gunnison River. There is a brown BLM "Hartman Rocks Recreation Area" sign on Highway 50 marking the turn. Drive 2.4 miles further to the signed lot for Hartmans on the right. If you want to skip the 6 miles of pavement on this loop, drive 3.1 miles past the main parking area to the end of the pavement on County Road 38 and park just past the cattleguard. Bambie's Trail starts here on the right.

Mileage Log:

0.0 Ride out of the parking area and turn right onto County Road 38. Follow this road until the pavement ends.

3.1 Pavement ends. Cross a cattleguard and immediately turn right onto Bambie's Trail 23. Climb up this beautiful canyon on the mostly gradual trail.

3.9 Top of the mesa. Follow the trail right, passing two singletracks to the left (the first leads to a dirt road in a very short distance and the second heads out past Wiensy'z Trail and on to The Outback Trail) and descend straight ahead.

4.1 Ride straight ahead, passing the start of the unmarked technical Sawtooth Trail on the right.

4.5 Pass the other end of the Sawtooth Trail on the right, then ride through a gate.

Please close it behind you. Turn right on the road at the end of the trail, and climb the hill, underneath the powerline.

4.6 At the top of the hill cross another cattleguard, then turn immediately left onto another doubletrack. (Trail 16, Skyline, starts just to the left of this road.) This road is fast fun!

5.5 Cross the signed Trails 15(left) and 17(right.) Continue on the road, climbing, and then descend gradually again.

5.9 Unmarked singletrack on the right. Take this or the road, they rejoin in a short distance.

6.1 Turn left onto the smooth Trail 14, Sea of Sage.

6.2 Stay left when another trail comes in from the right. Zoom down this incredibly smooth and fast trail.

7.3 End Trail 14, turn immediately sharp left on Trail 16, Skyline. This is just before trail 14 drops into a wash and joins Trail 9 to the right and a dirt road straight ahead.

7.5 Turn left at the T-intersection with another singletrack.

7.6 Turn right at the fork. This section of Trail 16, Skyline, is a little more technically difficult. (The left fork is marked Trail 15 and is a smoother and shorter way to return. If you decide to take Trail 15, just follow it ½ mile until it intersects the dirt road you were on earlier, turn right and follow it one mile back to Bambie's Trail 23, turn left and retrace your tracks back to your car.)

8.9 If you continued right on Skyline at the last fork, stay left and ride along the fenceline. Don't go through the gate or turn sharp left on a singletrack spur.

9.2 End of Trail 16. Turn right on the dirt road under the powerline and cross the cattleguard. Ride down the hill to Bambie's Trail, just before the fence and road intersection.

9.3 Turn left on Bambie's Trail, and retrace your tracks back to County Road 38, turn left and ride back to your car.

13.9 Back to the main parking lot at Hartman's. 🚲

Rocky Ridge, The Luge, Josies, Joshos, Rattlesnake

Description: This is a wonderful singletrack loop in the high desert at Hartman Rocks in Gunnison. Hartman Rocks is a great, but often overlooked area to ride. The landscape is quite spectacular and the trails are made with biking in mind. This loop is a combination of incredibly smooth, fast trails and short, technical granite sections. Some of my favorites! Hartman Rocks is often excellent riding when storms are dumping snow or rain on all the surrounding mountains, and Hartmans remains in a donut hole. For the least amount of stopping, read ahead through the entire description and plot your route out on your Hartman Rocks map ahead of time, then just go. The flow of trails is 9 to 13 to Josies (unmarked) to 15 to 17 to 8 to 7 to 2.

Distance: 14.3 miles, 2 miles of dirt road and 12.2 miles of singletrack

Time: 2-3 hours

Difficulty: Intermediate with dispersed, short expert sections

Technical Skill: Intermediate to expert

Aerobic Effort: Moderate

Elevation: Top: 8,360' **Gain:** 2,100'

Season: April through late October, when dry and gates open.

Finding Route: Moderately difficult. There are many turns and not all are marked. All the numbered trails have sign posts, use these to help you be sure of your location. The numbered trails also have names, but these names are not on the signs.

Maps: Hartman Rocks Trail and Bouldering Map, available at Gunnison bike shops.

Location: To get to the main parking lot for Hartman Rocks, drive or ride 1.4 miles west on Highway 50 from its' junction with Highway 135 in Gunnison. Turn left on County Road 38 (Gold Basin Road) just before the highway crosses the Gunnison River. There is a brown BLM "Hartman Rocks Recreation Area" sign on Highway 50 marking the turn. Continue 2.4 miles on County Road 38 to the signed and fenced in parking lot for Hartman's, on the right.

Mileage Log:

0.0 From the parking lot take the trail that starts just to the left of the bathrooms, through a gap in the fence. Ride over a couple very short roller coaster hills and head left into the open area and up an old rutted dirt road that is now closed to cars and trucks.

0.4 Turn right at a T-intersection with a dirt road on the benched out area and shortly begin climbing again.

0.6 Turn left on the well signed Jacks Trail singletrack and switchback up to the top of the mesa.

1.0 Top out and cross a cattlegaurd at the end of Jack's Trail. Turn left on the dirt road and ride downhill. Pass a wide open parking area and Trail 4 (signed at the back of the parking area) at the top on the right, then stay left, passing another dirt road on the right as you descend. Continue on the main road and pass three dirt road spurs on the left. Ride straight across the valley and climb out the other side, somewhat steeply. Pass another dirt road on the right as you begin to climb.

HARTMAN ROCKS
Rocky Ridge, The Luge, Josies, Joshos, Rattlesnake
Ride Information

1.6   Pass a dirt road on the right at the top of the ridge, then turn left on the next dirt road spur. Follow this along the ridge top, passing another spur to the left that deadends.

1.8   Pass signed Trail 7, Beck's, on the left, and turn right immediately on Trail 9, the Rocky Ridge singletrack. Enjoy a nice spin up, crossing a dirt two-track right away. There are some moderately technical obstacles along the ridge top on this trail, then a fast, smooth descent on the other side of the small ridge.

3.1   Turn right at the fork in the trail and cross two dirt roads immediately. This fork is easy to miss, it is just before the main trail turns left and descends into a sandy wash.

3.3   Merge onto a singletrack coming in from the right. Ride over the right end of an earthen damn, passing a wide motorcycle trail over the damn on the left. Parallel the cottonwood draw. When the trail splits in 1/10th of a mile, turn right and climb up a short loose hill. This is the Middle Luge, Trail 13, and you are in for a smooth, fast descent!

4.6   The trail continues across a dirt road and is numbered 12. Turn left here on the dirt road, cross a cattleguard, and turn immediately left on an unsigned singletrack, locally known as Josie's. When the trail splits in 2/10ths of a mile, stay left. Enjoy all the short fun technical sections on this trail.

6.5   The trail ends on a dirt road. Turn right on the road and then immediately left on the continuation of the singletrack. Roll through the sagebrush, then ride left up alongside a dry creek.

7.2   The trail splits, stay left and continue up alongside the dry drainage, then cross it.

7.8   The trail ends on a dirt road, turn right and ride over the cattleguard and climb gradually on the road, passing the other end of the dam you crossed earlier at mile 3.3.

8.1   Turn right off the road onto a rutted doubletrack spur and climb.

8.3   Cross the main road (this road heads back to Kill Hill and the base area) and continue straight on the unmarked singletrack. Ride straight ahead when a singletrack merges in from the left in 1/10th of a mile.

8.5   Turn left at the fork onto signed Trail 15, Broken Shovel.

9.0   Ride straight across the road and onto signed Trail 17.

9.8   Turn left on the continuation of Trail 17 when it intersects the powerline road. This next section is an incredibly smooth and fast descent, followed by a technical climb.

11.2   Reach the end of Trail 17. There are awesome views here. Continue straight across the road to signed Trail 8, Rattlesnake. Stay right when you reach the top of the small ridge and a trail comes in on your left. This is a fun and quite technical trail. (Or just zoom straight ahead down the road if you are ready to get back, and turn right when it T-intersects the main road and climb over the hill to the parking lot.)

12.5 Turn right on the doubletrack and then immediately left onto the signed continuation of the singletrack. In 1/10th of a mile at the end of the singletrack, turn left on another doubletrack and climb. Follow this doubletrack to the next signed singletrack on the right, Trail 7.

13.0 Turn right on Trail 7, Becks, and zoom down the winding hill!

13.4 Cross a dirt road and continue straight across onto Trail 2. Climb up the doubletrack and then ride onto the slickrock, heading slightly left through a rock gap, then right. Follow the tracks left and up a couple ramps to the top of the saddle, where you can see the base area.

13.6 From here, descend and stay right when the trails fork and ride through another gap, then through a fast dip. Turn left after the dip for some steep slickrock drops. At the bottom of the drops, head left and pass the bottom of Jack's Trail. Continue to the next trail on the right, just before the main kill hill road, marked with a tall green user sign. (You can also go right at the top just after the fast dip on a trail descending into the gulley. This is the easier way. If you go right, stay left when the trail forks and descend to the base area.)

13.9 Turn right and giggle all the way to the base.

14.3 Back to the car! 🚲

Rocky Ridge Trail, Hartman Rocks

Photo by Xavier Fane

HARTMAN ROCKS
Aberdeen Loop

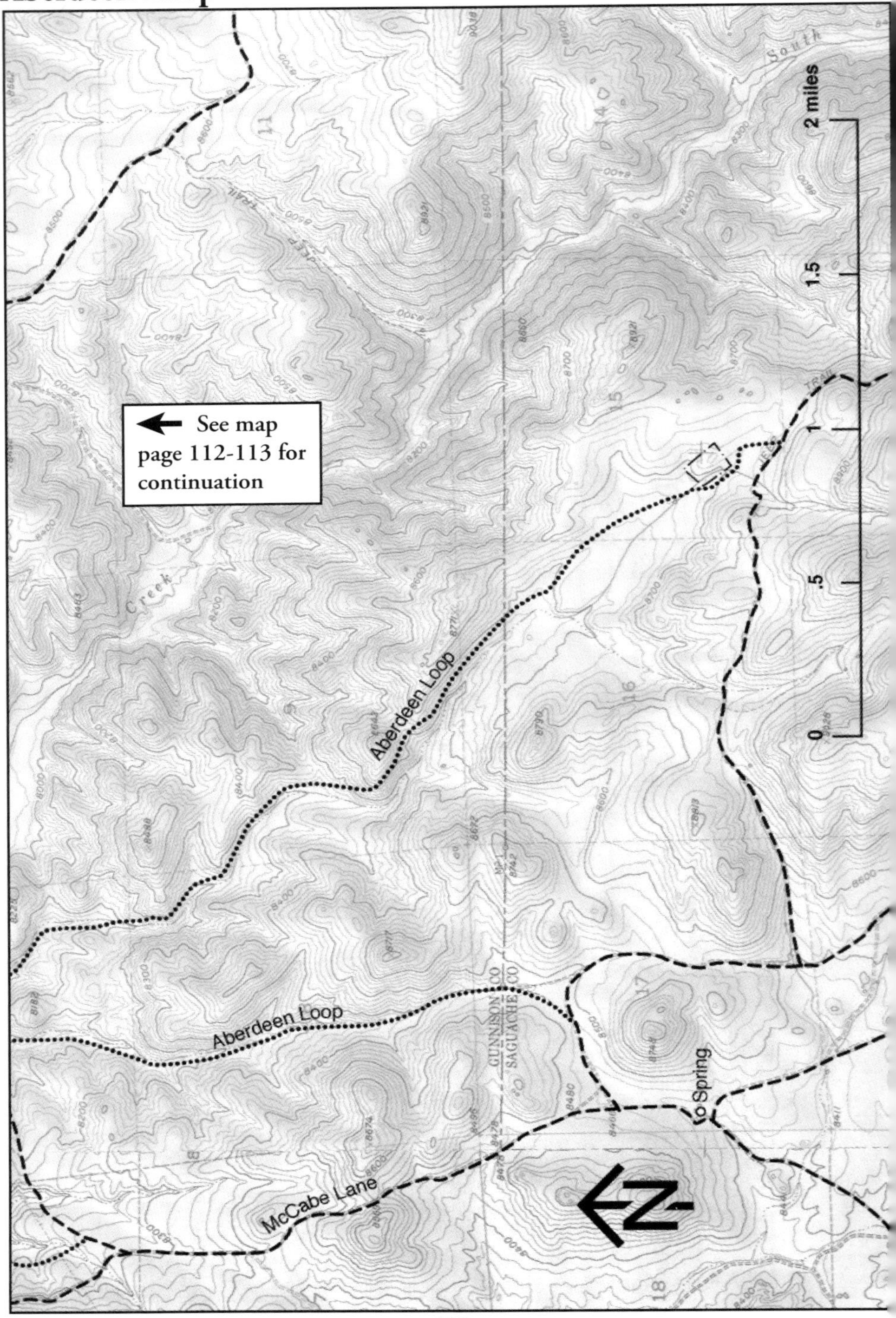

← See map page 112-113 for continuation

Aberdeen Loop

Aberdeen Loop

McCabe Lane

to Spring

GUNNISON CO
SAGUACHE CO

2 miles

1.5

1

.5

0

Description: This loop combines some of the most beautiful singletrack Hartman Rocks Trails with the more remote Aberdeen Trail. The loop starts with an enjoyable, moderate climb up Bambie's Trail through a beautiful, granite boulder strewn canyon. It then follows a dirt road to the technical Outback Trail and drops down to cross South Beaver Creek. The climb up the Aberdeen Trail from here is long and smooth, and riders are treated to views of the fourteener, Uncompahgre Mountain. The Aberdeen Trail has a much longer climb and descent than the more popular numbered Hartman Rocks Trails. It is more difficult to navigate beyond the numbered trails, as nothing is marked. The loop finishes by climbing out of South Beaver Creek on a steep dirt road, and continuing on the Enchanted Forest and Dave Moe Trails (these trails as well as the Outback Trail are part of the famous Rage in the Sage Race course) before returning on Bambie's Trail. This is a great loop with a bit of everything that Hartman Rocks has to offer: smooth, fast singletrack, technical granite sections, and awesome views and scenery. To save a lot of stopping at the many trail intersections, read ahead through the entire description and plot it out on your map ahead of time, then just go!

Distance: 17.5 mile loop, 7 miles of doubletrack and 10.5 miles of singletrack.

Time: 2-3 hours

Difficulty: Advanced intermediate with expert sections

Technical Skill: Advanced intermediate with expert sections

Aerobic Effort: Moderate

Elevation: Top: 8,720' **Gain:** 2,015'

Season: April through October, closed 6/15 - 8/31 for Sage Grouse protection.

Finding Route: Moderate to moderately difficult

Maps: Hartman Rocks Trail and Bouldering map, available at Gunnison bike shops.

Location: To get to Bambie's Trail, drive or ride 1.4 miles west on Hwy 50 from its' junction with Highway 135 in Gunnison. Turn left on County Road 38 just before the Highway 50 crosses the Gunnison River. There is a brown BLM "Hartman Rocks Recreation Area" sign on Highway 50 marking the turn. Continue 2.4 miles further to the signed lot for Hartman Rocks, on the right. Either park here and ride or continue driving three miles farther to the end of the pavement. Bambie's Trail 23, starts just past the cattleguard and pavement end on the right.

Mileage Log:

0.0   Begin riding up Bambie's Trail. This is a great climb.

0.8   Stay right, passing a closed trail on the left corner, just as you reach the mesa top.

0.9   Turn left at the next intersection and ride through a gate on a doubletrack. Ride straight ahead and west on the doubletrack, crossing a prominent dirt road. Stay on the doubletrack heading west for 9/10ths of a mile to signed Trail 21, The Outback.

1.0   Pass a faint doubletrack spur on the right.

1.3   Stay on the main road, passing Trail 22, Wiensy'z and a grassy doubletrack spur, both on the right.

HARTMAN ROCKS
Aberdeen Loop
Ride Information

1.5 Cross an unmarked singletrack, 9-0. Continue straight on the road.

1.8 Turn left off the doubletrack onto the Outback Trail, 21. This is a fun and technical trail through the granite boulders and Ponderosa Pines.

3.1 After topping out on a rocky flat area and starting down, turn left on the first doubletrack you come to and ride toward the powerline.

3.2 Turn left at a T-intersection with another doubletrack, cross a cattleguard, and descend. This road is quite steep in places.

3.4 Stay on this road, passing unmarked trails on the left and right.

3.6 Stay right as the road forks.

3.7 Stay right as the road forks.

3.9 Turn right and ride up a short steep hill, then descend to cross South Beaver Creek.

4.1 Cross South Beaver Creek and continue up on the road, passing a doubletrack spur to the left.

4.2 Turn left on the unmarked Aberdeen singletrack. This trail climbs gradually for two miles through the sage.

5.3 Cross a dry ditch and stay on the trail.

6.4 Arrive at a doubletrack. Turn sharp left on this road and climb gradually.

7.3 Stay left, passing a doubletrack spur. Climb and top out, then descend.

8.3 After descending to a low spot, turn left in the grassy drainage. Ride to the left to go around the fenced in area. Begin descending the trail at the other end. The trail zooms down the drainage through the sage. A couple spots are quite eroded and drop off, be careful.

10.9 End of the Aberdeen Trail in the cottonwoods. Turn left and ride down the creek on an old doubletrack.

11.0 Turn right and cross South Beaver Creek again. Retrace your tracks to the top of the hill, staying left at the spur roads until the mesa top at mile 11.9.

11.9 Ride straight ahead at the top, passing a doubletrack spur on the left.

12.0 Pass the doubletrack you came in on earlier on the right.

12.1 Turn left on the singletrack.

12.2 Cross a road, stay on the signed singletrack Enchanted Forest, Trail 20. This is right next to a huge powerline pole. Descend, watching your speed as there is a sharp right at a fence in 2/10ths of a mile.

12.4 Turn left and ride through the gate, passing doubletracks to the right on both sides of the fence. Descend on the singletrack to the left.

12.7 After winding through the woods, turn right and climb a steep doubletrack (now closed to trucks so it is turning into a singletrack) hill.

13.0 At the top of the hill, turn left on the doubletrack. Climb briefly, then descend to a rocky outcrop area and a singletrack, Trail 19, on the right.

13.3 Turn right on the signed singletrack, Trail 19, Dave Moe's. This is a fun technical singletrack! Be careful in 6/10ths of a mile of an off angle bridge, marked with a caution sign.

14.5 End of Dave Moe's Trail on the road. Turn right and climb on the road, passing a singletrack on the right, then one on the left in a short distance (Josie's.) Continue on the road.

15.4 Cross a cattleguard and then pass a spur road on the left. Continue straight ahead.

16.1 Turn left at the next road spur just past some water tanks and corrals, and immediately turn right on the signed singletrack Trail 23, Bambie's. Ride straight ahead on this trail, passing both entrances of the Sawtooth singletrack on the left. Climb gradually.

16.7 Ride straight ahead on Trail 23, passing the turn you took earlier to the right. Turn a corner to the left and descend the way you rode up.

17.5 End of the trail, at your car. Or turn left to return to the main parking area if you rode out. 🚲

SIGNAL PEAK

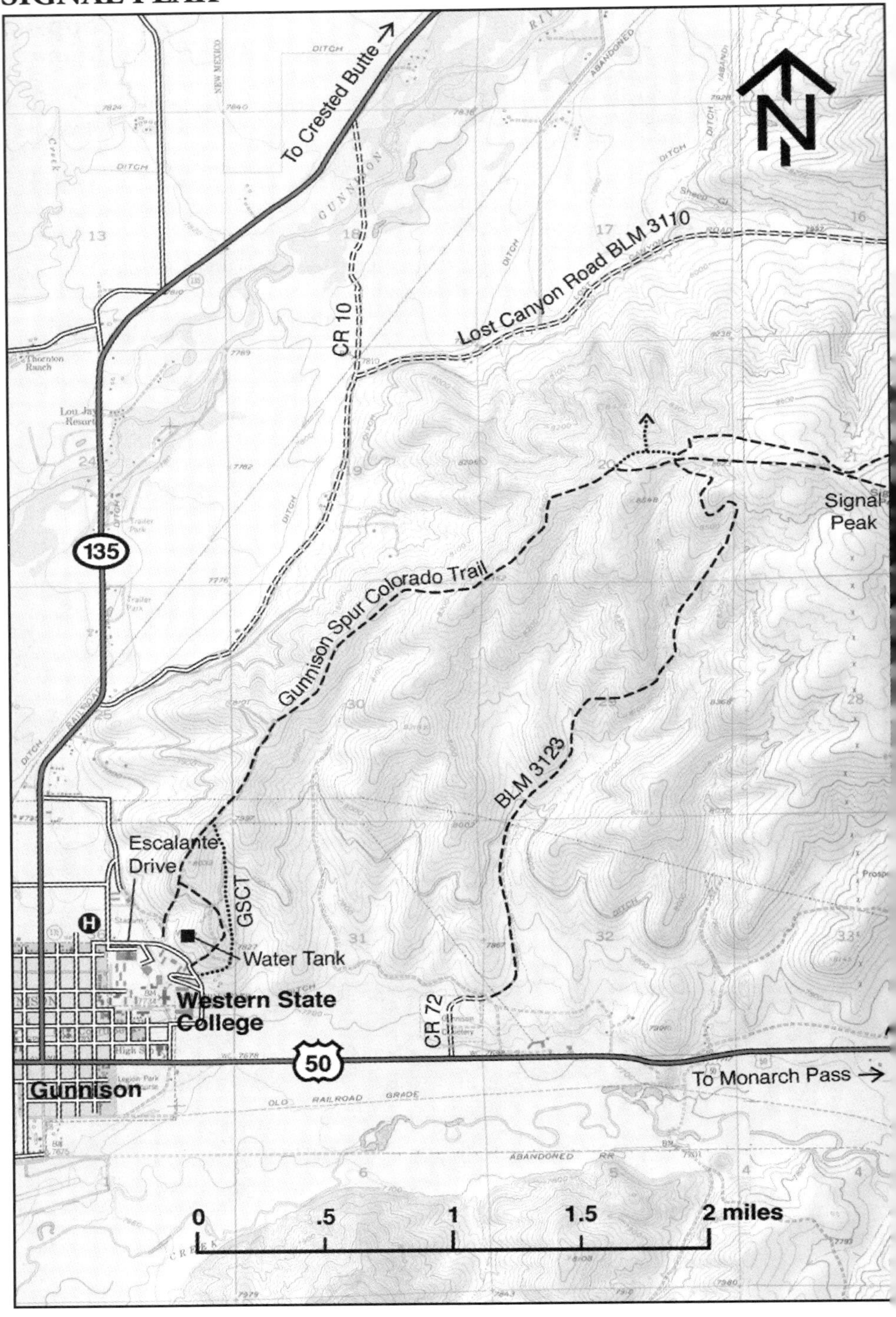

To Crested Butte

CR 10

Lost Canyon Road BLM 3110

Signal Peak

135

Gunnison Spur Colorado Trail

Escalante Drive

GSCT

BLM 3123

Water Tank

H

Western State College

CR 72

50

Gunnison

To Monarch Pass →

| 0 | .5 | 1 | 1.5 | 2 miles |

Description: Signal Peak is a steep hill climb through the sagebrush to beautiful views, right out of the town of Gunnison. It is a great early season hill climb, open much earlier than the Crested Butte rides. Zoom down the descent the way you rode up, or explore the maze of roads and trails beyond this point. It is possible to ride to Lost Canyon or Taylor Canyon, see your Latitude 40 Aspen/Crested Butte/Gunnison map to plan your adventure. Be sure to respect private property in this area.

Distance: 9 mile out and back: 2.5 miles of singletrack and 6.5 miles of doubletrack.

Time: 1½-2 hours

Difficulty: Advanced intermediate

Technical Skill: Advanced Intermediate

Aerobic Effort: Moderately high

Elevation: Top: 8,800' **Gain:** 1,200'

Season: Late April-October

Finding Route: Easy. Many turns are not signed, but the route is straightforward.

Maps: Latitude 40 Aspen/Crested Butte/Gunnison

Location: Start at the upper parking lot at Western State College. To get here, drive or ride north on Highway 50 (Main Street in Gunnison) to Denver Avenue. Turn right and go two blocks to Colorado Avenue and turn left, then turn immediately right on Escalante Drive. Climb up the tree-lined street and around the top of the college, passing the water towers on the left. When you start to go downhill, there is a large parking lot on the right. Park here if you drove. The Trail begins directly across the street by a stair-step to cross the fence. The beginning is marked by the small Colorado Trail symbol on posts and a large Colorado Trail map.

Mileage Log:

0.0 Cross the fence and ride past a large Colorado Trail map. Turn immediately left on the singletrack with the Colorado Trail symbol.

0.1 The singletrack intersects a dirt road. Turn right onto the road and ride a short distance to the corner where the marked Colorado Trail continues.

0.2 Take this singletrack and climb gradually. (The road takes you to the same place, but the trail is more fun and scenic.)

0.4 Stay right.

0.6 Ride straight ahead. The trail to the right is closed, please respect this private property.

0.7 Turn right onto the ridge-top road and climb toward the large red and white radio tower.

1.2 Stay right on the road, passing two spur roads to the left, riding around the base of the radio tower. Look for the Colorado Trail symbol. Descend away from the tower and then climb again, staying with the rocky ridgetop.

3.5 Pass an unmarked singletrack to the right, and climb very steeply.

3.7 On the left near the fence corner, a singletrack takes off left. Take this gradual singletrack through the sage.

SIGNAL PEAK
Ride Information

4.1 The singletrack splits. Turn right and climb up to rejoin the road.

4.2 Turn left onto the road and climb. (Another road goes straight ahead and down.)

4.3 Left at the road split onto the more gradual climb.

4.5 Reach a level spot just below Signal Peak. The views here are amazing! The Fossil Ridge is straight ahead, to the left you see the West Elk Mountains, the Anthracites, Carbon Peak, and Whetstone Mountain in the distance. From here return the way you came up.

9.0 Back to your car. 🚲

Hartman Rocks

Flag Creek, Reno-Flag-Bear Deadman Gulch

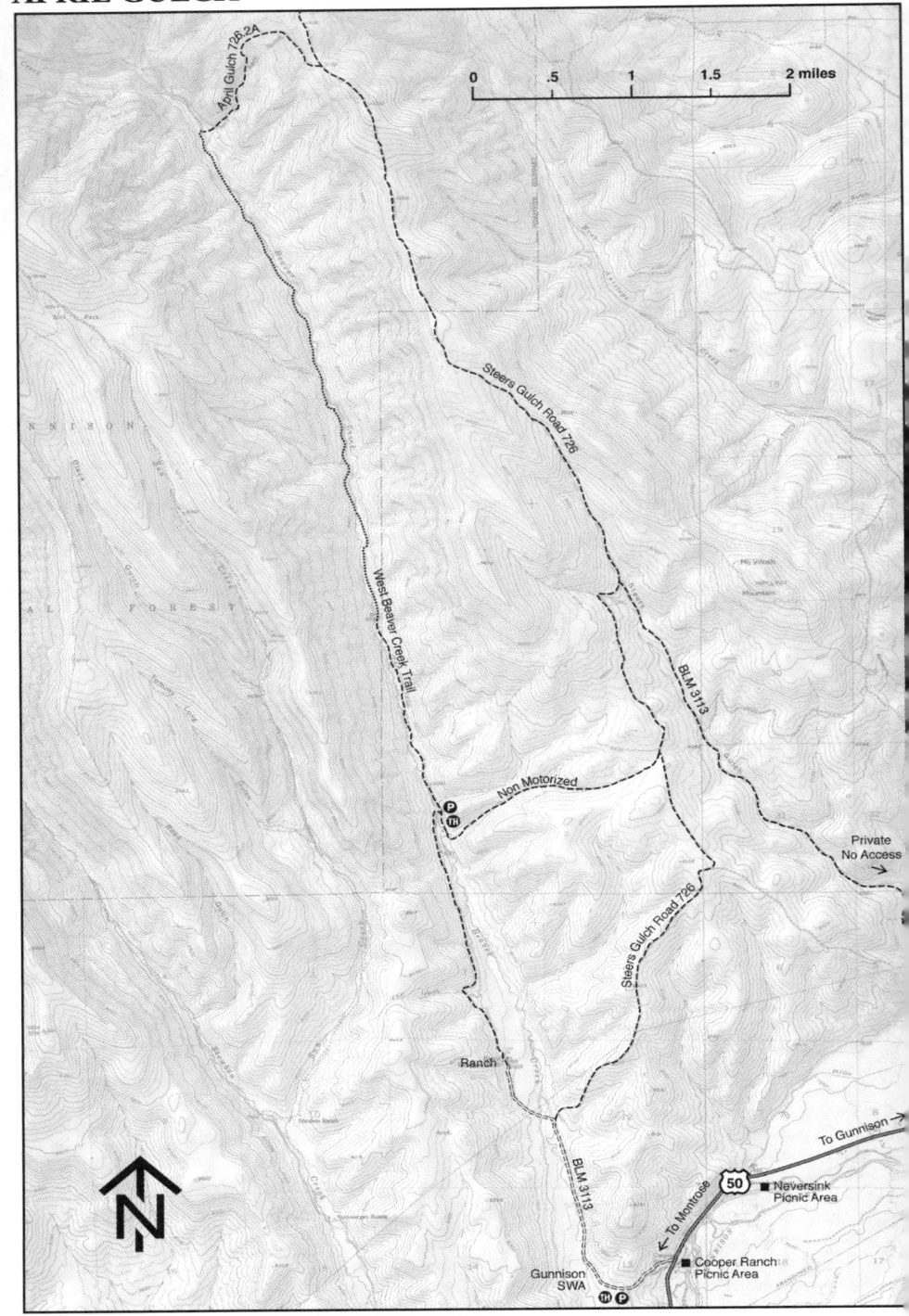

Description: April Gulch is a high mountain ride in Gunnison, starting down low in the rolling sage hills west of Gunnison and climbing high into beautiful aspen and Douglas Fir forest. Much of the ride is on dirt road, but the West Beaver Creek Trail descent is a wonderful, rolling singletrack. (An out and back on the West Beaver Creek Trail would be a great ride with a lot less climbing and more singletrack.) The road up to April Gulch is smooth and of moderate to steeper grades, a great workout that is open earlier than many climbs of this type in the Crested Butte area. The beginning of the descent is in horrible shape, some will walk most of a mile. It is a steep old road that is rutted and washed out and filled with large loose rocks. Some will love the challenge! Unfortunately most of the elevation gained is lost in this one descent, but the rest of the ride is quite good. The rolling singletrack at the bottom is awesome! The ride finishes with a fast road ride out.

Distance: 23 miles, 4 miles of singletrack, 19 miles of dirt road.

Time: 3-4 ½ hours

Difficulty: Advanced intermediate with a one mile expert descent.

Technical Skill: Advanced intermediate with one mile of expert descent.

Aerobic Effort: Moderately high

Elevation: Top:10,131' **Gain:** 2,780'

Season: May through mid-October

Finding Route: Moderate

Maps: Latitude 40 Aspen/Crested Butte/Gunnison

Location: To get to the beginning of the April Gulch ride, drive west on Highway 50 from Gunnison, 7 miles from the intersection of Highway 50 and Highway 135. The turn is 7/10ths of a mile past the Neversink Picnic Area, which has a large sign. When you see the State Wildlife Area sign on the right and the Cooper Ranch Picnic Area on the left, turn right and climb the hill on BLM Road 3113. There is a parking area on the left in ½ mile.

Mileage Log:

0.0   Turn left out of the parking area and descend briefly on BLM 3113, then roll along next to hay meadows.

1.3   Turn right and begin climbing on the dirt road on the right, Forest Service 726, Steers Gulch Road. There is a sign 1/10th of a mile up. Follow this road for several miles. (To do the out and back on the singletrack, turn left here, ride through the ranch and up the dirt road to the signed beginning of West Beaver Creek Trail. It is just after a wide crossing of the creek, 2.7 miles from Steer Gulch Road.)

5.2   Pass through a seasonal closure gate and continue climbing.

5.6   The road forks, stay left and continue climbing.

6.4   Stay left on the main road to switchback up, passing a spur to the right.

7.4   The road flattens through the aspen forest and then climbs again. Stay on the main road through here.

8.6   Views on the left of big mountains. Stay left on the main road, passing a spur on the right.

APRIL GULCH
Ride Information

8.7   Stay left on the main road along the ridge, passing a spur to the right.

8.9   Stay right on the main road, passing a spur through a fence on the left. Begin descending and ride through a gate, passing a Steers Gulch Road 726 sign.

9.6   Continue down, passing a faintly visible spur on the left. You may not even see this. Continue on the road around to the north side of a hill. Climb slightly and then roll along the flat and fast road.

11.4   Turn left at the unmarked fork in the road. This is a very prominent fork with views to the left. Just after starting on the left fork road there is a large sign about Colorado Cutthroat recovery. Begin descending gradually at first, then more steeply. Soon the road becomes very rutted and then quite rocky and steep. Hang on or walk!

13.1   Cross Beaver Creek at the bottom of the hill and head left, then immediately right. The trail is on the right on the open hillside. Climb away from the creek, but continue down the drainage. The trail climbs and descends through beautiful aspen groves and dark forest.

16.1   Switchback left down to the creek and cross a bridge. Ride left up the creek briefly to the continuation of the trail that switchbacks right and up the hill.

17.2   The singletrack ends, roll onto an old doubletrack. There is a sign here, West Beaver Creek Trail, facing the opposite direction. Continue downhill.

18.8   Stay left along the hillside through the grassy meadow area.

19.0   Ride or more likely, walk, up and down a rocky hill at the end of the trail. Stay to the right and cross the wide creek on the road. Climb gradually and then roll down the fast road on the sage covered hillside.

20.4   Stay on the main road, passing spurs to the left and right.

20.6   Stay on the main road and pass another spur.

21.0   Ride through the ranch and down the gravel road, ride left and cross the creek, then swing right.

21.7   Pass Steers Gulch Road on the left, continue straight alongside the hay meadows to return to your car.

23.0   Back to your car after a short hill climb. 🚲

Barret Creek Trail

NEEDLE CREEK RESERVOIR
Dutchman Creek Trail, Right Hand to Barret Creek

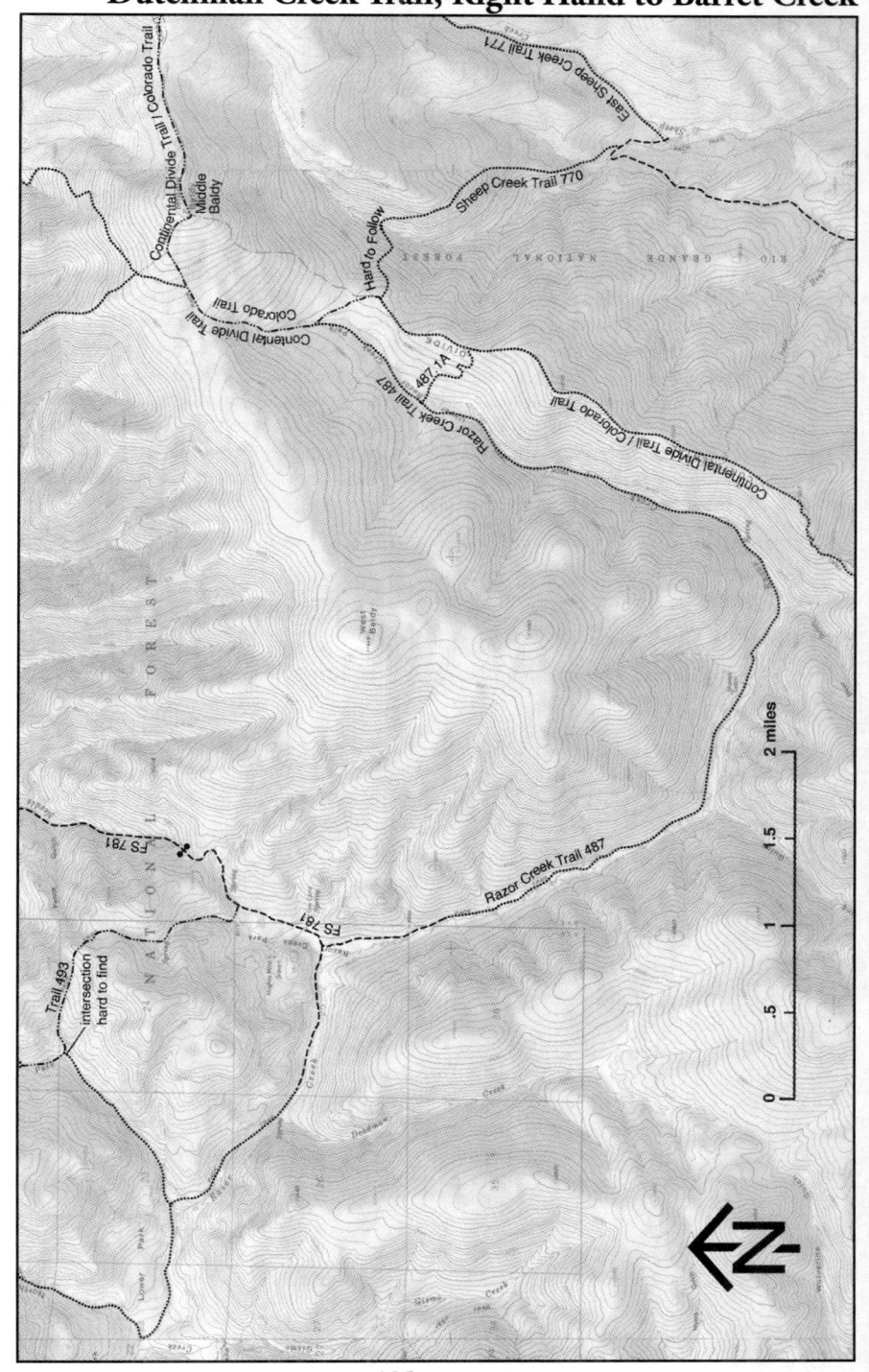

DUTCHMAN CREEK TRAIL

See map pages 134-135

Ride Information

Description: This is a little known, adventurous ride in the dark timbered and sagebrush covered Cochetopa Hills east of Gunnison and south of Doyleville. The trails here are rugged, isolated and difficult to follow. They are for expert riders only due to the difficult nature of the trails. This loop begins with a sustained climb on Forest Road 781, and then follows Razor Creek on an enjoyable, long and gradual singletrack climb through mountain meadows. From here the trail follows the Continental Divide and Colorado Trail. The descent begins with a rough traverse and a narrow and very rocky descent on the Dutchman Creek Trail. The last half of the descent is smooth and fast, along Dutchman Creek. Finally a climb up and over a big ridge on forest doubletrack brings you back to your car. This loop connects with several other trails including the Colorado and Continental Divide Trails between Marshall Pass and North Cochetopa Pass, for numerous different explorations. All of these loops are rugged and isolated, getting lost or hurt can have serious consequences. Don't ride here without the recommended maps or alone. It is quite likely you will not encounter any other people. It is a good possiblitity you will get lost or turned around here, so be prepared with extra food, water, and maps; and start early. Don't ride here during hunting season, it is packed with hunters and unsafe. Bow season seems to be mostly quiet and safe, however. For another loop in this area, see Right Hand to Barret Creek.

Distance: 26 mile loop, 12 miles of forest road, 6 miles of singletrack, 8 miles of four-wheeler track.

Time: 4-6 ½ hours

Difficulty: Expert to Epic

Technical Skill: Expert, these trails are muddy, very rocky, rooty and rugged.

Aerobic Effort: High

Elevation: Top: 11,400' **Gain:** 3,940'

Season: Mid- June through late September

Finding Route: Moderate to very difficult in places.

Maps: National Geographic/Trails Illustrated La Garita/Cochetopa Hills is best, and Gunnison Basin Public Lands map, 2002 or newer is helpful.

Location: To get to the trailhead, drive 18 miles east of Gunnison on Highway 50, and turn right onto County Road 45 in Doyleville. (A small group of ranch houses comprise all of Doyleville.) Continue one mile until the road forks, and turn left on County Road 46 toward Needle Creek Reservoir. Drive 1.6 miles until the road forks again, and turn right onto County Road 47, still following signs to Needle Creek Reservoir. This road turns into County Road 23YY. In another 1.6 miles, turn left on County Road 24UU. Drive 8/10ths of a mile and turn right on an unnumbered road marked only with a Needle Creek Reservoir sign. Drive 1.8 miles, going through and shutting two gigantic game protection gates, to the junction of the next road on the left, Forest Road 750. This road is somewhat obscure, the right fork off of it leads to a private home. Park here on the right, across from Forest Service Road 750, in a wide spot.

Mileage Log:

0.0   Turn right out of the parking spot and begin riding up Forest Service 781 toward the reservoir.

1.6   After descending to the creek, pass a spur on the left to a nice campsite in the aspens.

1.8   Pass a campsite with a bathroom on the left, cross Needle Creek and climb more steeply. Stay on the main road.

2.2   Pass Needle Creek Reservoir.

2.7   Pass Right Hand Trail on the right. (This is an optional route to begin the ride, but adds an hour to the ride and is overgrown and confusing in one spot.) The road continues to climb, more steeply as you near the top of the climb in three miles.

5.6   Top out and ride through a gate. Please close it. Descend on the road.

6.1   Pass the Right Hand Trail coming in on the right.

6.5   Pass a faint spur to a cabin on the left, stay on the main road.

6.7   Pass a faint spur to a cabin on the right, stay on the main road.

7.2   Stay low and right through a rocky and wet section, passing a spur to the left. Continue up the Razor Creek drainage.

7.7   Begin the Razor Creek Trail at the end of the road. This climbs gradually for the next several miles, next to Razor Creek. The trail is rocky in spots and sometimes muddy, but otherwise fairly smooth. Unfortunately four-wheelers are gradually (and not legally) widening this trail.

13.0   Reach an open meadow.

13.3   Continue straight ahead, passing the Razor Creek Spur Trail 487.1A to the right. (This trail climbs steeply up to the Continental Divide/ Colorado Trail. It is a fun option for another ride.)

14.4   Join the Colorado Trail at a signed intersection. Turn left and climb on the wide four-wheeler track, at first in the dark forest, then into a nice high altitude meadow.

15.3   Turn left at a signed fork in the trail, starting the singletrack Dutchman Creek Trail. To the right, the Continental Divide/ Colorado Trail continues to climb.

15.5   Ride straight ahead on Dutchman Creek Trail, passing the Left Hand Trail to the left. Begin a very rocky descent through tight trees.

16.8   The trail becomes smoother and is much faster.

19.4   Turn right and cross Dutchman Creek, then turn immediately left at the T-intersection. Hicks Creek comes in from the right. (Hick's is an awesome, smooth descent for another day.)

19.9   Cross the creek again and follow it down, passing a doubletrack spur on the left.

21.6   Cross the creek and ride onto a doubletrack, Forest Road 750.2A, where the trail ends. Zoom down this.

22.8   Just before the remains of an old cabin and a spur that lead to it, stay left on Forest Road 750.2A and climb very briefly. It is easy to get lost beyond this point as the roads are braided and mostly unmarked. Follow the directions closely.

23.0   Turn right onto an old doubletrack off the corner of the road before it starts to climb steeply. If you are climbing steeply, you have gone too far. Follow this old doubletrack around the corner to the left. It disappears briefly but reappears in a rocky section. Continue up the draw on it.

23.1 Pass a Forest Road that drops steeply in from the left, and ride to the right through a gate. Cross Owens Creek and head left up the creek. Soon you will turn right and climb the ridge that is between you and your car on Forest Road 781.

23.9 Turn right at the first road fork and climb away from the creek.

24.4 Stay left on this road as you near the top of the ridge, passing a grassy spur to the right.

24.6 Stay to the left on the main road, passing a weather station to the right. Ride up the hill. There are nice views along the edge of the ridge.

24.8 Ride through an old gate, staying left on the main road.

25.0 Reach a saddle, turn right and descend quickly on signed Forest Road 750.

25.9 Ride through a gate and left, continue descending.

26.2 End Forest Road 750 at a T-intersection with a private road. Turn right.

26.3 Back to your car.

Options: There are a lot of fun trails to explore in the Needle Creek Resevoir Area, all of them rough and isolated and many hard to follow. Here is a brief list of the main trails if you want to check the area out. You must be very good at reading maps and route finding, and be well prepared if an emergency situation arises. Always take extra food, water, and clothing when riding here, and both of the recommended maps in the above description. The area is confusing with many roads and trails, and only the main system trails marked. Many of the trails disappear for a brief time as well.

Right Hand Creek Trail 493: This is a fairly smooth and enjoyable singletrack ride up from Needle Creek Reservoir, although quite steep toward the top. It is a great downhill. The trail connects to Razor Creek Park but is grassy, overgrown and hard to follow where it traverses Barret Park. After the intersection with the Barrett Park Trail, turn left and descend briefly to cross a small creek. The trail resumes on the other side of the creek. From here it is all wide four-wheeler track with short, steep climbs back to Forest Service 781.

Barret Park Trail 494: A nice traverse through an open park and a steep, narrow singletrack descent. Big rock walls and fast, rolling singletrack down lower. Easy to get lost getting back to Needle Creek Reservoir. Not a great climb.

Upper Razor Creek Spur: Steep but short connecter singletrack from Upper Razor Creek Trail to the Colorado and Continental Divide Trails.

East Sheep Creek Trail: A beautiful and very continuous and challenging climb that goes on forever. Trail disappears in the upper meadow, look to the left if for some reason you are riding this. Fun descent but again, hard to follow.

Continental Divide and Colorado Trails: This is a good section, rideable from Marshall Pass all the way to North Cochetopa Pass. The trail is mostly rough, sometimes smooth, often rocky. Shuttle needed to ride the entire trail. A lot of it has been widened to a four-wheeler track. Only for the adventurous rider.

Baldy Lake Trail: If you want a longer version of the Dutchman's loop. Add 1-2 hours for this. The trail is very rocky up top and the route descends next to a beautiful high alpine lake. The lower part of the descent is quite fun and fast. A left on the Hicks Gulch Trail at the bottom of the Baldy Lake Trail is one of the best and only smooth trails in the area. This connects straight into The Dutchman Creek Trail.

Left Hand Trail: Very rough descent, hard to follow at the bottom. Not a good ascent.

Long Branch Trail: Narrow and very rocky descent, followed by four-wheeler track. Not a good ascent.

Big Bend Trail: Very rocky, rutted and difficult descent. Difficult to negotiate back to the road down lower. Access from Sargeants is closer. ᕫᕫ

RIGHT HAND & BARRET CREEK
See map pages 134-135 ———————————— **Ride Information**

Description: The Needle Creek Reservoir area is isolated and different for the adventurous expert rider. It is little known to mountain bikers, but is heavily used in the fall by hunters. The trails are rugged and rough, and it is quite easy to get lost here. Don't expect smooth and easy riding here. This second loop in the Needle Creek Area combines a beautiful climb up the Right Hand Creek Trail that is sure to challenge even the strongest riders, a stroll through open high altitude mountain meadows, and a steep and narrow downhill luge ride through the pines. It mellows at the bottom and follows Barret Creek down to a series of dirt logging roads that climb back to Needle Creek Reservoir. It can be quite confusing on these roads, and most are not marked. There are many spurs that are unmarked and not on maps. Be sure you are good at navigating if you attempt this ride. Do not ride here alone or without the suggested maps, and be prepared. It can also be quite hot here, take plenty of water.

Distance: 12 mile loop, 6.5 miles of singletrack, 5.5 of dirt forest road.

Time: 2-3 hours.

Difficulty: Expert

Technical Skill: Expert

Aerobic Effort: High

Elevation: Top: 10,400' **Gain:** 3,100'

Season: June through late September.

Finding Route: Difficult to very difficult.

Maps: National Geographic/ Trails Illustrated La Garita/Cochetopa Hills. The 2002 or newer Gunnison Basin Public Lands Map is helpful.

Location: Follow the directions in Location for Dutchman Creek Trail. Continue driving 1.8 miles farther on Forest Road 781 to the bathroom/campsite beyond the starting point for Dutchmans and park here.

Mileage Log:

0.0   Turn left out of the parking area, cross Needle Creek and begin riding up Forest Road 781 toward Needle Creek Reservoir.

0.4   Ride past the reservoir.

RIGHT HAND & BARRET CREEK
Ride Information

0.9 On a corner with a camping area to the right, turn right onto the signed Right Hand Creek Trail. This is near the top end of the reservoir. This rolls along nicely down low, but becomes steeper and more challenging as you ascend.

1.6 Stay left along the creek, passing a grassy fork to the right.

3.3 Gain the top, then zoom down a short, fast descent to a signed intersection in open meadows.

3.6 Turn right on the signed Barret Creek Trail and climb through the meadows to a saddle. (Left is the continuation of the Right Hand Trail.)

4.6 Stay right and descend on Barret Creek Trail, passing the North Gulch Trail at the top on the left. The narrow singletrack down Barret Creek will keep you on your toes. It passes some beautiful rock walls.

6.8 Climb out of the creek bottom, then stay left on the Barret Creek Trail at the top of the hill. Descend through the aspens.

7.1 Stay left in the willow bottom, and cross the creek. Turn immediately right after crossing and ride down the creek.

7.6 The Barret Creek Trail ends on a dirt road. Continue on this road briefly.

7.7 Turn right at a T-intersection with Forest Road 782, turn right and ride down to the creek. Cross and climb out of the creek.

8.0 Turn right on the first unmarked road and climb gradually.

8.4 Stay right at an unmarked fork in the road and climb through a gate.

8.6 Stay left at a road spur and climb.

9.2 Pass a spring and cattle trough and continue climbing around Big Hill, then descend. A series of short, steep climbs and descents lead around the mountain and through a clearcut. Stay on the main road through here to return to Forest Road 781 via a steep descent right and down toward the reservoir. There are user created spurs cutting steeply down and right and back toward the reservoir also. You can see the reservoir from the top of the descent.

11.9 Turn left on Forest Road 781 and descend.

12.1 Back to your car. 🚲

Barret Creek Trail

CANYON CREEK (WHITEPINE)

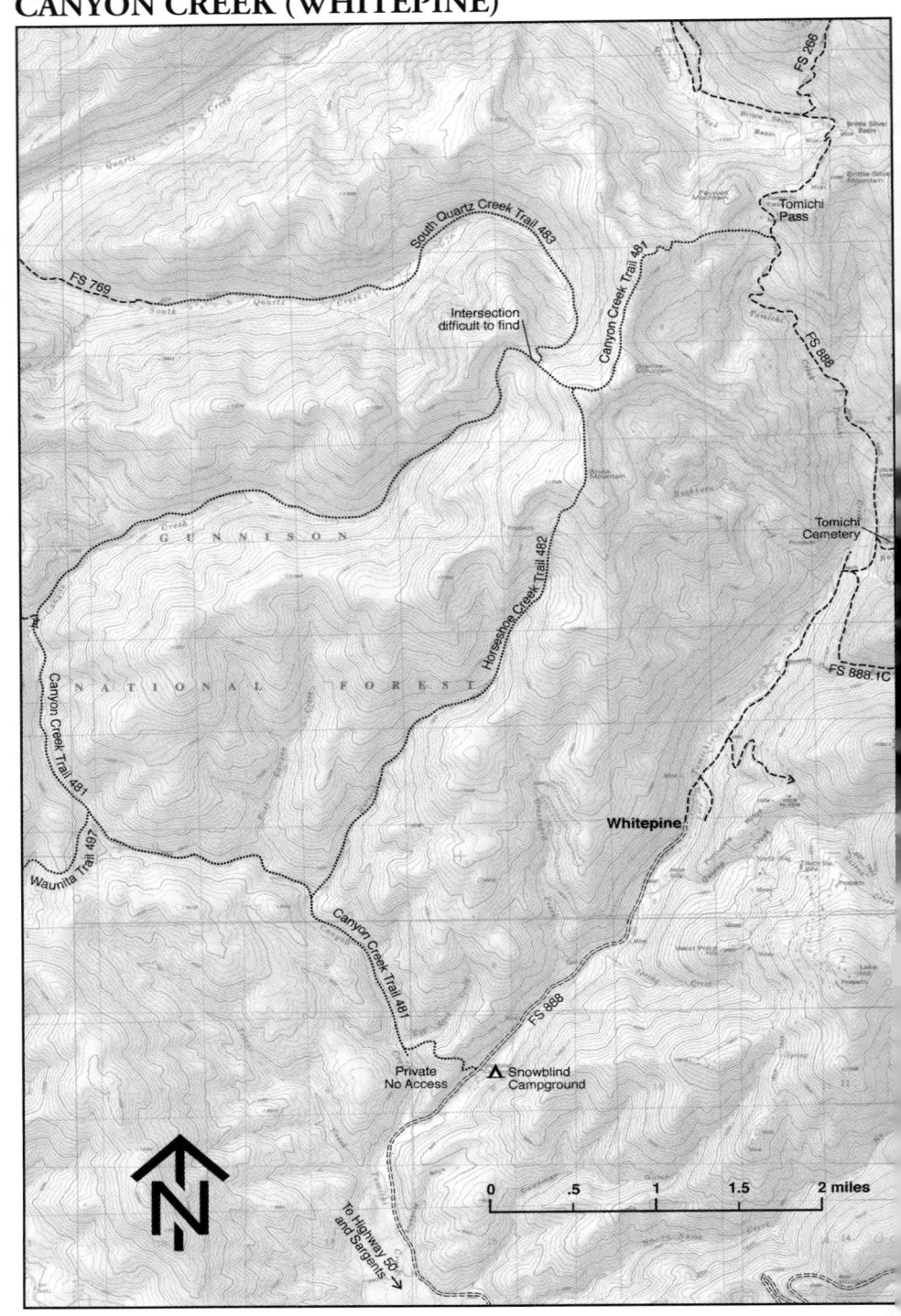

FS 266

FS 769

South Quartz Creek Trail 483

Canyon Creek Trail 487

Intersection difficult to find

Tomichi Pass

FS 888

Tomichi Cemetery

FS 888.1C

GUNNISON

Horseshoe Creek Trail 482

NATIONAL FOREST

Canyon Creek Trail 481

Waunita Trail 497

Whitepine

Canyon Creek Trail 481

FS 888

Private No Access

△ Snowblind Campground

N

0   .5   1   1.5   2 miles

To Highway 50 and Sargents →

Description: Canyon Creek is a challenging ride with an incredible and very long descent. It is located 31 miles west of Gunnison and 27 miles east of Salida. It combines a grueling road climb and hike-a-bike with one of the sweetest, fastest descents in Gunnison County! The loop starts with a flat and smooth road and becomes progressively more steep and rocky, climbing mostly within a dark pine forest. Once the four-wheel drive road rolls into open meadows, it is just a short distance to the Canyon Creek Trail, but the climbing isn't over yet. At the start of the singletrack, riders hike-bike for ½ hour to reach spectacular, high alpine views on an unnamed peak. Roll along the ridge to a saddle, and then from here it is all downhill: at first steep, rutted and technical, then fast, smooth and winding, with a few more rocky and rutted sections (motorcycles and mud) thrown in for surprise. End with a short steep climb and descending switchbacks right to the Snowblind Campground. The campground is a perfect place to stay for this ride, as you need a very early start to avoid lightning and thunderstorms. There are also campsites a little farther up the road, but be careful to avoid all the private property in this drainage.

Distance: 20 mile loop, 7.4 miles of dirt road, 12.6 miles of singletrack

Time: 3-5 ½ hours

Difficulty: Expert to Epic

Technical Skill: Expert

Aerobic Effort: Strenuous

Elevation: Top: 12,600' **Gain:** 3,800'

Season: July through early October

Finding Route: Easy to moderate, all junctions are marked on the trail. The road climb has several unmarked spurs, but the route is straightforward.

Maps: National Geographic/Trails Illustrated Salida/St. Elmo/ Shavano Peak is best, 2002 or newer Gunnison Basin Public Lands map has the route but less detail.

Location: Start at the Snowblind Campground. To get here from Gunnison, drive 31.5 miles east on Highway 50 and turn left on County Road 888 toward White Pine. The turn is one mile past the tiny town of Sargents. To get to County Road 888 from Poncha Springs (5 miles west of Salida,) drive 27 miles west on Highway 50 from the junction of Highways 50 and 285 over Monarch Pass. At the western base of Monarch Pass, turn right on County Road 888. Drive 10.4 miles to the Snowblind Campground. There are a couple spots to pull off the road near the campground, or more up or down the road. Only park in the campground if you pay for a spot and camp, they are strict about extra cars and parking.

Mileage Log:

0.0 Start the ride by continuing up County Road 888. Stay on this road for 7.4 miles.

2.1 Ride through the old mining town of White Pine.

4.1 Turn right and ride more steeply toward Tomichi Pass, passing a private drive on the left. Stay with the main road. This section is quite rocky.

4.2 Stay left on the main road, passing a spur road to the right.

4.4 Stay left on the main road, passing a spur road to the right.

CANYON CREEK (WHITEPINE)
Ride Information

4.5   Turn left at the old cemetery, staying on County Road 888 toward Tomichi Pass and descend a little, then climb again.

4.7   Stay left, passing a spur road to the right.

7.5   Tomichi Pass is now in sight and the road travels through open meadows. Turn left onto the signed Canyon Creek Trail 481.The trail is rideable for a short distance, then turns to a ½ mile or so hike-a-bike to the summit. (Note: The ½ mile hike is not included in mileage beyond this point, as it will not read on your computer.)

8.6   Top out and enjoy amazing views here. Continue on the trail, now heading downhill and contouring. (Note: The South Quartz Creek Trail turns off right within the next mile, but the entrance is difficult to find so it shouldn't confuse finding the descent on the Canyon Creek Trail. The forest service has plans to improve this area, so at some point it will be signed and easier to find.)

9.4   Stay right, passing an unmarked singletrack on the left.

9.6   Stay right and pass the Horseshoe Trail. (The Horseshoe Trail is a very steep and loose descent, and much shorter than Canyon Creek.) Begin the Canyon Creek Trail descent down the face of a small cliff. Roll through an open meadow below this and start a fast descent. There are several technical sections mixed in with the otherwise very fast descent, so be aware.

14.1   After an incredible descent, arrive at some corrals and a large hunting camp area. Turn left as the trail widens to doubletrack and cross Canyon Creek. Ride up a road a few yards, then turn right on the continuation of the singletrack. This section is continuously smooth and fast!

16.0   Stay left, passing the signed Waunita Trail on the right.

17.5   Stay right, passing the bottom of the Horseshoe Trail coming in on the left.

18.8   Turn hard left, passing a closed trail through private property, and stay with the Canyon Creek Trail. Climb a loose, sandy grunt of a hill then zoom down switchbacks.

20.0   Back to the campground! 🚲

The start of the Canyon Creek Trail

The Canyon Creek Trail

MONARCH CREST TRAIL & AGATE CREEK

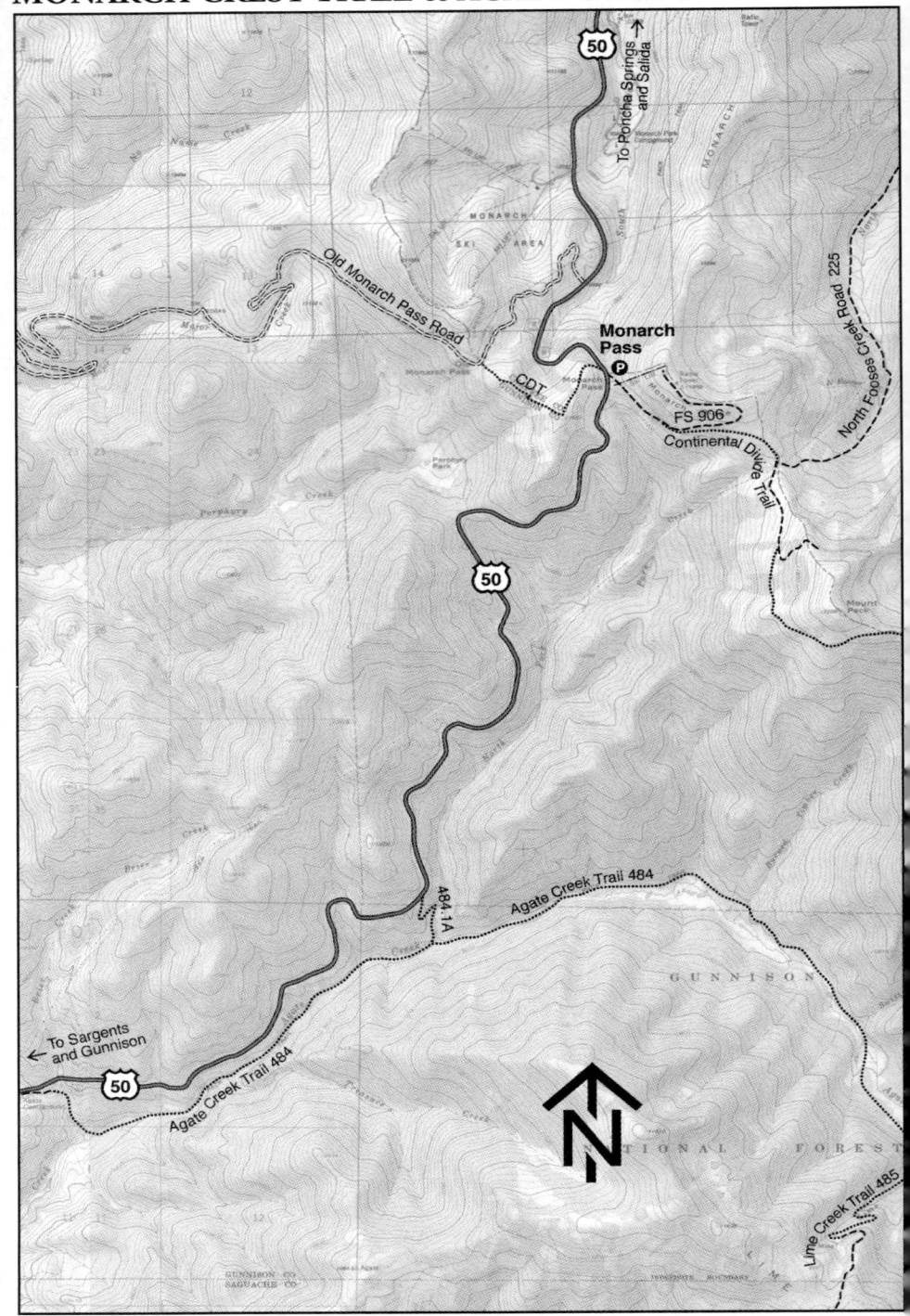

GREEN CREEK & SOUTH FOOSES CREEK TRAILS

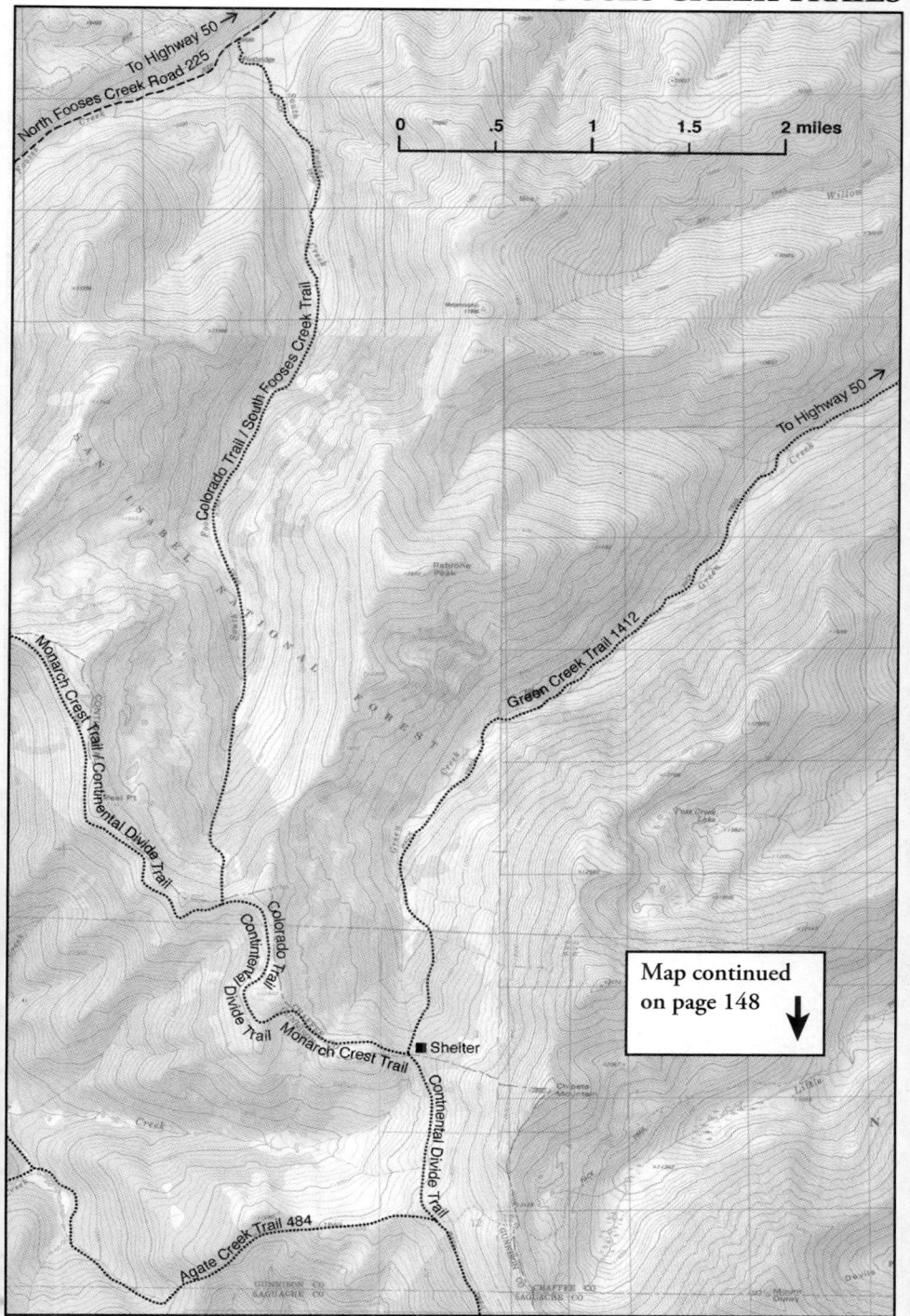

To Highway 50 →

North Fooses Creek Road 225

0   .5   1   1.5   2 miles

Colorado Trail / South Fooses Creek Trail

SAN ISABEL NATIONAL FOREST

To Highway 50 →

Green Creek Trail 1412

Rabione Peak

Monarch Crest Trail / Continental Divide Trail

Colorado Trail

Continental Divide Trail

Monarch Crest Trail

■ Shelter

Continental Divide Trail

Map continued
on page 148 ↓

Agate Creek Trail 484

GUNNISON CO
SAGUACHE CO

CHAFFEE CO
SAGUACHE CO

N

SILVER CREEK & RAINBOW TRAILS

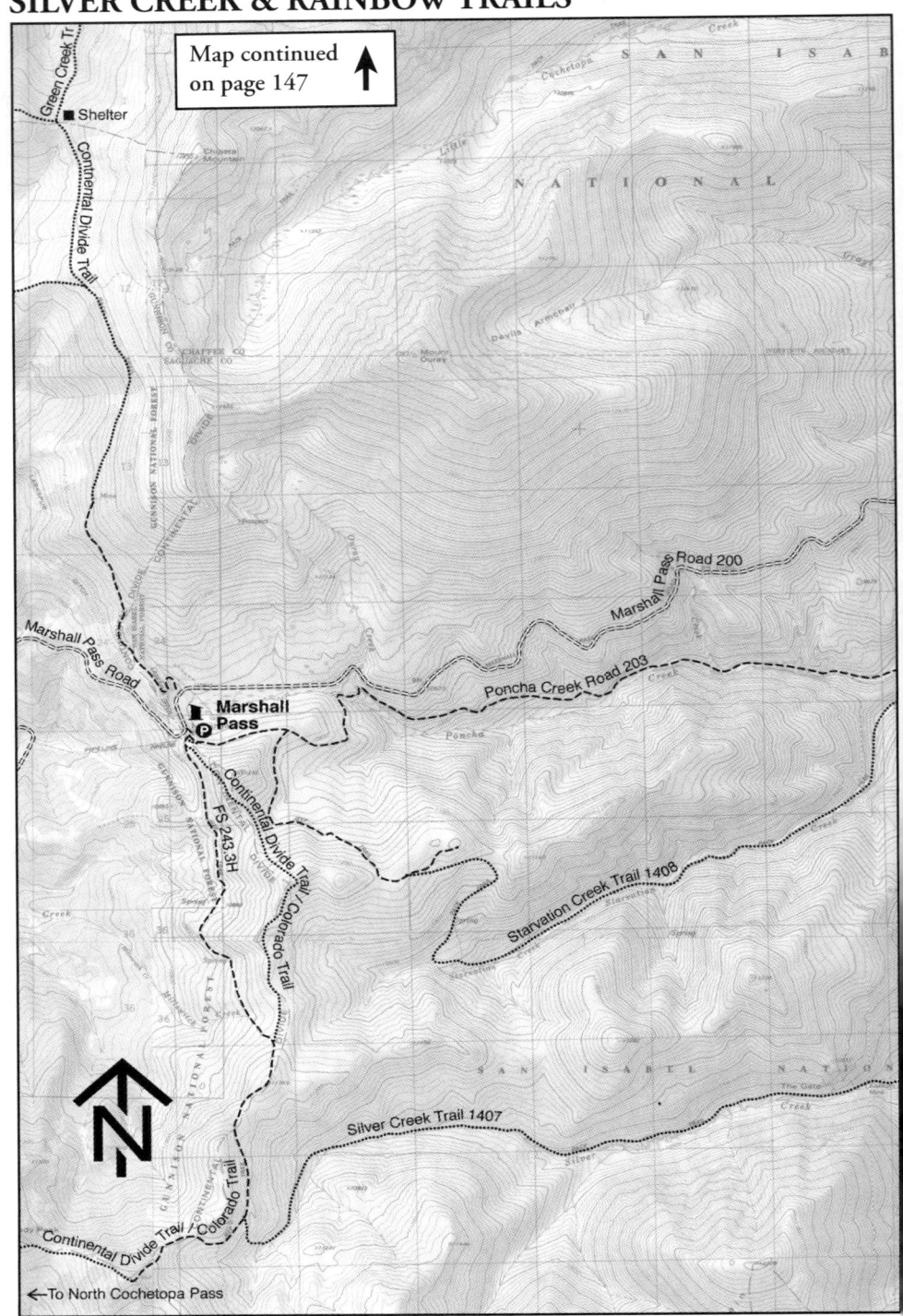

Map continued on page 147

Green Creek Trl

■ Shelter

Continental Divide Trail

SAN ISAB

NATIONAL

Marshall Pass Road 200

Marshall Pass Road

Marshall Pass P

Continental Divide Trail / Colorado Trail

FS 243.3H

Poncha Creek Road 203

Starvation Creek Trail 1408

GUNNISON NATIONAL FOREST

SAN ISABEL NATIO

N

Silver Creek Trail 1407

Continental Divide Trail / Colorado Trail

←To North Cochetopa Pass

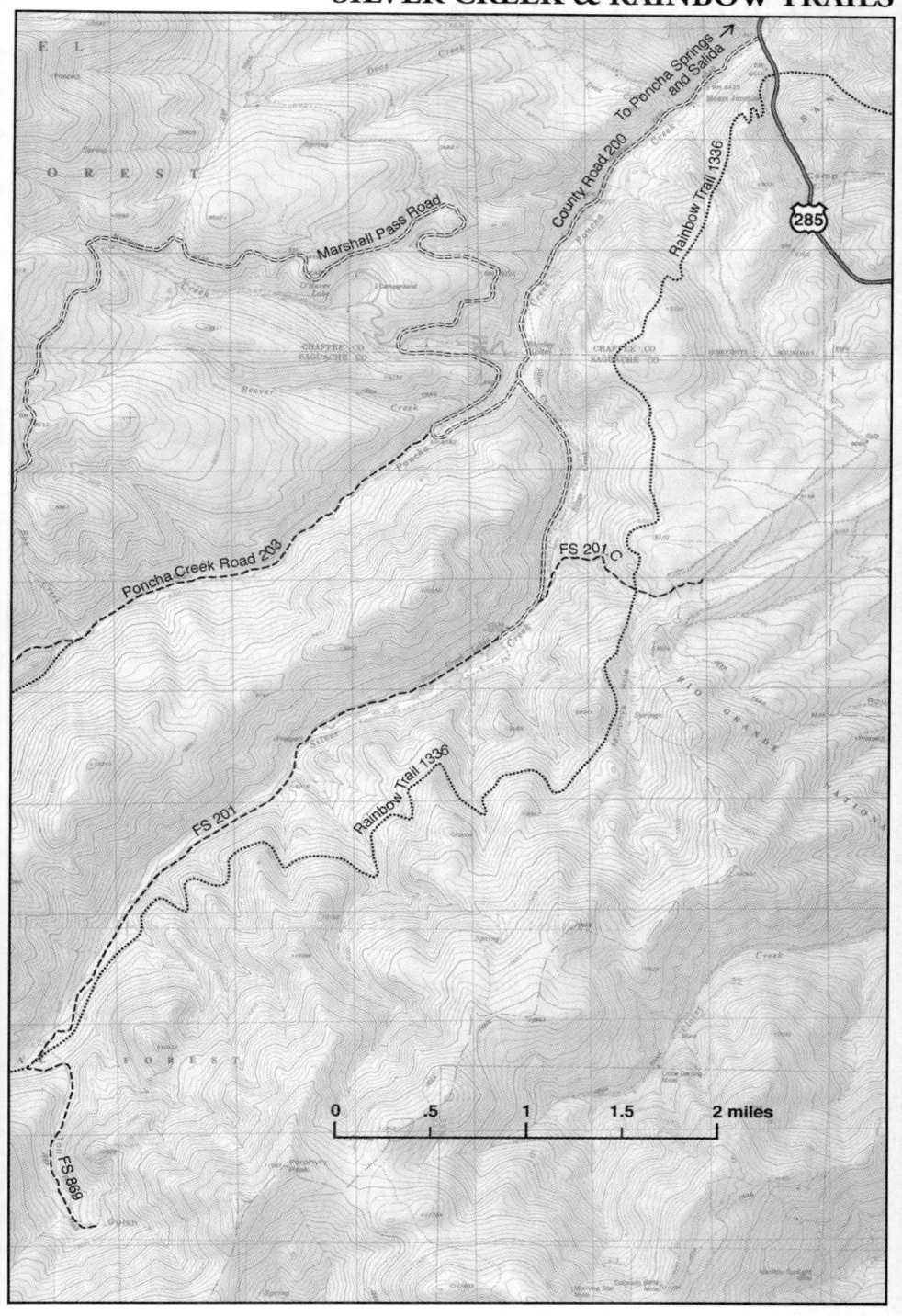

THE MONARCH CREST & RAINBOW TRAILS
Ride Information ——————————— *See map pages 146-149*

Description: The Monarch Crest Trail is a true cross-country classic, not to be missed! It is unbeatable for views and great singletrack as it follows a high altitude ridge just below 12,000' on a mostly gradual section of the Continental Divide Trail. The trail loses a lot more elevation than it gains with a shuttle, but don't let it fool you, it is still a very good workout. It starts at the top of Monarch Pass (11,312 feet) and climbs gradually and rolls along flat singletrack for the first six miles to the summit of an unnamed peak. This section is amazing! This high altitude exposure makes it imperative for an early start on most summer days due to the chance of lightning and thunderstorms. From the highest point in the ride it has fast descents and short climbs until the long and fast Silver Creek descent. From here, descend Forest Service 201 or take the Rainbow Trail. The Rainbow Trail is all giggles, up and down, and very fast! I suggest riding it at the end because it is an awesome trail and doesn't take much longer than descending Forest Road 201. It does climb 1,500', however, so it requires more effort. There are several options for descending off the Monarch Crest Trail for a shorter or easier ride, also. See options, below. A shuttle is available from the High Valley Center in Poncha Springs, see listing in the back of this book for more information.

Distance: 36 miles with a shuttle, 28.5 miles of singletrack, 2.3 miles dirt road, 5.2 miles pavement. See options, below, to shorten the ride.

Time: 3-6 hours

Difficulty: Advanced intermediate to expert, depending on where you descend.

Technical Skill: Advanced intermediate up to Silver Creek, the Silver Creek descent is expert. Exit before Silver Creek on Marshall Pass Road to avoid the expert section.

Aerobic Effort: Moderately high. Very high altitude.

Elevation: Top: 11,920' **Gain:** 3,600' **Gain with exit at Forest Road 201, skipping the Rainbow Trail:** 2,100' **Loss:** 7,800'

Season: July through September

Finding Route: Fairly easy, well marked. Note: The Monarch Crest Trail is not on signs along the route, this is the local name. Riders follow the Continental Divide Trail (CDT) all the way to the Silver Creek Trail (the Colorado Trail comes in at South Fooses Creek and continues along the CDT, so CT symbols also mark the way from South Fooses Creek to the Silver Creek Trail.) Follow the Rainbow Trail to Highway 285.

Maps: Monarch Crest Trail by Absolute Bikes, available from Absolute Bikes in Salida (see listing in back.) Also available at the High Valley Center and The Monarch Crest Store at the top of Monarch Pass. National Geographic/Trails Illustrated La Garita/Cochetopa Hills is also a good map for the area.

Location: Begin on the summit of Monarch Pass, 40 miles east of Gunnison on Highway 50, or 17 miles west of the intersection of Highways 50 and 285 in Poncha Springs. Park a car in Poncha Springs on the east side of the pass (there is a parking lot right by the junction of Highways 285 and 50 at the Visitor Center) and drive 19 miles west on Highway 50 with bikes and riders to the summit of Monarch Pass.

Mileage Log:

0.0   Begin riding up the paved Forest Road 906 behind the tramway building on Monarch Pass. Right away the road turns to dirt.

0.3   Turn right onto the signed Continental Divide Trail (CDT) singletrack.

1.0   Turn right on the doubletrack and begin climbing. (North Fooses Creek Road descends to the left.) Pass a road to the right that descends along the powerline.

1.6   Turn right onto the signed CDT singletrack, just inside the dark trees.

3.0   Pass a sign for Middle Fooses Creek.

5.2   Ride straight ahead, passing the signed South Fooses Creek on the left. This is also the Colorado Trail from the north. (See South Fooses Creek for a description of this trail.)

5.9   Reach the high point and start a fun descent.

7.0   Pass a small shelter and the Green Creek Trail to the left. (See Green Creek Trail for a description of this trail.) Stay right on the Continental Divide Trail and climb into the woods.

8.1   Ride straight past the Agate Creek Trail, which is on the right, the sign facing backwards. (See Agate Creek for a description of this fun descent.)

9.6   Top out at an old quarry and ride straight ahead and down the doubletrack. Be careful of the huge berms and steep corners on this descent.

11.0   Turn right on Marshall Pass Road and ride past the bathrooms. Continue uphill to the next left, just before the summit of the pass. (A left on Marshall Pass Road is the easy way down to Poncha Springs.)

11.3   Turn left onto a steeper, rutted doubletrack at the fork, just before the summit of the pass. As the doubletrack levels, stay to the right, passing a signed dirt road heading down to Starvation Creek and an inviting singletrack that leads back to the Starvation Creek Road, both on the left. Ride around the corner to the left and turn left onto the signed Colorado Trail that leads to the Silver Creek Trail. This is a confusing area, look for the large Colorado Trail sign and be sure you are CLIMBING on singletrack toward Silver Creek within 1/10th of a mile after turning off Marshall Pass Road.

13.8   Turn left and merge onto a forest road for a quick but steep climb.

14.6   There is a nice overlook for lunch on the left.

15.0   Turn left onto the Silver Creek Trail 1407, and start a long, fast and technical descent. Don't miss this signed turn! (The Colorado and Continental Divide Trails continue straight ahead and up.)

19.5   Cross the creek and ride down next to it and sometimes in it for a short distance.

19.7   Stay left when the road splits and ride downhill briefly on Forest Road 201.

19.8   Turn right on the Rainbow Trail and head toward Highway 285. This trail is all fast, rolling and fun! (Forest Road 201 descends quickly to Marshall Pass Road to skip the Rainbow Trail.)

Ride Information

26.6 Road crossing. Ride straight ahead to finish the Rainbow Trail. A left on this road is also a quick but steep exit if needed, but the trail is not much longer or more difficult.

29.4 Ride straight ahead on the singletrack.

30.8 End of the trail on Highway 285. Carefully cross and turn left and ride downhill. Stay on the shoulder to avoid high speed downhill traffic! In Poncha Springs, stay left to ride back to the visitor center and your car.

36.0 Back to your car.

Options: The Monarch Crest Trail is a fun out and back as well, and you don't have to deal with a shuttle. Go as far as you like, up to the Silver Creek Trail, and return the way you came. See Green Creek, Agate Creek and South Fooses Creek for other trail descents. For an easier way down, roll down Marshall Pass Road to Poncha Springs. This is flat and easy. Exit at Forest Road 201 just before the Rainbow Trail to shorten the ride. 🚲

AGATE CREEK
Ride Information
See map pages 146-147

Description: Agate Creek is well loved because of the fun roll along the high ridge of the Monarch Crest Trail that it's route follows, endless singletrack, and a very long and fast downhill! This shuttle ride loses a lot more elevation than it gains. The beginning of the route on The Monarch Crest Trail climbs gradually along mostly smooth and easy singletrack on a huge, open ridge on the Continental Divide, just below 12,000'. This section is spectacular! A couple more descents and short climbs lead to the Agate Creek descent. The Agate Creek Trail at first descends a very steep singletrack for 2 ½ miles. At the bottom it turns to follow Agate Creek on a gradual, smooth, and very fast winding trail. The trail crosses the creek several times. Many of these crossings are not rideable and must be waded. This is a great trail with a little bit of everything! It can also be ridden as a loop by riding up the Old Monarch Pass Road on the west side of Monarch Pass (see option, below.) Be sure to start early to be off the high ridge before afternoon thunderstorms set in.

Distance: 18.4 miles, 17.2 miles of singletrack, 1.2 miles of dirt road if done with a shuttle.

Time: 2 ½ - 4 hours

Difficulty: Expert

Technical Skill: Expert

Aerobic Effort: Moderate

Elevation: Top: 11,920' **Gain:** 1,300' **Loss:** 2,700'. **Gain if ridden as a loop with Old Monarch Pass Road:** 3,600'

Season: July through September

Finding Route: Easy. Remember the Monarch Crest Trail is a local name for the first section of this ride, so you will not see it on signs. Look for the Continental Divide Trail (CDT) symbols up to the Agate Creek Trail.

Maps: The Crest Trail by Absolute Bikes, see bike shop listing in back. Also available at the Monarch Crest Store on Monarch Pass at the start of the ride, or at the High Valley Shuttle, also see listing in the back. National Geographic/Trails Illustrated La Garita/Cochetopa Hills is a good map of the area also.

Location: Start the ride on the summit of Monarch Pass, on Highway 50, 40 miles east of Gunnison and 19 miles west of the intersection of Highways 50 and 285 in Poncha Springs (5 miles west of Salida.) For the shuttle, park 7 miles west and down from the summit of Monarch Pass or three miles up the pass from Sargents (33 miles east of Gunnison) on the right where the trail ends. This is an unmarked road pullout. Drive a shuttle with bikes and riders to the top of Monarch Pass.

Mileage Log:

0.0   Start riding up the road right behind the Monarch Crest Tramway, Forest Service Road 906. The road is paved at first and then turns quickly to dirt.

0.3   Turn right on the signed Continental Divide Trail (CDT) singletrack.

1.0   Turn right onto the doubletrack and begin climbing. (North Fooses Creek Road heads left and down.)

1.6   Turn right onto the Continental Divide Trail (CDT) singletrack, just inside the dark trees.

3.0   Ride straight ahead and pass a sign for Middle Fooses Creek.

5.2   South Fooses Creek (also the Colorado Trail) is on the left. Keep riding straight ahead on the CDT/Colorado Trail.

5.9   Reach the high point on the ridge. Fun descent!

7.0   Pass a shelter and the signed Green Creek Trail to the left. Stay right on the Continental Divide Trail/Colorado Trail and climb.

8.1   Arrive at the intersection with the Agate Creek Trail. The sign faces backward from the way you arrive. Turn right and begin a long descent.

10.6   Bottom of the steep descent, turn right and cross a creek. The trail rolls along Agate Creek, crossing it several times.

11.1   Ride straight ahead, passing the Lime Creek Trail on the left.

15.2   Stay left, passing the signed Agate Spur Trail on the right. This is shortly after a creek crossing.

17.6   Turn right and cross the creek again and climb. Straight ahead is private.

18.1   Reach the end of the trail. Ride straight ahead on the dirt road.

18.4   Intersection with Highway 50 and your car.

Option: To ride the Agate Creek Trail as a loop, park a car at the corner of County Road 888, one mile east of Sargents. Take County Road 888 4.5 miles to the corner of Old Monarch Pass Road and turn right. Climb up this road approximately 10 miles to the signed Continental Divide Trail, just beyond the pass sign. Follow this east to Monarch Pass and continue the ride as described above. 🚲

SOUTH FOOSES CREEK
Ride Information

See map pages 146-147

Description: South Fooses Creek is a section of the Colorado Trail that descends on a fast and smooth singletrack from The Monarch Crest Trail to Highway 50. The Monarch Crest Trail has wonderful views as it rolls along an open ridge just below 12,000'. South Fooses Creek offers a very long, varied descent of technical and smooth trail through aspen and old growth forest in a high walled canyon. The lower descent is similar to Agate Creek, except the creek crossings are on bridges. It is a relatively quick loop if a shuttle is used, and quite fun! It loses a lot more elevation than it gains, making it quite easy aerobically. To make the ride longer, continue across Highway 50 and continue north on the Colorado Trail to The Shavano Trailhead, and then descend County Road 250. Plan by leaving a car at the visitor center in Poncha Springs or on County Road 250. Riding up The South Fooses Creek Trail and descending Green Creek or Silver Creek is a fun loop option. The ascent is challenging but nearly all rideable. For an intermediate option on this trail or to avoid the shuttle, park at the trailhead on County Road/Forest Service 225 and ride an out and back as far as you like on this winding, beautiful trail through the forest. The road leading up to the trailhead is quite bumpy, park down lower to avoid the worst sections.

Distance: 14 mile shuttle ride, 4 miles of dirt road and 10 miles of singletrack.

Time: 1 ½-2 ½ hours

Difficulty: Advanced intermediate to expert. The beginning of the descent is quite steep and technical.

Technical Skill: Advanced intermediate with short expert sections.

Aerobic Effort: Moderate

Elevation: Top: 11,920' **Gain:** 700' **Loss:** 3,100'

Season: July-early October

Finding Route: Easy. The Monarch Crest Trail is a local name for the beginning of this ride and it is not on the signs along the route, remember to follow signs for the Continental Divide Trail (CDT.)

Maps: The Crest Trail, an Absolute Bikes Ride Guide, available at Absolute Bikes, see listing in back. Also available at the High Valley Center and the Monarch Crest Store at the top of Monarch Pass. National Geographic/Trails Illustrated La Garita/Cochetopa Hills is also a good map for the area. San Isabel National Forest Map has the loop, but with less detail.

Location: Leave one car at the bottom of County Road 225, 10 miles up Monarch Pass on Highway 50 from the junction of Highways 285 and 50 in Poncha Springs (5 miles west of Salida.) There is a parking area on the left side of the highway. Continue 9 miles farther to the top of Monarch Pass with bikes and riders, and start the ride here from the large parking area on the left. A shuttle is available from The High Valley Center, see listing in back.

Mileage Log:

0.0 Begin riding up the paved Forest Road 906 behind the tramway building on Monarch Pass. Right away the road turns to dirt.

0.3 Turn right onto the signed Continental Divide Trail (CDT) singletrack.

1.0 Turn right on the doubletrack and begin climbing. (North Fooses Creek Road descends to the left.)

1.6   Turn right onto the signed Continental Divide Trail singletrack, just inside the dark trees.

3.0   Pass a sign for Middle Fooses Creek.

5.2   Ride across a short grassy area to where the signed South Fooses Creek Trail begins with a steep descent into the north facing drainage. This is also the Colorado Trail. After 2/10ths of a mile, the grade of the trail lessens. Enjoy the roll through the dark forest. The trail is straightforward all the way to the bottom, with no junctions. Cross the creek on bridges several times on the lower section.

6.5   The trail levels and is faster.

11.0   Cross another bridge to the left and reach the end of the trail. Turn right and then veer left on Forest Service Road 225C.

11.2   Turn right toward the South Arkansas River on Forest Service Road 225. Zoom down this road, being careful of cars and other users coming up. Pass several less used spurs, and a small lake on the left. Just stay on the main road.

14.0   After crossing two bridges, turn right at the T-intersection and ride up to the Highway on County Road 225.

14.1   Back at the highway and your car. 昕

See map pages 146-147

GREEN CREEK TRAIL
Ride Information

Description: The Green Creek Trail is a moderate length ride that starts on the summit of Monarch Pass, between Salida and Gunnison. It is just one of many excellent singletrack options for descending from the popular Monarch Crest Trail. (The Monarch Crest Trail is a section of the Continental Divide Trail.) With the use of a shuttle, the ride loses a lot more elevation than it gains. It begins by rolling along for several miles on the awesome Monarch Crest Trail, just below 12,000'. It then descends to the northeast on a very long and fast singletrack to Highway 50. What a hoot! The Green Creek Trail is rocky, technical and steep up top, then becomes fast and rolling but never entirely smooth down lower as it follows the creek. The ride requires a shuttle, or for a long loop, ride up South Fooses Creek (The Colorado Trail) and down The Green Creek Trail. Shuttles are available from The High Valley Center, see listing in the back of this book.

Distance: 18.3 mile shuttle ride, 13 miles of singletrack, 5.3 miles of dirt road.

Time: 2-3 hours

Difficulty: Expert

Technical Skill: Expert

Aerobic Effort: Moderate

Elevation: Top: 11,920' **Gain:** 700' **Loss:** 3,900'

Season: July through early October

Finding Route: Easy. Remember to look for the Continental Divide Trail (CDT) signs for the first 7 miles. Even though the beginning of this ride is commonly known as the Monarch Crest Trail, it is not on the signs along the route.

GREEN CREEK TRAIL
Ride Information

Maps: Monarch Crest Trail, an Absolute Bikes Ride Guide, available at Absolute Bikes in Salida (see listing in back.) The map is also available at the High Valley Center and The Monarch Crest Store at the top of Monarch Pass. This is the most complete map of the area. National Geographic/Trails Illustrated La Garita/Cochetopa Pass is a good map of the area also. The San Isabel National Forest Map also has the loop, but with less detail.

Location: Leave a car at the bottom of County Road 220. This is about 7 miles from Poncha Springs, on the west side of Highway 50, on the way up to Monarch Pass. It is just before you reach Maysville. Just down the hill from the highway is a wide parking area. Drive a second car with riders and bikes 12 miles to the top of Monarch Pass. Start here at the scenic tramway.

Mileage Log:

0.0 Begin climbing on the paved Forest Road 906 behind the tramway. Shortly it turns to dirt.

0.3 Turn right onto the signed Continental Divide Trail (CDT) singletrack.

1.0 At the end of the singletrack, turn right on the doubletrack and begin climbing. (North Fooses Creek Road descends to the left.)

1.6 Turn right onto the signed Continental Divide Trail singletrack, just inside the dark trees.

3.0 Pass a sign for Middle Fooses Creek.

5.2 Ride straight ahead, passing South Fooses Creek (also The Colorado Trail coming from the north) to the left.

5.9 Reach the high point on The Monarch Crest Trail and start a fun descent.

7.0 On the left there is a shelter and the signed Green Creek Trail. Turn left before the cabin and descend into the meadow. The trail reappears in a few yards. There are no forks on the trail, so just have fun!

14.3 End of the trail. Turn left and descend the dirt Forest/County Road 221.

15.3 Pass a road that climbs to the left, staying on County Road 221.

16.7 Continue straight down on the main road, passing spurs.

17.0 Arrive at the end of County Road 221 and a T-intersection. Turn left on County Road 220.

18.3 Back at your car at the start of paved County Road 220. 🚲

THE RAINBOW TRAIL
Ride Information

Description: This section of The Rainbow Trail connects Silver Creek and Highway 285 near Poncha Pass, just a few miles outside of Salida. It is absolutely one of the most fun and fast, contouring singletracks I've ever ridden. It rolls up and down on awesome singletrack through the forest and high altitude meadows. Ridden as a loop with County Road 201 and Highway 285, it is a great advanced intermediate loop. The loop starts with a moderate climb up County Road 200 and County Road/Forest Service Road 201 to the Rainbow Trail. From here, it rolls up and down, in and out of drainages. There are several short, steep climbs and lots of high speed, low angle descents. The last descent to Highway 285 is loose, steep and technical. It is the only expert section. For a big day, ride The Rainbow Trail after The Monarch Crest Trail.

Distance: 19 mile loop, 8 miles dirt and paved road, 11 miles singletrack.

Time: 2-4 hours.

Difficulty: Advanced intermediate with one expert descent.

Technical Skill: Intermediate with one short expert descent

Aerobic Effort: Moderate

Elevation: Top: 9,500' **Gain:** 2,500'

Season: May through October

Finding Route: Easy

Maps: The Crest Trail, an Absolute Bikes Ride Guide. Available at Absolute Bikes in Salida, see listing in back.

Location: Drive south on Highway 285 from Poncha Springs 5.3 miles, toward Poncha Pass. Park on the left, just across from the end of The Rainbow Trail. This is 2/10ths of a mile past the turn on the left to Marshall Pass and O'Haver Lake.

Mileage Log:

0.0   Ride down Highway 285 to the turn to Marshall Pass and O'Haver Lake.

0.2   Turn left and spin up Marshall Pass Road, County Road 200.

2.6   Continue straight onto County Road/Forest Service Road 201, as County Road 200 turns right to O'Haver Lake on the right.

2.8   Continue straight on County Road 201, passing the Shirley Site Parking.

2.9   Ride straight ahead on the main road.

4.2   Ride straight ahead on the main road, passing a left turn over a bridge.

4.5   Stay right and climb on Forest Service 201, passing a left turn to Silvan Lakes, a housing area and lakes. The road gets a little more rough.

5.9   Ride straight ahead on Forest Service 201 along Silver Creek.

6.9   Ride straight ahead on the main road.

7.9   Cross a creek and climb more steeply. Just as the road turns sharply right, look for the signed Rainbow Trail on the left.

8.2   Turn left on the Rainbow Trail and begin the fun!

15.0 Road crossing. Stay on the singletrack and climb. This road leads back down to mile 4.2 in the description, above.

17.8 Ride straight ahead on the singletrack.

19.2 End back at your car. 🚲

Monarch Crest Trail

South Fooses Creek Trail

COLORADO TRAIL
Cottonwood Pass to Princeton Hot Springs

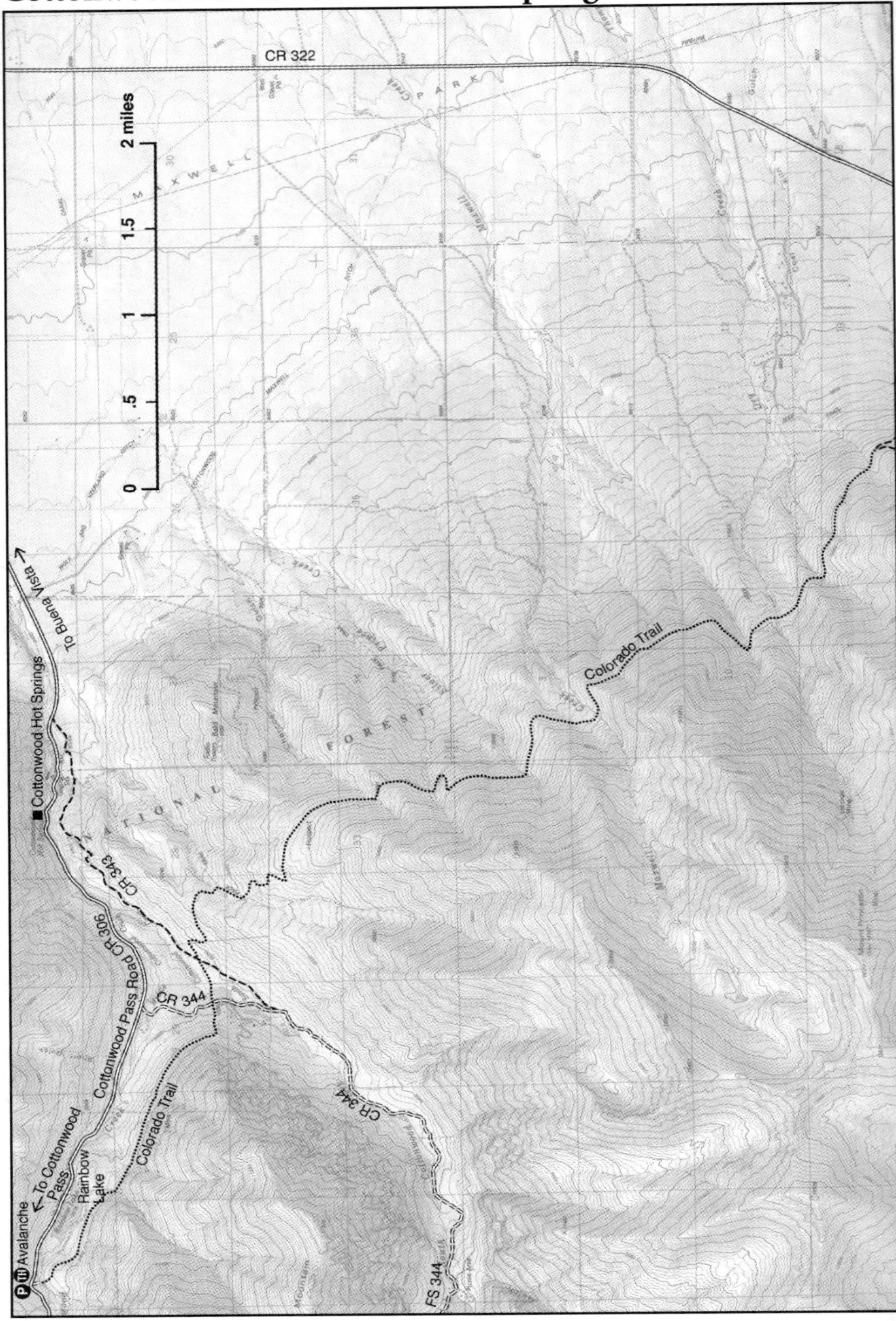

CR 322

PARK

2 miles

1.5

1

.5

0

MAXWELL

To Buena Vista

Cottonwood Hot Springs

Colorado Trail

FOREST

NATIONAL

CR 306

CR 306

Cottonwood Pass Road

CR 344

Colorado Trail

CR 344

Rainbow Lake

To Cottonwood Pass

Avalanche

FS 344

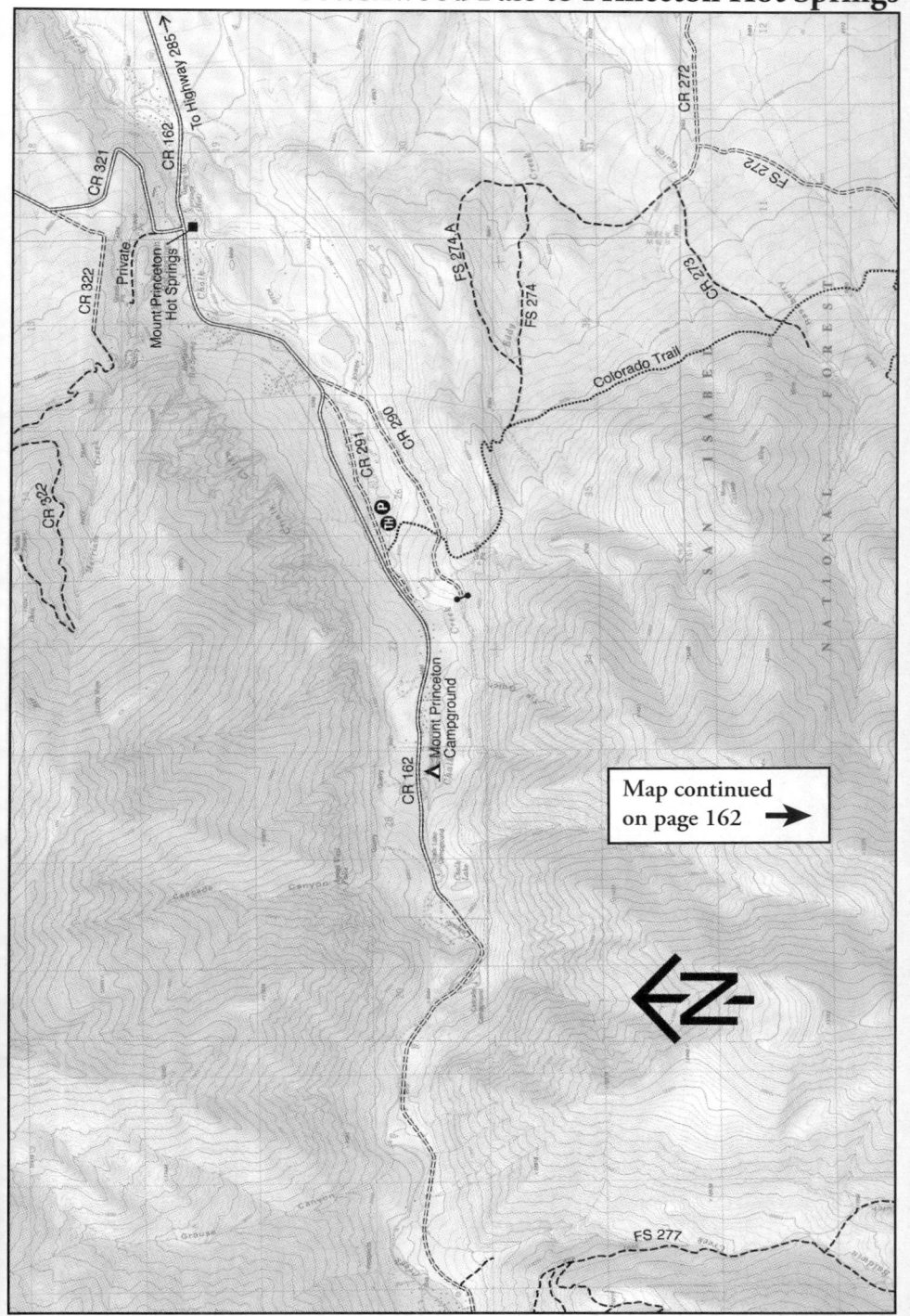

To Highway 285 →

CR 162

CR 321

CR 322

Private

Mount Princeton Hot Springs

CR 322

CR 291

CR 290

CR 162

Mount Princeton Campground

FS 274-A

FS 274

CR 272

FS 272

CR 273

Colorado Trail

SAN ISABEL

NATIONAL FOREST

Map continued
on page 162 →

FS 277

COLORADO TRAIL
Raspberry Gulch to Monarch Pass Road

FS 272
Wagon Loop 1427
Browns Creek Trail 1429
FS 275
Colorado Trail
FS 255
Colorado Trail
Little Browns Creek Trail 1430
Browns Creek Trail 1429
Mount Shavano Trail
2 miles
1.5
1
.5
0
FS 278

Map Continued
Page 161

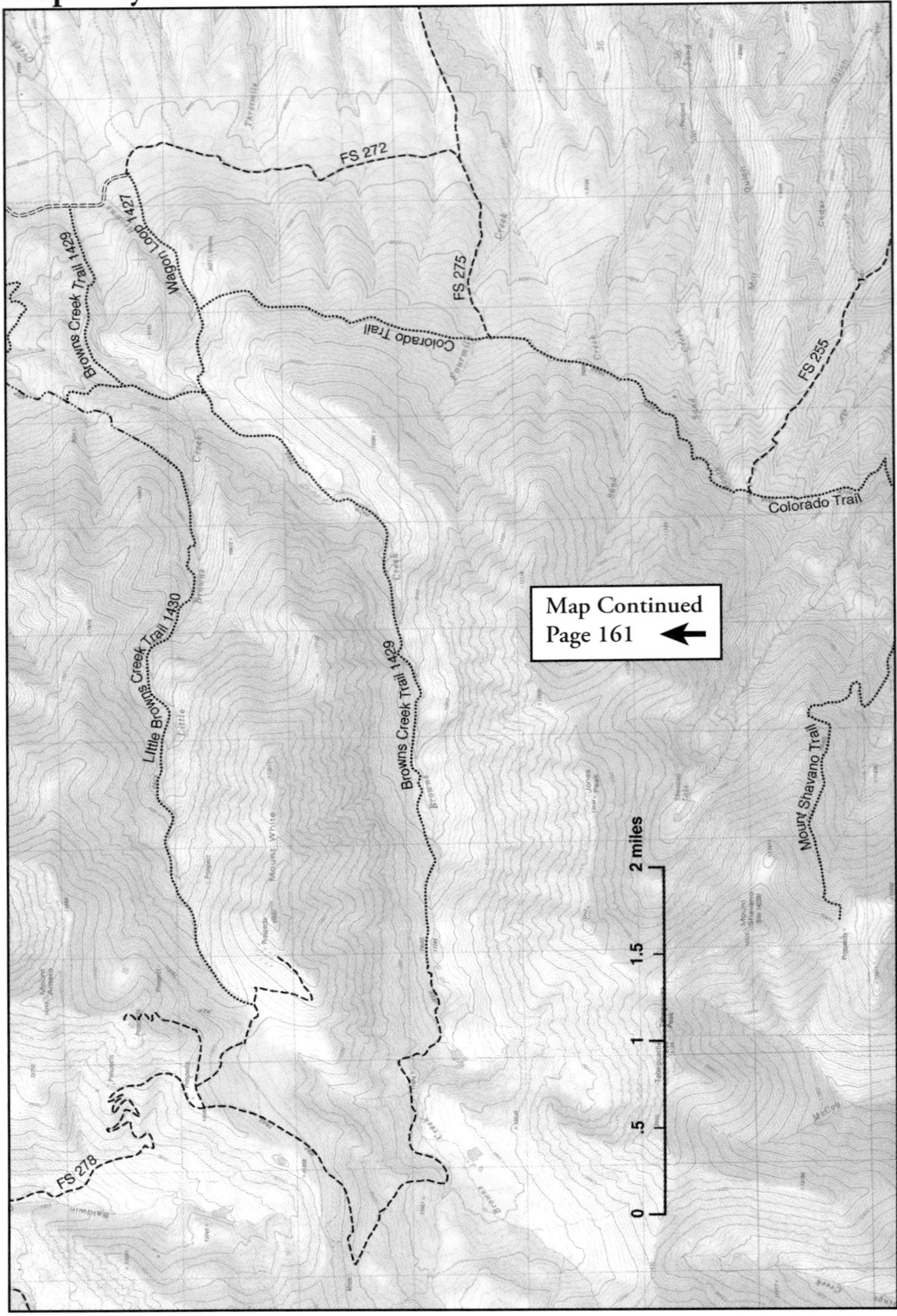

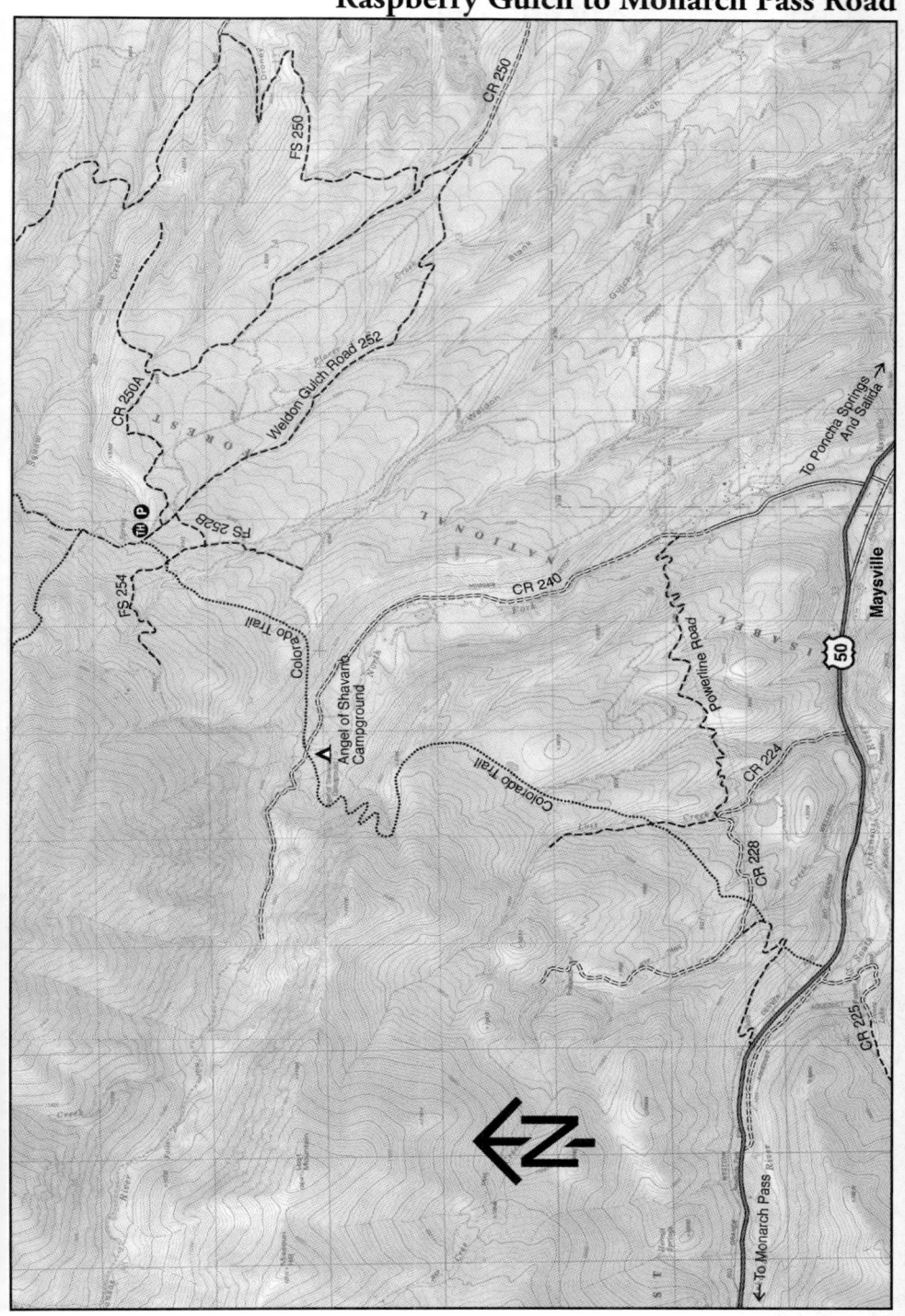

COLORADO TRAIL
Cottonwood Pass to Princeton Hot Springs
Ride Information ————————————— *See map pages 160-161*

Description: The Colorado Trail outside of Buena Vista is a beautiful, all singletrack traverse around the base of the Collegiate Peaks. It rolls through varying ecosystems of high desert and montane on excellent singletrack. Riders enjoy views of the Upper Arkansas Valley from high open meadows. This section of the Colorado Trail combines a long and somewhat grueling climb with miles of smooth and rolling singletrack. It can be ridden as an out and back as described here, or as an out and back from the other direction (an easier option, as long as you don't descend the long hill into Middle Cottonwood Creek,) or as a shuttle ride, or as a loop from the Mount Princeton Trailhead. See options, below, for these variations. This ride opens earlier than the high rides near Crested Butte. In midsummer, the Upper Arkansas Valley can be quite hot so a ride this section in the early morning hours. Bring extra water.

Distance: 21.2 miles out and back, all singletrack

Time: 2 ½ - 4 ½ hours

Difficulty: Expert, intermediate in reverse

Technical Skill: Expert, intermediate in reverse

Aerobic Effort: High, moderate in reverse

Elevation: Top: 10,000' **Gain:** 2,100'

Season: Mid-May through October

Finding Route: Fairly easy, most intersections are well marked. Always look for the small Colorado Trail symbols on trees.

Maps: The National Geographic/Trails Illustrated Buena Vista/Collegiate Peaks has the first section of the trail, National Geographic/Trails Illustrated Salida/St. Elmo/Shavano Peak has the second half and the next section of the Colorado Trail to Monarch Pass.

Location: Park at the Avalanche Trailhead, 9 miles west up Cottonwood Pass Road (County Road 306) from Buena Vista, or 10 miles down from the summit of Cottonwood Pass on County Road 306, 50 miles from Crested Butte via Taylor Canyon Road and Cottonwood Pass Road.

Mileage Log:

0.0   From the bathrooms in the center of the Avalanche Trailhead parking area, find the Colorado Trail leading south toward Chalk Creek. Follow this down and cross the highway carefully.

0.1   Ride left through an informal camping area onto the signed Colorado Trail. Cross Middle Cottonwood Creek and climb and descend along this beautiful section of singletrack.

1.7   Stay right and high, passing an unmarked spur trail to the left.

2.4   Descend left around a switchback, passing a closed trail on the right that leads to private property.

2.5   Cross County Road 344 and ride straight ahead onto a doubletrack and down to South Cottonwood Creek.

2.7   Cross a bridge and follow the creek downstream.

3.0   Stay on the singletrack, passing an old doubletrack spur to the right.

3.1   Ride straight across a dirt road, County Road 343, and stay on the signed Colorado Trail. Begin climbing rocky switchbacks shortly.

3.8   Stay right, passing a smooth singletrack spur to the left, and continue climbing short rocky hills.

4.4   Stay left on the singletrack, passing a faint closed doubletrack on the right. (You may not even notice this doubletrack.) Ride through a small, steep dip and then begin climbing. Pay close attention through the next section as the trail goes on and off old roads, some that lead to private property. In the last couple of years these roads have been used and could deter you.

4.5   Ride a sharp right switchback onto an old roadbed that is now the trail.

4.6   Turn left off the old road onto the singletrack.

4.7   Stay left on singletrack. Soon climb steeply.

4.8   Top out and enjoy a flat section of trail, then climb a steep, sandy switchback and hill.

5.2   Top out. The trail rollercoasters along for the next several miles, it is quite fast and smooth!

9.2   Cross an old doubletrack, ride straight ahead on the singletrack.

9.3   Cross a creek and climb some short hills.

10.6   Reach the end of the singletrack on County Road 322. Return the way you came, or turn left and descend the steep dirt road to your car if you shuttled, see option 1.

Option 1: To leave a shuttle car at the southern access on County Road 322 or to ride it as an out and back from there, drive to the Mount Princeton Trailhead. To get here, drive 16.3 miles north on Highway 285 from the junction of Highways 285 and 50 in Poncha Springs (5 miles west of Salida,) and turn left on County Road 162 toward Princeton Hot Springs. (County Road 162 is about 8 miles south of Buena Vista on the right.) Drive 4.7 miles on County Road 162 and turn right on County Road 321. Follow this uphill for 1.3 miles. Turn left at the sign for Young Life Frontier Ranch on County Road 322. Stay left after the yield sign and drive 9/10ths of a mile and bear right just after a corral on the right to the parking area. (Left leads to the Frontier Ranch.) Leave one car here and return to Highway 285 with bikes and riders, and drive north to Buena Vista, then turn left on Cottonwood Pass Road. Drive 9 miles to the Avalanche Trailhead. If you are riding the Colorado Trail as an out and back from the Mount Princeton Trailhead, ride up to the right through the small brown metal posts on County Road 322 toward Mount Princeton from the parking area. This switchbacks up to the signed beginning of the trail in 1.1 miles, on the right of a sharp switchback.

Option 2: Loop the ride from the Mount Princeton Trailhead by following the directions in option 1 to access the trail on the southern end, and ride north toward Cottonwood Pass on the Colorado Trail to County Road 343. Follow this to Cottonwood Pass Road and turn right. Continue downhill and turn right on County Road 339. Follow this to County Road 326 and turn left. Follow this to County Road 321, where a right will return you to County Road 322 and your car. I don't recommend riding this section of the Colorado Trail as a loop that involves riding up Cottonwood Pass Road, as it is narrow and has quite a lot of traffic in the summer.

COLORADO TRAIL
Cottonwood Pass to Princeton Hot Springs
Ride Information

Option 3: To combine this ride with the Colorado Trail from Princeton Hot Springs to Monarch Pass (an epic day,) leave a car on Monarch Pass Road 9 miles up from Poncha Springs (8 miles down from Monarch Pass.) There is a parking area on the south side of the highway, next to the start of County Road 225. Follow the directions in Location, above, to the Avalanche Trailhead on Cottonwood Pass Road. On the ride, once you reach County Road 322 at the end of the above description, turn left and descend 2.5 miles to County Road 321 (Passing the Young Life Frontier Ranch in 1.1 miles and then a private road to the right in 2 miles.) Turn right and descend on County Road 321 1.3 miles to the intersection with County Road 162, across from Mount Princeton Hot Springs. Turn right and ride up this paved road 1.4 miles and turn left on County Road 291. Continue 1.1 miles farther to the Chalk Creek Trailhead and the continuation of the trail. From here:

Mileage Log:

0.0 Begin by crossing Chalk Creek and climbing gradually. Stay right past the walk-in camping.

0.5 Cross a dirt road and look for the continuation of the trail just to the right.

0.7 Begin climbing. Parts of this are hike-a-bike.

1.7 Top out and begin a steep descent.

2.0 Stay right.

2.4 Stay right.

2.8 Cross a private road, continue on the trail. From here, follow the description for Colorado Trail, Raspberry Gulch to Monarch Pass from mile 3.2. 🚲

COLORADO TRAIL
Raspberry Gulch to Monarch Pass Road
Ride Information ——————————————— *See map pages 161-163*

Description: The Colorado Trail has many beautiful sections throughout the state, and this is no exception. It is a great cross-country ride, traversing around the base of the Collegiate Peaks between Buena Vista and Poncha Springs. The trail rolls along through pine and aspen forest, crosses creeks and traverses sunny meadows. It is constructed for biking, well maintained, and mostly smooth singletrack. The trail is very rideable, although it has several challenging climbs. It is easy to shorten the ride by exiting at the Mount Shavano Trailhead at mile 14.2, as beyond this the trail climbs a lot toward Monarch Pass. For a longer day, ride it from Mount Princeton Hot Springs or combine it with the Cottonwood Pass Section, see Colorado Trail, Cottonwood Pass to Princeton Hot Springs. There are several options for riding this section of the Colorado Trail in reverse, which is also great riding. Access it from Monarch Pass, the Angel of Shavano Campground, or from County Road 250 and The Mount Shavano Trailhead. See options, below, for details. Or, ride the Monarch Crest Trail and South Fooses Creek and continue across Monarch Pass. Follow the Colorado Trail to The Mount Shavano Trailhead, and then descend to Poncha Springs where you leave a car. Call the High Valley Center shuttle service for a ride to any of the trailheads, see listing in back. Always bring extra water on the Colorado Trail, it can be quite hot here in the summer.

Distance: 22 mile shuttle ride, 3 miles of dirt road, 19 miles of singletrack.

Time: 3 ¼- 5 hours

Difficulty: Expert. For an easy intermediate loop on this section, ride the first 4.8 miles of this description, then take Forest Road 273 left to return to Forest Road 274, turn right and retrace your tracks back to your car.

Technical Skill: Expert

Aerobic Effort: High

Elevation: Top: 10,170' **Gain:** 4,400'

Season: Mid-May through October

Finding Route: Fairly easy, always look for the Colorado Trail symbols on the trees.

Maps: National Geographic/Trails Illustrated Salida/St. Elmo/Shavano Peak.

Location: Leave a car on Highway 50 where the Colorado Trail crosses it, 9 miles west of the junction of Highway 50 and Highway 285 in Poncha Springs, on the way up Monarch Pass. There is a parking area on the left side of Highway 50 next to the start of County Road 225. With bikes and riders, return to Highway 285 in Poncha Springs and turn left. Drive 12 miles north to County Road 270 and turn left toward Raspberry Gulch. This turn is about one mile after you pass the Centerville Gas Station and a rock shop on the left of Highway 285 and drive under some water pipes, and is marked on the highway with a small County Road 270 sign only. The turn is approximately 11 miles south of Buena Vista. Once you make the turn, drive straight on County Road 270 for 1.5 miles and onto County Road 272. Continue straight on County Road 272 for 8/10ths of a mile to a parking area on the left. Begin the ride here.

Mileage Log:

0.0   Turn left from the parking area and begin riding up County Road 272.

1.1   Ride straight ahead onto County Road 274.

1.4   Ride straight ahead, staying on Forest Road 274.

2.0   Turn left on Forest Road 274.2, passing Forest Road 274A on the right.)

3.0   Stay left as Forest Road 274A comes back in on the right.

3.2   Turn left on the signed Colorado Trail singletrack. This section is smooth and fun.

4.8   Cross Forest Road 273. The trail is rolling, and then begins a series of climbs in this section.

7.0   Turn left on the Colorado Trail singletrack after a heinous rocky hike-a- bike section. Little Browns Creek Trail is straight ahead.

7.3   Stay right and climb, as the Browns Creek Trail takes a sharp left and heads down.

7.5   Cross a creek and turn left on the signed Colorado Trail and Wagon Loop. Right and up is the Browns Creek Trail. Cross more creeks.

7.9   (approx. mileage) Stay high and right on the Colorado Trail as the Wagon Loop road heads down and left. The trail is rolling through here with some challenging climbs and fast descents.

COLORADO TRAIL
Raspberry Gulch to Monarch Pass Road
Ride Information

10.6   Stay high and right, passing an old doubletrack to the left.

13.6   The trail turns to an old doubletrack. Descend.

13.9   Continue straight, passing the Mount Shavano Trail on the right.

14.2   Arrive at the Mount Shavano Trailhead (also known as Blanks Cabin) and a large parking area in the aspens. Stay right on the trail and climb briefly. (This is a good exit to shorten the ride, plan by leaving a car in Poncha Springs.)

14.4   Cross a road and continue on singletrack. This is an awesome section, climbing and descending on fast and smooth singletrack.

16.3   Pass the Angel of Shavano Trailhead and begin climbing.

19.5   Continue straight ahead on the trail.

20.5   Cross a dirt spur road and continue on the singletrack.

20.7   Cross Cree Creek Road, continue on the singletrack.

21.2   Ride straight under the powerline and onto an old road, heading left and down a switchback.

21.6   Take a sharp left off the road and descend the singletrack. Look for the CT symbol. This turn is easy to miss.

22.1   End at your car on the Highway 50. Please cross this busy highway carefully!

Options: To shorten the ride if riding in a southerly direction, leave a car in Poncha Springs at the visitor center, at the corner of Highways 285 and 50, instead of on Monarch Pass. Or to avoid riding on Highway 50, leave a car parked on County Road 250 where the road crosses onto National Forest Service land. (County Road 250 turns off Highway 50 1.7 miles west of it's junction with Highway 285.) Exit the trail at mile 14.2 and descend County Road 250 to your car. To ride a little farther on the trail, leave a car in Maysville, 6 miles up on the way to Monarch Pass, and exit the ride at mile 16.3. Ride down County Road 240 to your car. I do not recommend riding down Highway 50 from Maysville, it is narrow and dangerous in spots. Leaving a car on County Road 250 is also preferable to the visitor center for the same reason. These are the same access points if you want to ride the trail in reverse. ⛢

Colorado Trail - Cottonwood Pass to
Princeton Hot Springs section

Colorado Trail -
Raspberry Gulch section

BEAR CREEK TO THE RAINBOW TRAIL

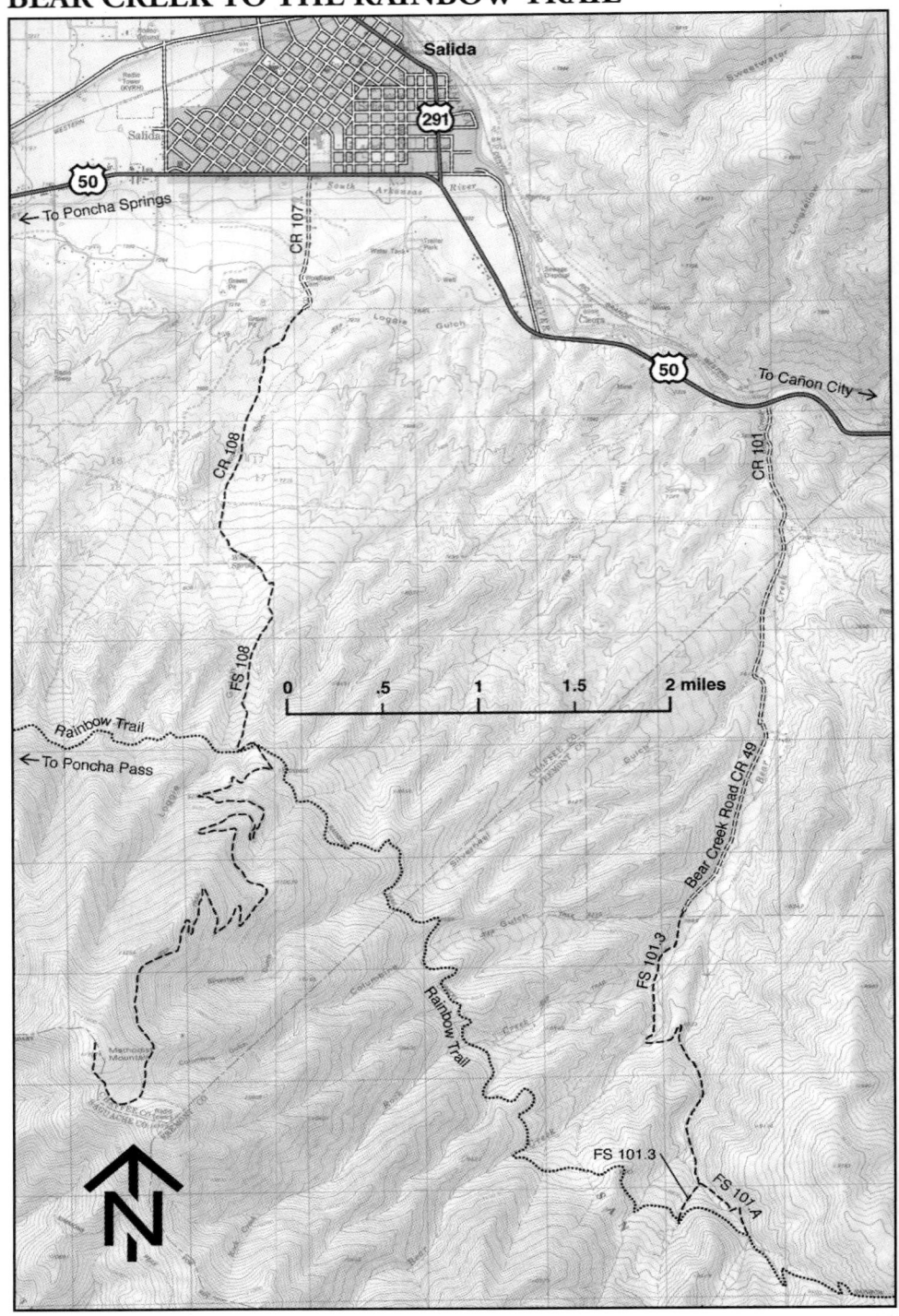

BEAR CREEK TO THE RAINBOW TRAIL
Ride Information

Description: This loop or out and back ride south of Salida includes a very smooth and beautiful section of the Rainbow Trail. It rolls through beautiful forest and open meadows on great singletrack. The climb up County Road 101 is quite steep and rocky in spots, a great workout. The vegetation changes from high desert pinon, juniper and cactus to lush mountain forest as you climb the road. Once the trail is gained, there is little elevation gain or loss. To shorten the climb, drive 3.3 miles up County Road 101 to a parking lot on the right, just before a cattleguard. Ride up to the trail and continue on it to County Road 108. Turn around and ride back to County Road 101 and down to your car. If you ride the loop, the descent on County Road 108 is very steep. It is quite arid here, and the trail opens sooner than the high Monarch Crest area trails. It can be very hot here in the summer months, ride early and take plenty of water.

Distance: 18 mile loop, 6 miles of singletrack, 2.5 miles of pavement, 9.5 miles of dirt road. As an out and back from County Road 101: 18-24 miles, 12 miles of singletrack, 6-12 miles of dirt road.

Time: 2 ½-4 hours.

Difficulty: Advanced Intermediate

Technical Skill: Advanced Intermediate

Aerobic Effort: High

Elevation: Top: 9,100' **Gain:** 2,500'

Season: May through October

Finding Route: Easy

Maps: San Isabel National Forest has the route, but no topographical detail.

Location: Begin this ride from the junction of Highway 291 and Highway 50 at the eastern edge of Salida. I like to start downtown at the park on F Street and ride southeast through all the interesting neighborhoods to the junction of the highways, and then have lunch downtown after the ride. There is parking across the river at the end of F Street. There is also parking at the Salida Forest Service Ranger District on Highway 50, one mile west of the junction of Highway 291 and Highway 50. (Or ride the ride as an out and back from County Road 101: Drive 2.5 miles to the beginning of County Road 101 and park in a pullout to the left of the highway. Ride up to the Rainbow Trail from here. To shorten the climb, turn right on County Road 101 and drive 3.3 miles up to a parking area on the right, just before a cattleguard and park here.)

Mileage Log:

0.0   Begin riding east on Highway 50 toward Canon City from the edge of Salida. Stay far to the right as this road can be quite busy.

2.5   Turn right and begin climbing on County Road 101. Climb steadily, and steeply up higher. (Up higher the road becomes County Road 49 when it crosses a county line, then Forest Service 101.3 beyond that when the road enters national forest.)

5.7   Cross a cattleguard after passing the alternate parking.

7.9   Ride straight ahead on the road, passing the County Road 101.A spur to the left. Continue to climb quite steeply.

8.3 Shortly after crossing a creek, the road ends. Turn right on the signed Rainbow Trail and begin the fun! Follow this smooth singletrack for the next 6 miles, passing two 4WD roads that descend to the right at mile 8.6 and 11.2. (The Rainbow Trail also continues to the left at the top of County Road 101/Forest Road 101.3. This direction is mostly steep and loose climbing and descending. It is a very difficult section.)

14.2 Reach Forest Service Road 108 at a big intersection with a trail register and parking. Turn around and retrace your tracks if you parked on County Road 101, or turn right and descend to Salida on Forest Road 108. Be careful, this road is very steep. (The Rainbow Trail also continues to Highway 285. This section is also a difficult ride with lots of loose rocks and steep climbs and descents.)

15.8 Forest ServiceRoad/County Road 108 becomes County Road 107. Veer right on the graded road and descend.

18.2 Back to Highway 50, turn right and return to your car if you parked in town, left if you parked at the Ranger Station. 🚲

The Rainbow Trail

Crested Butte has several dirt road options that are absolutely beautiful rides, without the technical aspect that many of the singletracks have. These are perfect for the beginning rider. Ride as far as you want, and then turn back. Latitude 40 Crested Butte/Taylor Park or Latitude 40 Aspen/Crested Butte/Gunnison will help you find your way.

Peanut Lake Road (County Road 4)

From the four-way stop at the corner of Elk Avenue and 6th Street (Highway 135,) drive or ride west up Elk Avenue to 1st Street and turn right. Continue down to Butte Avenue and turn left. When County Road 4 begins and the road turns to dirt, there are parking spots on the right a short distance up if you drove. Ride up this road as far as you like. A fairly easy and wide section of the lower loop begins just past the mine if you choose to ride farther. Only local traffic to the two residences are allowed on Peanut Lake Road, which makes it friendly for kids.

Slate River Road (County Road 734)

From the four-way stop at the corner of Elk Avenue and 6th Street, drive or ride north on 6th Street (Gothic Road) toward Mount Crested Butte for 9/10ths of a mile to Slate River Road. There is a narrow pullout here on the dirt road, but it is better to ride out to avoid congestion in the roadway. This is a beautiful, mostly gradual ride out for several miles, following the wetland sanctuary of the Slate River. It is not unusual to see birds, waterfowl, and coyotes along here. The road becomes steeper once it passes the Pittsburg townsite, several miles up. The mountains rise steeply on both sides of the valley, making this a breathtaking ride. Traffic is moderate on this road.

Washington Gulch Road (County Road 811)

From the four-way stop at the corner of Elk Avenue and 6th Street, drive or ride north on 6th Street (Gothic Road) toward Mount Crested Butte to Washington Gulch Road, on the left. There are pullouts at the top of the first hill. For a more peaceful and safer experience, ride here on the bike path. (See Bike Path to Upper Loop and Tony's Trail.) This road is gradual and rolling for several miles. Traffic is moderate on this road.

Brush Creek Road (County Road 38)

Brush Creek Road is two miles south of Crested Butte on the left, off Highway 135. Once you get past 6/10ths of a mile of pavement, there are places to pull off and park. Riding out on the easy singletrack that parallels Highway 135 is another option. (See Skyland to the Upper Loop and Tony's Trail.) Brush Creek Road has wonderful views of the East River Valley, and White and Teocalli Mountains. Six miles up is a wide creek crossing, and then the road becomes steeper. At the Brush Creek Trailhead, 2.4 miles up Brush Creek Road on the left, there is also an out and back doubletrack ride out of the back of the parking lot. This is a little more challenging, but traffic free and very quiet. Watch out for horseback riders here. Brush Creek Road has a moderate amount of traffic.

Cement Creek Road (County Road 740)

Cement Creek Road is located 6.8 south of Crested Butte off Highway 135. Drive 1.8 miles to a parking lot off to the right. The road ride follows a steep walled canyon through Douglas Fir Forest along Cement Creek. This lower section of road sometimes has heavy traffic and a lot of dust. There are several spots to pull off up farther, as well. 6.8 miles up is the Deadman Gulch Trailhead, this gets you past most of the traffic. The upper Cement Creek Valley is wide open and beautiful.

EASY ROAD RIDES

Gold Basin Road

Gold Basin Road, County Road 38, is the paved road that passes Hartman Rocks Recreation Area just outside of Gunnison. After 5.5 miles it turns to dirt and meanders through the sage and pinon-juniper hills. Traffic is light on Gold Basin Road. This road is 1.4 miles west of the intersection of Highway 135 in Gunnison (Main Street,) and Highway 50 (Tomichi Avenue.)

McCabe Lane

McCabe Lane is located 3 miles west of Gunnison on the left, just past the Mesa RV resort. Drive ¼ mile to a parking area on the left by the Gunnison River. Ride out past ranches into the sage covered BLM hills. At a fork just past a gravel pit, go left or right and ride as far as you like, returning by the same route. If you continue right and ride through another ranch, a left on the next major fork in the road is the continuation of McCabe Lane. It is easy to get lost out here, be sure to return via your same route. There are no great maps of the area and everything is unmarked. Traffic is very light on these roads.

Marshall Pass Road

Marshall Pass Road, or County Road 200, is a nice ramble along creeks and through meadows just outside of Salida. It is gradual and smooth and climbs all the way to Marshall Pass at nearly 11,000'. Explore the lower side roads as well. Drive south from Poncha Springs 5.1 miles toward Poncha Pass. Marshall Pass Road is on the right. There is moderate to heavy traffic at times on the roads in this area.

ADVANCED ROAD RIDES

Paradise Divide

This is a long and beautiful road ride out of Crested Butte. It is quite steep toward the far end of the loop. It is perfect for a fit rider who doesn't want to ride singletrack. There are a few options to riding a loop around Paradise Divide. Ride up Slate River Road to the Pittsburg townsite, and stay right on Forest Road 734. Follow this up the steep switchbacks to the fork in the road. From here turn right on Forest Road 811 and roll back to Crested Butte. For a little longer loop, stick with road 734 until you arrive at Schofield Pass. Here, turn right and follow Gothic Road all the way back to Crested Butte. Or ride the loop in reverse. This ride is 23 to 28 miles, climbs to 11,200', and takes 2½-4 hours. Take along the 5th edition Latitude 40 map for Aspen/Crested Butte/Gunnison or Latitude 40 Crested Butte/Taylor Park Trails Map.

Pearl Pass To Aspen

This ride is a classic, first ridden in 1976 by a group of local rowdies on their one-speed "klunkers." On comfortable mountain bikes with gears, it is still a challenging ride. Start by riding south two miles from Crested Butte to Brush Creek Road. Turn left and follow this 8 miles to a signed fork, and stay right on Brush Creek Road. Continue 3 miles further and turn left on Middle Brush Creek Road. Continue riding and hike-a-biking on this road until you reach Pearl Pass at 12,700'. Straight down the other side on Forest Road 102, to Castle Creek Road, turn left and ride into Aspen! Take along the Latitude 40 Aspen/Crested Butte/Gunnison. See information in the back of this book on a one way shuttle to or from Aspen.

ADVANCED ROAD RIDES

Crested Butte To Marble

Follow the description for riding Trail 401 to Schofield Pass, but continue on Gothic Road 317 to Crystal, and on to Marble. This is 25 miles one way, takes 3-6 hours, and climbs to10,700'. This is a beautiful tour. The road is quite rocky and challenging on the Marble side, but smooth on the Crested Butte side. Traffic can be heavy up to Schofied Pass, light beyond that.

Gunsight Pass Road

Gunsight Pass Road is located 3.4 miles out Slate River Road on the left, just outside of Crested Butte. It is also accessible from the Lower Loop (see Lower Loop, mile 4.3.) This is a continuous 5 mile climb up to the saddle just below the summit of Mount Emmons, the last ½ mile being hike-a-bike. This climbs to 12,100' and takes about 3-4 hours out and back from Crested Butte. There are beautiful views from the top!

Poncha Creek Road (Forest Service 203)

This is a beautiful and challenging road climb up to Marshall Pass, just 5 miles south of Poncha Springs on Highway 285. It begins just a few miles up Marshall Pass Road, and follows Poncha Creek up through mixed stands of aspens and firs. There are great views from Marshall Pass. Make a loop with Marshall Pass Road, Forest Service 200.

Marshall Pass Road/Silver Creek Road

Marshall Pass Road, or County Road 200, is a nice ramble along creeks and through meadows just outside of Salida. It is gradual and smooth and climbs all the way to Marshall Pass at nearly 11,000'. Drive south from Poncha Springs 5.1 miles toward Poncha Pass on Highway 285. Marshall Pass Road is on the right. Be sure to park up the road, past the private property. Forest Service Road 201 that follows Silver Creek up is another gradual, mostly smooth ride in the same area. It is accessed off Marshall Pass Road. Stay left at mile 2.4 and continue on to park at the Shirley Site, just a little farther up on the left. There is moderate traffic at times on the roads in this area.

LOCAL SERVICES
BIKE SHOPS
Crested Butte and Mount Crested Butte

The Alpineer, 419 6th Street, Crested Butte. 970-349-5210. Sales, demos and rentals, parts and service, maps and local trail information, camping equipment. Gary Fisher, Santa Cruz, Marin, Moots, Pearl Izumi, Patagonia, Marmot, Cloudveil. www.alpineer.com

Back Alley Bike Supply, 312 Belleview, Crested Butte. 970-349-0331. Town bikes to mountain bikes in a brand new location! Sales, parts and service. Function Before Fashion handmade clothing and packs.

Crested Butte Sports, 35 Emmons Road, Mount Crested Butte. At the ski area, next to the Nordic Inn. 970-349-7516. Sales, parts, service. www.crestedbuttesports.com

LOCAL SERVICES

Gunnison

Tomichi Cycles Inc., 104 North Main Street, Gunnison. 970-641-9069. Gunnison's premier cycling center. Rentals, repairs, maps and local information. Full line of active clothing. www.tomichicycles.com.

The Tune-up, 222 North Main Street, Gunnison. 970-641-0285. Bike pros since '76! Santa Cruz, Trek, Klein, Specialized and Litespeed

Rock 'n Roll Sports, 608 West Tomichi, Gunnison. 970-641-9150. Sales, service and gear for mountain, road and cyclocross. Yeti, Giant, Bianchi and Gary Fisher. Also climbing, backpacking, kayaking and ski gear.

Salida and Buena Vista

Absolute Bikes, 330 West Sackett Avenue, Salida. 719-539-9295. Sales, service, rentals, maps, trail and ride information, museum. info@absolutebikes.com. Next to Bongo Billy's Coffeehouse Cafe.

Otero Cyclery, 104 F Street, Salida. 719-539-6704. Since 1989, anything and everything for your bike. Experienced technicians, full service shop. Trek, Ellesworth, Kona, KHS. Check website for local trail and weather information: www.oterocyclery.com

The Trailhead, 707 U.S Highway 24 North, Buena Vista. 719-395-8001. Sales, repair, outdoor, camping and bike gear, maps and books, Trek bicycles.

GUIDE SERVICES

Crested Butte Mountain Guides, 970-349-5430. Behind the Post Office in downtown Crested Butte. www.crestedbutteguides.com. Custom guided tours with experienced guides, all abilities welcome. 15 years experience. Mountain biking, rock climbing, backpacking, kayaking, skiing, mountaineering and ice climbing. Whatever you can dream up, CBMGs can make it happen!

SHUTTLE SERVICES/ PUBLIC TRANSPORTATION
Crested Butte

Mountain Express Bus, Crested Butte to Mount Crested Butte, 970-349-7318. Bus stops and information located at the 4-way stop by the Visitor Center, in front of Clarks Market, in front of the Nordic Center, at the corner of 2nd and Elk Avenue, and at the ski area.

Dolly's Mountain Shuttle, Local Crested Butte: 970-349-2620, Local Aspen: 970-948-9893.Check visitcrestedbutte.com and click on shuttle for more information. From Aspen, $50/person with a $250 minimum (5 people.)

Poncha Springs and Salida

High Valley Shuttle, 6250 Highway 285 in Poncha Springs, 719-539-6089. 1-800-871-5145. www.monarchcrest.com. Shuttles to The Monarch Crest Trail, Rainbow Trail, Bear Creek, Colorado Trail (Raspberry Gulch,) Silver Creek, Marshall Pass. Custom shuttles within a 25 mile radius.

RESTAURANTS
Crested Butte

Donita's Cantina, 330 Elk Avenue, downtown Crested Butte. 970-349-6674. Across from the Mountain Bike Hall of Fame and Museum. Great Mexican Food and Margaritas!

Lil's Land and Sea, 321 Elk Avenue, Crested Butte. 970-349-5457. Serving Crested Butte's best sushi for 11 years. In addition to the freshest fish and seafood, we serve elk, beef and pork tenderloin, duck, pasta dishes, vegetarian entrees, fresh salads, sandwiches and burgers. Kids menu and amazing homemade desserts. Dinner only, patio dining.

Paradise Café, Beautiful midtown Crested Butte, 303 Elk Avenue. 970-349-6233. Breakfast, lunch, deck seating.

Camp 4 Coffee, 402 ½ Elk Avenue in Crested Butte (across from Mountain Earth Foods on the Third Street.) 970-349-5148. Also in Crested Butte South and Mount Crested Butte. Great coffee and espresso drinks, espresso shakes, homemade chai tea, breakfast burritos, biscuits and croissants, smoothies, doughnuts, muffins, sandwiches.

The Ginger Café, 313 Third Street, in the heart of Crested Butte. 970-349-7291. Offers pan asian cuisine, specializing in Thai and Indian. Fresh fish, fusion dishes, and original cocktails. Voted best vegetarian of the butte 2005. Reservations recommended. Open 11 am -10 pm daily.

The Buckaroo Beanery Coffeehouse, 601 6th Street, Crested Butte. 970-349-5252 Fresh roasted coffees, espresso, pastries, smoothies, panini sandwiches, internet access.

The Secret Stash Coffeehouse, Pizza, & Lounge, 21 Elk Avenue, Crested Butte. 970-349-6245. Unique atmosphere. Pizza, sandwiches, salads, calzones, backyard deck. Open late!

Last Steep Bar and Grill, 208 Elk Avenue, downtown Crested Butte. 970-349-7007. Lunch and Dinner, open 11 a.m. until late! Voted best Bloody Mary 3 years runnin'!

Teocalli Tamale, 311½ Elk Avenue, Crested Butte. 970-349-2005. Healthy Mexican grill. Good and healthy burritos, tacos, tamales, margaritas and beers. Fast service! Take a burrito on your ride!

Pitas in Paradise, 212 Elk Avenue, Crested Butte. Brand new location and great food! 970-349-0897. Beer Garden, Free Internet, Giros, Filafel, Greek Salads, Espresso Bar.

The Brick Oven, 229 Elk Avenue, Crested Butte. 970-349-5044. Huge sunny deck and gazebo bar, Pizza, Subs, Salads.

Gunnison

The Firebrand Delicatessen, 108 North Main, Gunnison. 970-641-6266. Extra Special Breakfast Specials, Vegetarian Fare, Soups, Salads, Muffins, Cookies, Beer.

Café Silvestre, 903 North Main, Gunnison. 970-641-4001. Authentic Mexican Food, homemade tortillas, margaritas, family-run.

LOCAL SERVICES

Katie's Cookery, 112 South Main, Gunnison. 970-641-1958. Lunch, dinner, outdoor seating, full bar and live music. Good food!

Mochas Drive Thru Coffeehouse, 710 North Main, Gunnison, 970-641-2006. Open 6am-9pm, in the Mountain Meadows Mall. Smoothies, great coffee, pastries, ice cream.

HEALTH FOOD STORES
Crested Butte

Mountain Earth Whole Food Grocer, 405 4th Street, Crested Butte. 970-349-5132. Organic and Natural Foods and Deli Items: Wraps, Chili, Tuna, Salads, Soups.

Gunnison

Gunnison Vitamin and Health Food Store, 722 N. Main, Gunnison, in the Mountain Meadows Mall. 970-641-5928. Organic Groceries, Sports Nutrition, Vitamins, Supplements.

LODGING
Crested Butte And Mt. Crested Butte

Elk Mountain Lodge B&B, 2nd and Gothic, in town Crested Butte. 970-349-7533 Crested Butte's Historic Inn. www.elkmountainlodge.net

The Nordic Inn B&B, 14 Treasury Road, Mount Crested Butte. 970-349-5542. AAA, Kitchenettes available, next to the CBMR bike trails. www.nordicinncb.com

Gunnison

The Mary Lawrence Inn B&B, 601 North Taylor, Gunnison. 970-641-3343. "Your Victorian home away from home." Private baths, full breakfast, outdoor hot tub.

Massage Therapy

Samantha Corn, 970-275-4724. Specializing in therapeutic deep tissue and recovery massage.

US Forest Service, 216 N. Colorado, Gunnison, - 970-641-0471

US Forest Service, 325 W. Rainbow Blvd., Salida, -719-539-3591

Hartman Rocks

ABOUT THE AUTHOR

Holly Annala lives in Crested Butte, Colorado with her husband, Rob Mahedy. She has spent all but two years of her life in Colorado, growing up on a ranch in Durango. She has always loved the outdoors. Holly has been mountain biking the four corners area for 20 years. This is her third mountain bike guide, following Mountain Bike Crested Butte Singletrack and Hartman Rocks in Gunnison and Mountain Bike Summit County and Vail Singletrack. She is happiest out on the trail and camping around the west. For questions or comments, please write her at hollyannala@yahoo.com.